L-earn-ing Every Stroke

A 1,500 -mile Kayak Adventure along the Florida Coast

Jeffrey "Treehouse" Buncie

i

To the sun, winds, and tides: Fuck you, you know what you did; to crab trap ball Wilson, with whom I hope this publication will once again reunite me, and to my Moms and Pops, who accepted all the drunken phone calls along the way.

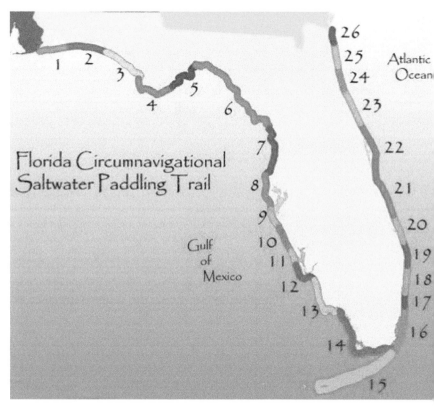

Photo credit: https://floridadep.gov/parks/ogt/content/florida-circumnavigational-saltwater-paddling-trail

Contents

1	Preparation to the Border	1
2	Pensacola to Emerald Coast	7
3	Panama City to St. Joseph Island	20
4	The Forgotten Coast & St. Marks	30
5	The Big Bend	48
6	The Nature Coast	65
7	Pinellas, Tampa, Sarasota and Venice	77
8	Charlotte Harbor to Estero Bay	94
9	Ten Thousand Islands	102
10	The Everglades	116
11	Florida Keys South	128
12	The Dry Tortugas	145
13	Florida Keys North	159
14	Biscayne to Ft. Lauderdale	179
15	Pompano to the Indian River	191
16	The Space Coast	201
17	Tomoka Basin & Timucuan Trails	214
18	Fort Clinch	226

Join Me

Have you ever had to ask yourself, "How the hell did I end up here?" The little devil hanging over my shoulder brought me a moment of uncertainty. There I was, overlooking the Weeki Wachee River from a shaded bench at the Bayport Boat Ramp, where a large oak helped me escape the morning sun. I sat in the shade, choking down a foul meal-replacement shake. Every swig of the putrid liquid punched the back of my throat, triggering my gag reflex. Over and over again, I swallowed the grainy sauce-like beverage. My eyes stared blankly at a water-logged cell phone. Resting on the splintering bench, I wished the magical phone fairies to create power, so I could navigate my way along the Florida coast. One gulp away from regurgitating breakfast, and staring at a blank phone, a wicked thought crept from the shadows of my mind. On the brink of defeat, one negative thought away from calling the whole thing off, I heard a voice in the distance.

"You OK? Do you need some help?"

Across the park, loading a skiff boat onto a trailer, was a man in his early 30s with ruffled, shoulder-length hair, sporting a bandana, Costa sunglasses and a beard rivaling Jeremiah Johnson himself. I looked up at the man with his lovely wife sitting at the wheel and their 4-year-old son, rocking turtle arm wings, standing on the boat. When they saw my dismal expression, they took a chance and extended a helping hand. The ball was in my court -- If I had the willingness to set aside my pride and accept their offer.

That was one of the hardest lessons I had to face -- dropping my pride and accepting people's generosity was not in my vocabulary. But, at that moment, on that day, one step from defeat, I was a broken man who took this leap of faith. Once I realized the journey was bigger than me, the story began to write itself. The adventures became more exciting, opportunities seemingly endless and the tales a lot more interesting.

I invite you to join me on this 1,500-mile paddling adventure circumnavigating the Florida peninsula. Be there when I encounter the wildlife, such as curious hammerhead sharks, majestic rays and the alligators of the Everglades. Dive into the culture of the Florida coastal towns and witness the generosity of its people. Hang with me in the Dry Tortugas, where a group of campers get stranded and come together as a family. Learn from my mistakes and laugh with me along the way. Most of all, I challenge you to follow the progression of a prideful, stubborn man regaining his faith in humanity.

Big Lagoon State Park kayak ramp

Why Would I Do a Thing Like That?

Imagine paddling to a small plot of land isolated and surrounded by the warm, emerald waters of the Gulf of Mexico. You approach a sliver of dampened sand smoothed over by the gently crashing waves. Your paddle interrupts a school of bait fish skimming the water below; the nose of your kayak runs aground, cutting a small notch onto the unscathed beach. You lift your left knee out of the boat to catch your balance before the crashing waves pull your aft sideways. Your foot breaks the plane and splashes into the rippled sand below. Following quickly with your right, you are now equally balanced and begin to shuffle toward the blank canvas. While stepping aground, your foot sinks slightly into the cool, salt-soaked sand, freeing small bubbles into the atmosphere. Muscle memory kicks in as you grab the nylon tow cord and give it a good heave to secure your vessel. The work is done and a feeling of gratification brings a smile upon your salty, sunburned face.

After catching your breath, the moment begins to sink in. A warm gulf breeze swoops across the island, cooling the hard-earned sweat beading down your salt-caked body. You feel the soft crystals of pristine white sand between your toes, then realize your footprints are the only visible disruptions upon the beach. For the twisted-mind folk, like me, a fleeting thought of claimed land rights runs through your mind as if you landed on the moon itself. The possibilities that wait are endless, with choices abound.

Once you set camp among the swaying palm trees, hidden behind the scrambling shrubs of the coin vine, you are left with only time to fill. If you are a sportsman, you can take a moment to throw a line in the flats and try your luck with game fish, such as the tarpon. You just want to hang out? Work on your tan? The option is there -- and, if you hate tan lines, the intimate setting allows you to be discreet and free. I used to fill my time with snorkeling, swimming and spear fishing, although, the most-coveted times were the twilight hours, when I was able to enjoy an infamous Florida sunset while tipping back some of Kentucky's finest, toasting to another safe and successful day of paddling.

1

This was one of the experiences I had a year and a half before I attempted circumnavigating the Florida peninsula. I found a paddling trail along the southwestern waters of the Gulf Coast, the Great Calusa Blueway. Over the course of a weekend, I made a float plan and shipped out to paddle a 60-mile section. For the reasons listed above, I fell in love with the idea after spending a night on Picnic Island, overlooking the Sanibel Causeway. When I finished the section and returned to Ocala, Fla., I had a craving for more of these experiences. I hit the internet and did further research.

The Florida Greenways and Trails website directed me to the grand-daddy of all the paddling trails, the Florida Circumnavigational Saltwater Paddling Trail. Also recognized as the "CT," it is estimated to be a 1,515-mile sea kayaking trail that encompasses every Florida coastal habitat.

The idea of a paddling trail circumnavigating the Florida coastline was introduced in the late 1980s by a paddler. By 2005, the Office of Greenways and Trails began developing and mapping the new paddling trail. In 2007, the CT was designated a National Recreation Trail that was divided into 26 different segments. In 2009, it had its first thru paddler. Paddlers navigate 1,500 miles through salt marshes, mangroves, barrier island dune systems, marine sanctuaries, aquatic preserves, state parks, and national parks, such as the Everglades.

The Florida Greenways and Trails has created a fantastic website that includes all the information needed to make an attempt to paddle the trail. Would-be paddlers are able to print a complete set of maps, a well-laid out data book, scope out a suggested gear list, use the recommendations from prior long-distance paddlers or contact trail angels, who are willing to help you along your journey. [The term "trail angel" is widely used in the long-distance community, referring to people who are willing to go out of their way and carry out a small act of kindness. It could be as simple as giving you a lift into town for a resupply, allowing you to sleep in their yard, take a shower or cook you a meal, basically anything that makes your excursion that much easier.]

Using this website, I began my preparation. I printed out the complete set of color maps, cut them out and marked potential end-of-day (EOD) campsites. I studied each map as if I were about to take a statistics exam, spending hours on preparing a very detailed itinerary. The gear list became more like a Christmas list. I tacked the list on a wall in my room, next to a magic marker. With every new online purchase, I celebrated by drawing a line through the item, unwrapping

2

it, showing it off to my roommates, then placing it into the corner with the other newly acquired gear.

During these preparatory months, I had very little time for practice paddles, so I continued to study the data and well-thought-out itinerary. I was hell-bent on doing this as an unsupported paddle, so I chose not to reach out to any prior paddlers, trail angels or even let the Florida Paddling Association know I was attempting a thru paddle. I was running the show and I wouldn't have it any other way.

However, word got out; I couldn't hold it to myself any longer. Family and friends caught wind of it and the news spread like a Southern California wildfire. At the time, I was an educator on summer break, moonlighting as a bartender. One day, I received a call from my principal about my contract renewal. As the phone call progressed, I realized this was the defining moment. After some deliberation, I decided to pull the trigger and begin to cut ties with the societal world. Respectfully, I declined the renewal, ended the phone call, took a deep breath, then exhaled a gasp -- a somewhat uncertain "shit." Don't get me wrong, I was ready. I had all the necessary gear, a solid float plan and the finances were in order, but when I hung up the phone that day, everything seemed a little more real.

Enthused about the new turn of events, I started wrapping up loose ends. During the day, I would pull my kayak into the yard, wash it down and work on securing my gear and then put it all back inside before I went to serve adult beverages to the local patrons. The bar caught wind of my impending departure and began to mess around with my schedule. I took the initiative and cut ties with my last revenue stream in order to focus on the final steps.

August was coming to an end; I was unemployed and more eager to start than ever. As a symbolic gesture, it made sense to choose Sept. 1 as my send-off date. It was easy to remember and it was a holiday weekend.

Using the recommendation from the Florida Greenways and Trails website, I called the first few state parks and reserved campsites. The young lady on the phone told me which campsites were closest to the water and was excited to hear about my journey. The longer we talked, the more flirtatious the conversation became. By the time business was concluded, she wished me safe and happy travels. I was overcome with butterflies and goose pimples crept up and down my arms. It could've been caused by the flirtatious nature of the call, but I believe it had more to do with the overwhelming excitement of coming another step closer to beginning my adventure.

The next step was figuring out how I was going to get someone to drive me six hours to the Florida-Alabama border with a 16-foot kayak on top of their car. Six hours wasn't that difficult to sell, but when I reminded them about the drive back, prospective drivers became a little more hesitant. Luckily, I had the holiday weekend on my side. In 2014, Sept. 1 was part of Labor Day weekend, which opened a few more options to get me to the trailhead. Some close friends stepped up and offered me a ride, but traveling with the kayak eliminated many of them. Time was running out -- I went to my ace in the hole.

My good friend, Barry, happened to have the day off and was very receptive when I asked him to help a brother out. It seems fitting to describe our friendship by using the characters from the 1960s television show, "Gilligan's Island." It might be a little dated, but it's quite familiar. Barry is larger than life, at the time a 35-year-old, scruffed-up version of the character Skipper; a good-natured man with a strong, yet portly physique, sensitive about his hair loss, but confident and charismatic enough to still charm the ladies. He has a warm-hearted disposition and always watches over his best pal to make sure he doesn't do anything too stupid.

Whereas I would be the loyal, goofball, little buddy known as Gilligan. Try not to read too far into it, I wouldn't describe myself too much like Gilligan, other than the slender build and a touch of arrested-youth syndrome. I'm simply explaining the similarities of the friendship. The adventures we shared together in the past led us to this moment and my transportation problem was solved. I was to crash at his apartment the night before and we were to hit the road at daybreak on our six-hour tour.

The days leading up to my departure were spent sitting at patio bars and on lounge chairs, saying goodbye to my friends and sharing my anticipation. At last the day came where we would prep the kayak and strap her down to the car. It was quite comical. We had a 16-foot kayak strapped to the roof of a four-door coupe. The kayak's nose lined up evenly with the front bumper, but the tail went well beyond the rear end of the car. For safety reasons, I dug out an orange bandana and tied it to the back rudder system. Once the gear was loaded and the kayak secured, we took the night off and attended a few last-minute parties.

Throughout the evening, we played the game "just one more beverage, then we'll go," knowing damn well we were leaving at daybreak. That wasn't how it all went down. Last call came at 1:45 a.m., so we ordered our final rounds and went to Barry's apartment. Almost immediately, Barry passed out on his bed, leaving me to my thoughts, which were racing. I was amped and I had a full head of

4

liquor. There wasn't a chance in hell I was going to get any sleep. II sat on the outside patio, sipping bourbon as the sun breached the horizon.

Around 5 a.m., I walked back inside the apartment to start a pot of coffee. Not knowing when my next shower would be, I decided to at least wash the booze off me. By the time I got out of the shower, Barry was up and waiting; we hopped in the coupe and drove north.

The first couple hours was a quiet ride -- with the exception of what was racing through my head. It's an odd feeling, truly hard to describe, the anticipation spread through my body, causing a heap of nausea in my stomach. I sat there staring at the passing billboards, trying to keep my mind occupied. When we stopped for gas, I forced myself to eat crappy gas station food, even though I had no appetite. Barry sensed the tension in the air, every once in a while striking up a conversation about some off-beat topic. Somehow the conversation would steer its way back to the trip, causing me to deflect using one-word answers. From what I can remember, that's how most of the car ride went.

Signs for Big Lagoon State Park in Perdido, Fla., started to appear on the roadside. Suddenly, I remembered I didn't have any drinking water. In fear of the kayak ramp not having a spigot, we stopped at a gas station, where I purchased three liters, then drove to the park entrance. At the gate, after paying an entrance fee, the ranger gave us a map and directions. The road inside the park led us past a large campground, fishing docks, pavilions, and amphitheater and beach areas marked off for swimming. They might as well have been nonexistent for I had blinders on, much like a racehorse leaving the gates, concentrating solely on the road that led to the ramp.

Once we pulled into the parking lot, we pulled the kayak off the car. During the process, I realized both of the neoprene hull covers were missing -- and then the kayak slipped from my grip, ripping the rudder off the boat. There I was, holding the rudder in one hand as the boat lay on the hot pavement, connected only by the steel steering cables. I looked up at Barry, eyes wide and mouth open in disbelief.

We walked the kayak a couple hundred feet to the waterline. I grabbed a coil of paracord and lashed the rudder back to the boat. The rudder remained inoperable, but at least it wasn't going to hang in the water, adding to the kayak's drag. We made a few more trips to the car to grab the rest of the gear. Dripping sweat from my forehead, I stood at the ramp, looking down at the gear, trying to recall how I had stored it all securely back at the house in Ocala. Little by little, I stowed it away, thinking of what I might possibly need while I was paddling. Barry laughed as I sat cursing, wondering why I couldn't get it right. It took three different attempts to finally find enough space for all the gear.

The moment had arrived. Barry shook my hand, took a send-off photo, hugged me and wished me good luck. I pushed the kayak into the water, walked in knee-deep and attempted to sit in the cockpit. That was exactly what I did -- I attempted. The narrow body of the kayak did not allow me to climb in without water pouring over the sides and into the cockpit. "This is going to be a long day" I thought as Barry looked on with a grin and a chuckle. Trying not to allow this doubt to linger, I pulled the boat back up, sat in the cockpit while on the ramp and had Barry shove me off. Of course, Barry expressed his doubts, but I shrugged them off and said I would figure it out along the way. With a quick shove, I was free from the grip of the land and floating cautiously in the warm waters of the bay.

I chose to spend a little time playing around, getting acquainted with the movement of the boat. I quickly learned hip shifts or leans dictated whether or not I stayed afloat. When I felt comfortable, I yelled goodbye to Barry, then began the long paddle eastward. Well, I thought it was east; turned out I had paddled west toward Alabama. Good thing I was paying attention and noticed another kayak ramp that, according to my map, proved I was paddling west. Embarrassed, I circled back toward the ramp. Barry was headed for the car, but caught me trying to sneak past undetected. We shared another laugh, a few digs and some playful banter as I left the security blanket of society behind and embarked upon a journey into a world that is treasured, but often forgotten.

First time in the kayak at Big Lagoon State Park

6

Segments 1 & 2
Big Lagoon - Grayton Beach Park
81 miles

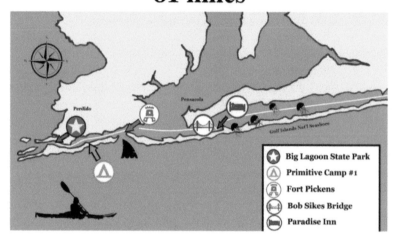

Big Lagoon State Park
Primitive Camp #1
Fort Pickens
Bob Sikes Bridge
Paradise Inn

Follow the white line for my actual paddling route

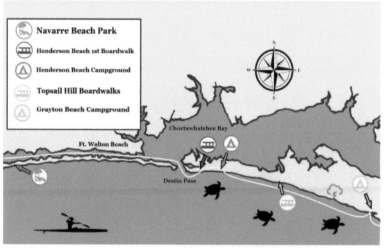

Navarre Beach Park
Henderson Beach 1st Boardwalk
Henderson Beach Campground
Topsail Hill Boardwalks
Grayton Beach Campground

All maps were hand drawn and created by the author
Jeffrey "Treehouse" Buncie

Bull Sharks and Jelly Orbs

Paddle in hand, eyes forward, gazing across the lagoon at the cordgrass dancing in the breeze, I sat waiting for a pleasure craft that was ripping up the calmness of the channel to pass. The oncoming wakes swept under the bow fluidly raising and lowering my boat. My uncertainty and inexperience handling a sea kayak caused me to shift my hips a little too far, compromising the buoyancy of my kayak. There was an uncomfortable amount of water in the cockpit -- and I had only been on the water for a matter of minutes. As the wakes slowed, I continued to paddle across to the beach in the hope of draining the water that was up to my calves.

Along the short paddle, my bear canister, which was intertwined with the deck net, popped out of the boat and other pieces of gear were falling into the water. Snatching up the gear that was bobbing up and down like the crab buoys around me, my kayak began to resemble a homebum's shopping cart. I finally reached the sandy beach with all the misplaced gear.

I banged my knee exiting the kayak and landed face-first in the bay. Grasping whatever part of the boat my one free hand could reach, I kicked as hard as I could to stay afloat. I don't know if you have ever been completely under water, with one hand clutching a paddle as the other holds onto a 16-foot kayak, but I'll tell you it's not a pretty situation. It's especially embarrassing when you're surrounded by multiple boats with half-naked, super-hot females watching. I quickly realized that however the situation was going to end, I would have to act like I meant to do it or laugh it off as a lesson of humility.

I made it to the other side, where I broke out my paracord and reassessed how my gear was to be secured. I was back on the water within an hour with the sun beating down on my pasty, shirtless body. The relentless afternoon sun was adding a red hue to my skin. I ignored the sensation, brushing it off as a short six-mile paddle and pressed on toward the primitive campsite at the east end of Perdido Key. Using a GPS app, I was able to pinpoint where the camp was, but the damage had already been done. My body was radiating heat and the ball of fire in the sky painted a new, brighter color upon my skin. After pitching my tent in a cove behind the sand dunes, I hid in the tent until the sun reached the horizon. It wasn't long before my eyelids became heavy and I drifted off to sleep.

An uncomfortable silence and sweat beading off my body brought me out of my slumber a while later. Feeling uneasy, I sat in my tent, listening to the splashes from the fish feeding in the cove. Hot, still air filled my tent. I unzipped the fly and stepped out to find a starlit sky. A feeling of peace and solitude made me forget -- for a moment -- how the sun had assaulted my body. The evening was mysteriously quiet with a strong moon etching its way through the darkness. I listened to the waves crash across the small barrier island.

Irritated from the stiff, salt-dried shorts across my waist, I realized how secluded the island was and decided to get rid of the cause of the irritation. My shorts came off and not just my mind was free. I enjoyed the cool ocean breeze as it soothed the damage from the sun, while taking a barefoot, bare-ass walk along the moonlit beach. Later, I headed back to the cove, unhinged the tent fly and crawled back into the tent, to return to dreamland.

The sun greeted the morning sky, heating the tent almost instantly. I lifted my head off the cool, damp sand pillow fashioned below the tent's footprint and crawled out to meet the day. Severely low on water, cooking some oatmeal was not an option, so I settled on a protein bar and a bagel. I broke camp with the hope that Fort Pickens, three miles east on Santa Rosa Island, would have potable water.

Rounding Robertson Island, the tide rolled in from the Gulf of Mexico. This would be the first fight I had with an unfavorable tide. I really could've used that rudder tied to the stern of the boat. Every three or four strokes, the movement of the water would cock the boat sideways, continuing the ongoing battle. Halfway across the bay, a dorsal fin appeared, circling round and round, directly where the tide was pushing me. I know enough about sharks to know if you can see dorsal fins stick that far out of the water, from that distance, it's a pretty big shark. Also, being an avid follower of the annual Shark Week festival on TV, the closer I got, I could identify the shark. By using the large dorsal, followed by a second smaller fin and the distinctly pointed tail thrashing through the water, I realized I was being pushed toward a bull shark.

I was also surrounded by hundreds of floating jellyfish. With every stroke I was flinging jellyfish orbs over my head, onto the boat and into the boat. These 6- to 8-inch in diameter jellies I later learned are known as moon jellyfish. They have a very mild sting, but at that moment, I didn't care if they had a sting of the infamous Portuguese man o' war jellies or not.

There were pink balls of jellyfish flying through the air as the tide pushed me closer to one of the most aggressive sharks known to those waters. My arms were moving as fast as a cheetah running through the Serengeti. I came within 20 or 30 yards of the shark before catching what I like to call the shelter of the island. The movement of the water slowed, allowing me to paddle quickly away from the feeding frenzy and jelly hoards. I rounded the island and beached as soon as I could. Two older fishermen were watching and chuckling away. Wiping the sweat from my brow, I joined them in laughing and inquired about a water spigot. They sent me to the restrooms, which provided shade and running water.

While I rehydrated and enjoyed a snack in the shade, I decided to stroll around the grounds. At first glance, the fort appeared barren with the remnants of maybe a few powder rooms. Further investigation led me to find the fort was named after the Revolutionary War hero, Andrew Pickens.

Fort Pickens, built to fortify and defend Pensacola Harbor after the War of 1812, was also used during the Civil War. Lieutenant Adam Slemmer of the Union Army defended the fort from the militia led by the designer of the fort himself, Colonel William Henry Chase. Slemmer was able to hold the fort and, despite many other attempted threats, the Union was able to hold the fort throughout the Civil War, thus making it one of three Southern forts to remain under the Union's control.

The fort is known across the long-distance community as the Northern Terminus of the Florida Trail. The time I spent there allowed me to appreciate both the present and the past. The moment was short-lived, however, because of the fear of my kayak and gear being stolen or the tide pulling it all out to the bay. I made my way toward the restroom and pushed off the beach.

Paddling along Gulf Island National Seashore was not as enjoyable as it sounds. The death-ball sun was in full force, scaring away the clouds and preventing any opportunity for shade. When the afternoon heat reached its peak, my body became overheated and I started seeing floating black dots, which progressed into a long, narrow tunnel. Again, I'm not a genius, but I was pretty sure I was entering the dangerous zone of heat exhaustion. I pulled onto the shore and tried to create some shade. By using the tent fly, I managed to create a sad-looking lean-to. After lying in its shade for a while, with my battery-operated fan doing nothing but circulating hot air, I elected to take my chance with the jellies and stingrays. Wearing a long-sleeve nylon shirt, I walked into the water, pushing aside the jellies and shuffling my feet to disturb the hidden rays, to let the water cool my core.

Once my vision returned to normal, I ate some mac and cheese, and continued toward Pensacola Beach. A storm in the distance motivated me to get to the end-of-day (EOD) goal. To wrap up the day, I paddled under the Bob Sikes Bridge near Gulf Breeze, took a hard right and made my way to a hotel right off the water, the Paradise Inn. The inn provided a dock, clean rooms at a reasonable rate, and an onsite bar and grill, and the staff was friendly and helpful.

They often say a way to a man's heart is a good meal; the way to mine is a tasty burger and a cold beer. The Paradise Inn had both -- and they were just steps away from my home for the evening. Ass-whipped, but with a full stomach, I returned to my room to do a food inventory, some minor repairs, charge my electronics and take a cold shower. Chores done, Day 2 on the water was finally over.

Hiding from the "Death Ball"   **Such a sad, sad lean-to**

Match Made in Pensacola

Rising with the sun and eagerly anticipating my return to the water, I enjoyed a quick continental breakfast, then pulled my kayak back into the water. My upbeat mood was dampened shortly after paddling out. A large advancing thunderstorm forced me to pull over at a picnic shelter on Navarre Beach, 11 miles east of The Paradise Inn. For the next few days, storms forced me to take many breaks and shelter on dry land. In a way, I looked forward to them. They made me pull over and rest my battered body.

The headaches came when the storms approached and the water of the sound would become a nasty bay chop. These moments forced me to sharpen my balancing techniques. At one point, it became so choppy and chaotic, I started talking to my kayak. Soon talking turned to singing, then all of a sudden, we connected and I felt like we were dancing. I couldn't help but sing a song, "Frank and Lola" by one of my favorite artists, Jimmy Buffett.

The song is about a couple having a second honeymoon in Pensacola. This particular song stuck out because at the time, I was paddling through Pensacola Bay and in the song, Frank is called Frankie. The coincidences didn't stop there -- Frankie has two syllables, such as my last name, Buncie (pronounced "Bun-cee"), plus it rhymes! Not too long after, the lyrics became Buncie and Lola, and we were on our first honeymoon in Pensacola. Seems odd enough, doesn't it? But my kayak and I shared a bond -- and that was how Miss Lola and I became a couple writing our history.

Over the next couple days, I was only able to paddle 33 miles through multiple storms, where I couldn't see past the bow of the kayak due to the hostile rain. I disregarded the cramps that crept into my muscles and dealt with the sun poisoning I acquired through the overcast sky. In addition to the uncomfortable, nauseating pain caused from overexposure to the sun, my face fluctuated from red to purple. There was no way to stop the damage. My lips cracked severely and the taste of iron lurked in my mouth. My new reflection in the water was that of a true castaway, stranded on the open water. All of this didn't stop me from moving forward, although it did cost a little more money. I accepted that if I was going to continue putting my body through hell,

I would at least escape the unfavorable evening weather and pamper myself with a comfortable hotel room.

Uncharted territory was the theme of Day 5, when I would surpass both my personal goals and experience level. For the first time, I would be on the water longer than four days -- and I was entering the open waters of the Gulf of Mexico. It sounds asinine to admit I was on this journey and had never been in open water, but I had the persistence of a naïve child learning to walk. I knew I would capsize or flip over a few dozen times, I just hoped I would be close to shore when it happened.

I went through the shallow rollers of the Choctawhatchee Bay and into what I thought was known as East Pass (Destin Pass). I ended up paddling past the Destin Bridge, which marked the inlet to the Gulf and found myself at a jet ski/kayak rental business, where I took a short break.

When I left the safe sands of the beach, it took me a matter of seconds to find myself in the next unfortunate situation. The outgoing tide had such a force, it swiftly pushed me into the outreaching dock, hastily pinning me up against the pylons. The water's python-like grip and I were in a battle for my freedom. The port side became the dock's pylons, lodging me against the wooden structure, which rendered the paddle useless. While I held the paddle on top of the dock, I grabbed the lowest decking board, attempting to pull myself forward, then in reverse. Both were unsuccessful attempts. I was, to say the least, not off to a great start. After what seemed like hours, but was actually a few minutes of struggling, a jet skier came to my rescue. The surge made the rescue more difficult by slamming his jet ski into the dock a few times, but he was able to pull my kayak free and I was able to paddle again. I expressed my thanks as he extended his sympathies, adding a simple "good luck" before driving away.

Into the pass I went. Large fishing boats whipped by me, picking up the wakes and bouncing my kayak around like a pinball. The struggle was real -- the water was very alive and, for an early Friday afternoon, there seemed to be a lot of boats running the pass. Still in a heightened state of fright from my prior situation, adrenaline kept my arms churning, while fear kept my eyes peeled. I watched the wakes pour over the deck of the kayak and into the uncovered cockpit. It was as if the Kraken itself was reaching up from the depths of the sea and getting Lola within its grip.

With every stroke my mind traveled deeper into an abyss. Would I be able to make it through the pass? That was when I realized how water reacts once disrupted by so many factors. Think about lying in a bathtub full of water. While lying there, you begin to move your arms up and down. The water has no place to go, so you receive a bounce back from the original displacement sent to the edge of the bathtub and back to the original object. The arms still exist and continue to move causing even more pandemonium. Now imagine a little plastic boat trying to stay afloat in the middle of all this … that was my position in the middle of Destin Pass.

For a moment, I stopped flailing about and took the time to embrace the chaos. I slowed my breathing and searched for a solution, using patterns to better understand the rhythm. Reaching down, I brought a handful of saltwater to my face and wiped away the fear.

By holding the paddle perpendicularly across the cockpit, I used small lengthy strokes to propel forward. The broader strokes added a lower center of gravity allowing me to stay upright. Slowly, I began to make headway. I attacked the wakes fearlessly, turning the bow into the mouth of the crashing beasts preparing for the next. Using zig-zag motions, I was able to navigate through following my instincts and got around the jetty into the rhythmic waves of the Gulf.

Three miles of serene paddling through the blue waters of the Florida Panhandle I arrived at what I thought was the campground boardwalk. What I *didn't* know is that there are multiple beach accesses to Henderson Beach State Park, the first state park at which I had reserved a campsite. Recognizable from the water by its five beach boardwalks, it is the first public beach when paddling from the pass. The fifth boardwalk leads you on a lengthy walk into the campground that features 60 sites with electricity, shower houses and fancy crushed shell/rock tent platforms setup for RV campers. No frills or thrills here -- other than the white sandy beaches, emerald waters and famous Florida sunsets.

Stoked to be less than a mile from the campground, yet still perturbed about choosing the wrong boardwalk, I enjoyed a breather on the beach. Upon trying to re-enter the kayak, I learned another lesson. Entering the cockpit on a calm surface was difficult itself, but attempting to time a break, hop in without scraping my shins and trying to paddle beyond the break before the next wave crashed and filled the cockpit, was a whole new ballgame. Failing miserably again and again, I looked at my hand cart, used for portaging, then prepared Lola for a walk on the beach.

Once I secured her to the cart and began to pull, I realized she was too heavy. The cart was useless on both the wet and the dry sand. I was going to have to drag Lola the remaining half-mile to get to the boardwalk. Devoting all the energy I had left, I committed myself to

14

getting Lola to that safe haven. I pulled Lola 10 yards at a time, often falling on my ass, only to stand back up and somehow repetitively hit the back of my ankles.

At last we reached the golden stairway in the sand leading to the campground. While preparing to leave Lola under the boardwalk, I had another thought. My mind was exhausted, but a burst of intuitiveness reminded me I would have to carry 30 to 40 pounds of gear over the boardwalk to the campsite. In a moment of ingenuity, I lashed the paddle to the hand cart, making a wheeled traveling suitcase. After the way it had gone, I wouldn't be lying when I say this was the proudest moment of the day. It all came together and I walked my tired body straight to camp. After cleaning up in a hot shower, I laid in the tent, trying to process the events of the day. Exhaustion soon had me asleep.

Pinned against a dock

Enjoying the seashore   **My travel luggage**

Newton's First Law

Much like an algebraic equation, lessons can be introduced, but retention and recall will lead you to the correct solution. I apologize for bringing algebra into the world of sunshine and seashells, but it holds value -- especially when you overlook a pivotal step once learned before. The previous day was the introduction as Day Six would take me through the process of retention and recall.

The walk back to the beach was an opportunity to pump up my psyche. When I arrived at the shore, the surf was calm, allowing me to jump in Lola and track the flat water at an impressive rate. It also allowed me to encounter my first green sea turtles. The elusive creatures were having a field day breaking the surface, then disappearing below, as if they were playing a game of peek-a-boo. The morning hours passed, with the surf picking up in the off-shore winds. A lack of confidence kept me on the water until I reached the first entry point of Topsail Hill State Reserve in Santa Rosa, Fla.

I stopped to explore the "must-stop" destination, according to the website's data book, a mile and a half before the campground. I was making excellent time, and it was a good time for an expedition.

The surf brought me in with the crests rolling over the stern. Slowing our momentum, the waves lined the cockpit, capsizing my poor Lola once again. After gathering my belongings and draining her, I enjoyed a hike along the camp's hiking trail. The barefoot hike through the sugar sand and sandspurs led me to a coastal lake, where I had a light lunch of protein bars and peanut butter.

The afternoon hours were coming to an end, leaving me with little time to catch the tram at the campground boardwalk. Topsail is an unique campground about a mile behind the dunes, so they provide a tram for the campers that runs every two hours -- and with the tram comes a schedule restricting the freedom of tiresome travelers. The last tram was at 7:30 and I sure as hell didn't want to walk the mile, so I hopped back into the kayak. Well, not quite. I tried a half-dozen times before my spirit was broken by the unmanageable surf.

The exhausting process of capsizing goes as follows: Standing in thigh-deep water, holding both sides of the cockpit with the paddle gripped on the opposite side of entry; counting the seconds between the sets of the oncoming waves, you propel your lower body out of the water and into a small 2- by 3-foot hole. Coordinating time and motion, as a bobsledder jumping into their sled, is the most important factor. If your fluidity is not on point, you are faced with two options: One, you scrape the skin off your knee and shins or two, you miss the timing all together and end up face-first in the water. If you find yourself in the cockpit, but miscalculate the immediate act of paddling, you end up with a cockpit full of water or capsize from the ambush of collapsing waves. If either happens, when you go over, your kayak and exposed gear gets hammered by the unforgiving surf.

When these unfortunate events happen, not only do you get tossed around, but you have to collect your gear, paddle and kayak, and then drag it ashore. Once you reach the shore, you have to flip it over to get as much water out as you can, then use a bilge pump (which I did not have) or a scoop (such as a cut-open 32-ounce Gatorade bottle) to scrape out the remaining water. So, here you are, you've gotten all the water out, tied your gear back on and approach the water, only to do it all over again. Not only is this time-consuming, but it is very physically demanding.

As I stated earlier, I went through this process a half-dozen times before having my spirit broken. On the last attempt, the crashing surf broke my seat, scraped my back, bruised my shoulder and skinned my shins. After collecting my gear, I sat in bewilderment watching the sun disappear.

Convinced I was not going to be able to beat the surf, the only logical conclusion I could reach was to pull the kayak behind me while walking it just beyond the break. We all know where pulling her on land got me, so I pushed her out and scuffled in waist- to chest-deep water. My motivation was fueled by Sir Isaac Newton's First Law of Motion -- an object in motion remains in motion.

The sun abandoned its post as I approached the boardwalk from the water. I was finally here, so I pulled Lola onto the beach, sat down and collected my thoughts. With a blank stare, I shook my head and snapped out of the stupor. Then I noticed my blue dry box, usually clipped to the deck net, was missing, presenting a new dilemma. That little box was my lifeline and the only box I trusted to keep my cell phone, cash, passport and other necessities safe from the water. I jumped up, looked around and frantically searched through the surf. It was only a matter of minutes before the light would be gone.

I ran along the surf, looking in the salty suds within the break and among the tidal pools. Down the beach, about a hundred yards or so, I saw the reflection of a foreign object floating just beyond the break. It was my dry box! Feeling like I was moving in slow motion, I ran through the surf toward it, like I was reuniting with a long-lost lover. After I dove after it, I raised it high above and yelled out a very cynical "Ha, ha!" mocking Poseidon, himself.

When I returned to Lola, a couple in their 40s approached me and asked if everything was alright. They had witnessed the events unfolding from afar. The gentleman, from Jacksonville, Fla., was fishing and offered me a beer while I explained to him and his lady friend from Albuquerque, what had happened. One beer became two, then three, while we shared pleasantries and conversation. They were camping at the campground, too, and after many offers to help me out, they wouldn't take "no" for an answer. Jacksonville helped me carry Lola up to the boardwalk and Albuquerque carried some gear. The 7:30 p.m. tram had long come and gone, so we walked to the camp. When we found the sign, I thanked them, we parted ways and I began my camp routine.

A blanket of mosquitoes forced me to skip dinner and settle for a few bars that I ate later in the shower house. With nothing to do but think, my stubborn mind refused to focus on all the shitty situations that had occurred thus far. I laughed them off as I walked back to the tent.

I woke up thirsty a while later and found Mother Nature providing a late-night light show in the sky. I admired the lightning storm through the early morning hours until it came time to pull my body off the ground. My body, on the other hand, had a different idea. Torn, beaten and battered, I decided to take a zero day. "Zero day" is a term used in the long-distance community to recognize a non-paddling day or zero miles progress made. That day, I slept in, rested my body, did some research on spray skirts and searched the internet for pointers on how to enter a sea kayak from deeper water.

Feeling confident and well-rested, I approached the next morning's surf with ease. For most of the day, I was able to pull over for shelter before the storms hit. As my confidence grew, I decided to push it a little further. Unfortunately, a band of storms rolled in a little quicker than I expected and my only land option was a barren beach with private property beyond the dunes.

The skies went from gray to a deep purple. I was stuck, with nowhere to go. The thunder crashed, lightning lit up the sky with sharp meticulous streaks, and the wind intensified the open water, picking up the wave heights to a point I disappeared behind them. Not knowing what to do, I landed on the beach and sat as low as I could next to Lola as the rain came. A bolt of lightning struck in front of me just as the waves broke. With no cover and no safety, I flipped Lola over and crawled underneath, supporting her weight with my body. For 20 minutes I was pinned, cheek-to-cheek with the sand, as the rain hit. Small splotches of sand spit up, stinging my face. The lightning was honing in on my body's energy and all I could do was wait it out, hoping I'd pull through so the journey could continue. Eventually, the storm passed. My gratitude for not being killed or injured was verbally discussed with Mother Nature and then I hauled ass to Grayton Beach State Park.

To enter the campground at Grayton Beach, you must enter through an inlet. What I didn't know was, at low tide, the inlet becomes a tidal pool leading to a coastal lake. After a short portage, I paddled up to the unmarked campsites along the water. I beached, walked up to the office and learned I was already at my reserved site for the evening. Back in August, when my first reservations were made, the young lady on the phone recommended site #20. She was right. It had a magnificent view overlooking the bay. The ranger told me a general store, where I could resupply my food rations, grab some sandwiches, cold beer and bait, if needed, was a mile up the road.

When I returned to the campground, I met a father and his son from Texas. The son, Brian, in his mid-20s, spoke with a long southern drawl, and was intrigued by the stories I shared. His slightly intoxicated father invited me to hang out for a few beers. A few hours later, quiet hours came around, so I bid them farewell and many thanks. Before I left, they shook my hand and said, "We will never forget this." During the walk back to my site, it hit me -- not only was I making personal memories, but I, too, was becoming a memory to others.

My time on the water now surpassed eight days. I had completed the first two segments, totaling around 80 miles or so, and persevered through the toughest of times. My body had felt the effects of color change. Feeling like a chameleon, I went through the progression of ghostly white to lobster red, overly poisonous purple to a new rusty tan. I fought the tides, challenged the sea life and faced thunderstorms. With every obstacle thrown my way I had gained confidence through experience. Staying on course, I remained motivated to face the upcoming segments. My thoughts led me to believe the worst had to be over, I mean, hell, what else could go wrong?

Segment 3
Grayton Beach - St. Joseph State Park
63 miles

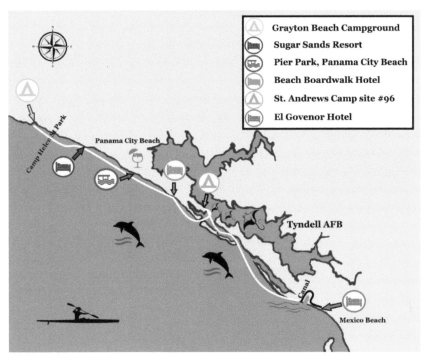

Grayton Beach Campground

Sugar Sands Resort

Pier Park, Panama City Beach

Beach Boardwalk Hotel

St. Andrews Camp site #96

El Govenor Hotel

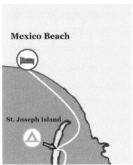

All maps were hand drawn and created by the author Jeffrey "Treehouse" Buncie

The Inch Became a Mile

Over the next 80 miles, the bountiful sea life along the sugar sand beaches of St. Andrews Bay put me in a euphoric trance. Surpassing milestone after milestone, I faced impassable breakers, tormenting weather and caloric deficiency. I paddled onward, placing a positive spin on the otherwise unfavorable outcomes. Sure as the sun would rise and fall with the day, mistakes were made and the calamity continued. There's just something about being able to keep pace with a bale of sea turtles or a manta ray darting out of the water, feasting on the floating plankton, that puts a smile upon your face and longing for more. The captivating sights kept my arms moving and heart racing as I continued the adventure along the Florida Panhandle.

After I left the tidal pool of Grayton Park, early morning storms didn't take long to push me off the water to a quaint beachside park, known as Deer Lake. Thankfully, the pavilions provided shelter from the bands of passing storms. Once the storms withdrew, I was lucky to return to the water before the winds elevated the mayhem of the crashing waves. Unfortunately, I was forced off the water yet again by another thunderstorm four miles later at Camp Helen State Park. Recognizable by the deteriorating pier standing high above the water, you can really get an appreciation for what a storm surge does to these beaches. The data book claimed there was a pavilion at the park, so I escaped the wrath of the storm while enjoying a carb-filled lunch and an afternoon nap.

Late in the afternoon, the storms dispersed, but left behind bombarding waves. Six, count them, six times, I attempted the entry, experiencing the emotions Tom Hanks portrayed in the movie "Castaway." You know the scene, the one where he tries to paddle over the breakers in his raft, but doesn't have his outhouse sail quite yet. The waves take him down crashing and his leg gets struck with coral. Yea, that was me, minus the coral, of course. In the process, Lola's seat got ripped off, leaving a nasty battle scar on my lower back. As the saltwater stung the fresh wound, I sat on the beach with the sun retreating behind the horizon.

I was finally able to lash the seat back on and miraculously paddle beyond the break into the moonlight. A few miles from the resort, I noticed my maps were missing. How could this be? Not only were my maps missing, my phone was inaccessible. I was flying blind and I'd be damned if I was exiting the water before I arrived at the resort. In the midst of dark, a rogue wave upended me and pushed me through the surf to the sand. A night fisherman witnessed the catastrophe, so I gathered my belongings and limped up to him for information. At night, along the beach, there are no indications of what building is a condo or what building might be a hotel. They all look the same -- windows glowing from the incandescent lights within. I had to break down and ask somebody. The fisherman confirmed I had reached the Sugar Sands Resort. After learning that, I was glad the rogue wave did me the solid, stopping me from paddling farther.

My next stop was the front lobby, where I met the friendly clerk, who couldn't grasp the concept that "I paddled here." The day ended with me laying in my fluffy bed after a soothing hot shower.

The next day gave me clear skies and the water was smoother than an oiled thunderbolt. Ahead of me was an easy four miles to reach Pier Park in Panama City, Fla., known for its fishing pier and hub of stores across the street. As I approached, I couldn't escape all the fishing lines coming from above, slightly perturbing the fishermen along the pier. I broke free from the entanglement, then beached next to a dad and his daughter. After a trust-building conversation, he said he would keep an eye on Lola while I went to the nearby shops and grabbed some lunch. Naturally, I didn't fully trust the people visiting the beach that day, so I grabbed my paddle and a day pack filled with my most expensive equipment, then headed to the pier bathrooms to clean up.

My excitement grew when I discovered there was a Margaritaville, Jimmy Buffett's own, across the street from the pier. I would treat myself to some fish tacos and a few margaritas. The lovely bartender, Jordan, and her coworkers did their job to keep me around. One by one, my story circulated around the restaurant, garnering endless questions and compliments. Time flew by, as the beverages came and went, it was getting late. I still had to acquire a waterproof phone case and visit the grocery, so I bid adieu to the staff and did my land-bearing chores.

When I returned to Lola, the dad and daughter had left, leaving Lola unattended, but she was all accounted for and intact. You would figure with all the problems I'd had entering the water prior to that day, there was no way I was going to successfully paddle off the beach in

22

my slightly inebriated state, right? Well, it surprised the hell out of me, too, but I was able to send off on the first attempt. The one kicker was actually a kicker. I sat down and paddled off, straddling Lola and using my legs as make-shift outriggers. Once I was beyond the break and paddling, I was able to bring one leg in at a time without dumping over. I felt like Albert Einstein -- until my arrogance must've shown through to Poseidon. The gusts blew through my windswept hair; the waves fiercely attacked Lola as if she was a Homeric ship sailing to Ithaca.

The next five miles proved to be the hardest I had to earn yet. My mind was so wrapped up in staying afloat, I ended up paddling past the Beach Boardwalk Resort by a half-mile. I dragged Lola out of the water and up to a cabana used to rent beach chairs. Debating what I should do, I approached the situation like I had earlier at the beach. I packed up, took my paddle and left a note apologizing to the cabana employees. The note stated I would return early in the morning to retrieve my kayak. I threw on my pack and started the hike back to the resort. The resort had an eerie "The Shining" feel. The employees were friendly, but there was something off, giving the lobby area a desolate feeling, which didn't bother me -- all I wanted by that time was a soft bed to lay my head.

**Those
damn ol'
yellow flags**

**Stuck in
another
lightning
storm**

23

The Mexico Beach Disaster

My stiff, plank-like body wasn't agreeing with me upon awakening in the morning. I had to follow through on my word to retrieve Lola before the cabana opened, so first thing, I hiked the half-mile back. In August, I had secured a waterside campsite at St. Andrews State Park, which was seven miles from the beach cabana. With a short day ahead of me, I was able to take advantage of and enjoy my surroundings.

The morning was filled with shifty sea turtles playing their games, an occasional jellyfish and fevers of stingrays gliding beneath me along the seafloor. I was enjoying the paddle immensely. In fact, I was enjoying myself so much, I paddled past the jetties beyond the inlet leading to the campsites.

After a well-earned breather from fighting the incoming tide on the rocks, I reentered the inlet and allowed the tide to push me into the bay. I was welcomed immediately by a majestic manta ray propelling his body above the flats of the bay. For a split second, time froze as he reached his jump's apex, glanced over and gave me a wink, just before returning below with a crowd-pleasing belly flop. Never in my life had I seen such a sight. I was impressed to the point I found myself shouting, "10! A flipping 10!"

Moments later, I was lost, peering across the water to the unmarked sites. Confused, I pulled up to an empty site and asked a neighboring camper where I could find site #96. He told me I was on site #96. "What an accidental win," I thought. He also told me the registration building was about three-quarters of a mile away and offered me a ride there on his golf cart. After the short ride, we came to a building occupied by an ill-tempered lady, sitting behind a counter, watching over the contents in the camp store. Her obtrusive attitude was nastier than the smell coming from the outhouses. I was flying too high to allow her to beat me down, so I checked in and started walking back to my site. There's not much to say about the park, I kept to myself and hung out at camp most of the day.

Later in the day, while walking back to my campsite after a hot shower, a lady rolled up in her golf cart and called my one-tent camp a "cute campsite." At first, she seemed interested as I told her some stories. As her questions progressed, she became oddly rude. After I had addressed each question, she would refute them, like I had given

24

her the wrong answer. The conversation came to a screeching halt when she called me a "trust-fund baby." She had found the one comment that ate me up inside. I knew I busted my ass for years to be able to give this thing a go, but something about her slowly chipped away at my euphoric state. I walked away, cursing her negative vibes, deeming her the "trust-fund bitch" and returned to my camp. Looking across the bay, I regained my peace as the sun set. I spent the evening relaxing in my tent, preparing for the 27-mile crossing of Tyndall Air Force Base, near Panama City.

This was a big day for me. The Air Force base is a strictly enforced, no-camping zone; therefore, making the paddle an all-or-nothing day. I don't believe I'd ever paddled this type of distance in one day. Taking these factors into account, it motivated me to get up at sunrise in order to get a jump on the restless afternoon waters I'd come to know.

The morning mirrored the prior day's paddle with sea turtle sightings. I was blessed with a group of four racing in the water beside me. Just when I thought the "10" couldn't be beat, I witnessed another manta breaching the flats, only to top his friend's belly flop with a back flip. What?! I was completely blown away. Riding high on the spectacular sights, I overlooked eating lunch. Making excellent time, I chose a beach in the distance to stop for lunch. This so-called beach became more like a mirage across a barren desert. My body was missing its required calorie count to push through the choppy bay water, so I had to choose a much closer, smaller, shadeless beach.

For three long days, my stove had not worked properly, mostly in the morning hours, but on this day, the day I would need the most energy, it chose not to work at all. Ravenously searching through my food bag, the only items I had left that didn't require cooking was a three-pound jar of peanut butter and a protein bar. Although I was making good time, I wasn't able to gather enough wood to have a fire adequate enough to warm water, let alone boil it. On the bright side, I had a spoon. I accepted the fact I would be eating peanut butter until I reached the other side of the Air Force base, so in the jar my spoon went.

The day, I'm sad to say, did not get any better from there. Once I was back on the water, the longer stretches started to take a toll on my lower body, numbing my legs from the tip of my toes to my hips. I had to stop multiple times, which slowed my progress. It was nearing 5 p.m. when I took my final break along the last stretch of breakers. I prepared myself for the last five or six miles, downed a few more spoonfuls of peanut butter and attempted to reenter. (Disclaimer: If you ever find

25

yourself along this journey, I would highly recommend you stay in your boat until you reach Mexico Beach, especially around this bend.)

The set breakers along this land made it impossible to reenter at this point. I cannot stress this enough. Sure, I was weak from the lack of calories and probably dehydrated from the long, hot stretches, but I busted out all my tricks and still found myself unable to reenter. Reaching for another trick I had in the bag, I decided to walk within the breakers with Lola following closely behind. I figured if I got to the bend, the breakers would lighten up and give me a shot.

After a long mile of wading through the surf, I arrived at the bend. To my dismay, the bend sheltered the winds I was now facing, making it even more impossible. The last mile between the breakers chewed up the twilight hours, so I prepared Lola for another shot of night-time paddling. Determined, I pulled out my Coast Guard-approved boat light, put the batteries in and was disappointed yet again. After a minimal time on the water, the connections had completely rusted out. Nothing was going right and I was faced with another challenge, but every man has his breaking point.

In the dark of night, I made the decision to pull Lola behind a restricted entry sign beyond the scrub. I stashed her with yet another note, saying that if found, she was my home and please do not steal, I will return in the morning. I Googled the address of the El Governor Hotel, hoping the space gods would find a route I could walk. A canal led me to a boat ramp along U.S. 98, which was a straight shot to the hotel. The hike was just over three and a half miles along a shoulderless highway. Once I reached the road, I strapped on my headlamp and walked until a gas station appeared.

The gas station was a mile from the hotel, but this birdie couldn't wait. I ate more terrible gas station food and downed a large fountain drink before heading back to the road. When I arrived at the hotel, I was lucky they had a room for the weekend. There was a triathlon kicking off the next day and the hotel was taking full advantage of the high demand. Still famished, I located a Subway a half-mile down the road, and after a shower and a change of clothes, I indulged. Two foot-long subs later, I was in a food-induced coma that sent my weary head to bed. The Mexico Beach disaster, as I would later call it, was finally over.

Up Where I Belong

Once upon a time, before the widely accepted Uber existed, a tougher time for travelers to get around existed. Not 12 hours before, I had walked three and a half miles and there I was again, retracing the steps to rescue Lola from the dunes of the Air Force base. Before leaving the hotel, I decided to reserve the room for another evening in order to prepare and reboot for the upcoming section. When I left the hotel, I saw the triathlon athletes were proudly sporting their medals around the town.

Following the road back to the ramp, I stopped for a coffee and passed a boat fishing by the holes of the flats. When I found Lola, she was undisturbed and the morning waters were calm. With little trouble at all, I was back on the water headed toward the hotel. Not long after, I saw the same fishing boat and I wondered what the three guys on the boat thought. The first time they saw me, I was on foot and now, out of the blue, I arrive by kayak? It would've been great to be a fly on that boat.

The three-and-a-half-mile paddle to the hotel was uneventful. When I approached the beach property, I attempted to exit among the surf like a pro. Think of a side-straddle horseback rider dismounting, both legs hanging over one side, allowing the waves to pull you in closer before launching to stand firmly on the seafloor before the force pulls you and the boat sideways into the break. I was set up for success, but once I launched -- kerplunk! I misjudged the depth of the water. It was so bad, I never even touched the seafloor. You know what happened next, don't you? The waves crashed and dragged me and Lola right up to the beach -- in front of the vacation goers sunbathing in the sand. The hotel had a spot under the second-story bar to stash Lola, so I gathered my gear to dry out, clean and do inventory.

Back in my room, I became confused as to what time of day it actually was. The town of Mexico Beach is on an imaginary line where you are able to time travel. The time zones fluctuate between Eastern and Central times. My room at the hotel allowed me to be a recurring time traveler. For example, when I was in the bathroom, it registered Eastern, and, if I stepped on the balcony, it registered a whole hour behind in Central. To get behind the mystery of the time zones, I asked at the front desk before walking to the grocery store next to the

Subway. The receptionist assured me the hotel followed the Eastern Time Zone, allowing a late check out the next morning.

While the laundry was drying, I resupplied for the next stretch, adding to my arsenal eggs, flavored drink packets and rubbing alcohol to back up my non-working stove. My room featured a full kitchenette, so I purchased sloppy joe fixings to catch up on my protein intake.

When I returned to the room, my mind was fixated on my daily chores and cooking up some grub. There was only one question -- I had a skillet, but no pot. How was I going to carry the eggs? I searched the room over and over, and came to a conclusion that would become a new life hack for my travels. I would use the coffee maker to boil the eggs, three at a time, since I was not carrying an egg protector. The day quickly came to an end -- as they always do when doing chores and relaxing indoors.

Ten miles was my goal for the day, including an open-water paddle to the secluded campsites of St. Joseph Peninsula State Park. A solid breakfast and a hot cup of coffee set me up for success for the upcoming paddle. I knew I wasn't going far, but with that break and the depth of the water, I had to ensure a solid disembarkation. The early morning beach walkers stood by to watch me paddle off into the distance. At these times, there is always an audience, where confidence must overcome the lingering doubt to ensure success. This time was a complete success, thanks to my outrigger approach, and soon I found myself looking back across the sand, leaving the luxuries of the hotel world behind.

Following the suggested routes on the maps in front of me, I saw there was a choice to paddle inside the bay or outside in the Gulf. I chose to take the inside route for two reasons. The first reason was evident as there were more campsites on the inside; the second had more to do with the luck I'd had inside the bays with the absolute mesmerizing wildlife encounters. My choice didn't disappoint me. Once across, I made the cut and found myself watching tarpon and sharks feeding among the flats. It was unfortunate there were no sea turtle sightings, but another manta scared the crap out of me by flying through the air not 10 feet from me, showing off his acrobatic nature with a tail-whipping back flip.

I passed the sign for the first campsite. The day was still young, so I continued to the second primitive campsite, indicated by a large brown-and-white state park sign. I steered left and beached to explore my home for the evening. Beyond the high dunes, a path led to the designated site under the trees to the left as another led right to the Gulf side camp. The bay site #2 was home to eight or nine large crabs. I watched them scamper off to their homes while looking over the site. Before setting camp, I explored farther and walked over to the Gulf camp. It really wasn't that far away and it was closer to the bay than the long walk through the sand from the Gulf. The site was equally nice, including a fire ring, but it was farther in the trees, restricting the breezes coming off the water. Another decision was made and I set camp with the crabs.

The sun began to set as I walked along the Gulf beach, kicking up the water that lapped over the shells in the sand. My mind was at ease. Throughout the section, I had gained a few more tricks to stow in my bag and I was well-prepared for the upcoming section. With another section behind me and a new set of maps awaiting, I became overwhelmingly giddy with anticipation. But at that moment, I simply enjoyed the subtle breeze as it blew across the colorful horizon.

Welcome to St. Joseph Island State Park

Segments 4 & 5
St. Joseph St. Park - Ring Dike Camp
160 miles

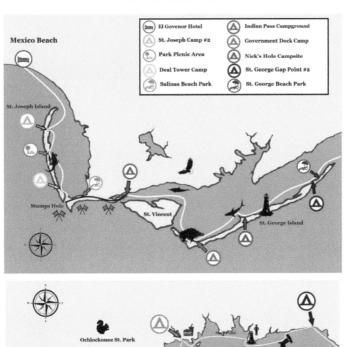

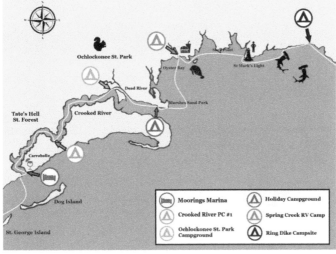

All maps were hand drawn and created by the author Jeffrey "Treehouse" Buncie

Double Red Flags!!!

If you take a close look at a Florida map and follow the panhandle from the western border, you'll see what looks like a hook leading into the Gulf of Mexico. About four miles from the mainland is a chain of barrier islands made up of St. Joseph, St. Vincent, St. George and Dog Island. Three of these islands may have made sainthood by name, but they all share one important factor -- they form a delicate aquatic preserve that is important and necessary to the local commerce and ecosystem.

These islands were but a fraction of what was ahead of me. The route would lead me from the forgotten coast and into the Crooked River. Paddling up the river provided opportunities to encounter wildlife, such as the Florida deer, feisty raccoons and the white squirrels of Ochlocknee. Out of the river and into the shallow waters of the St. Marks Refuge, rounding the point where the historic lighthouse stood, I would soon find myself heading farther into the sparse, historic, coastal towns of Old Florida.

The next 11 days and 160 miles found me paddling the next two sections of the journey. Huge mistakes would be made, dangerous wildlife encounters would happen and questioned motives by state officials would occur. In order to keep the stories flowing, let's take a visit back to the campsite on St. Joseph ...

Facing a brand new day, and a brand new section, I returned to the water. The high winds and rough waters quickly reminded my body it had been a long two weeks on the water. There was a picnic area about three miles from camp that would supply me with fresh drinking water, a shower if needed, a restroom that *was* needed and shelter. The skies were dark and gloomy, with rainstorms in the distance. When I arrived at the picnic area, the storm began to whip sheets of stinging rain at me. I ran to the shelter to avoid the storm, eat my boiled eggs and study the radar in order to gauge paddling times between the storms.

The rain subsided; I had a look around and found a six-foot alligator in the marsh at the park. It was a little hard for me to grasp. Did he swim across the saltwater? Are they slowly acclimating themselves? Will we finally have a real-life super gator vs. outlandishly large shark B-rated film? I mean, it's not that far off, if you think about the bull sharks slowly making their way into our river systems. My rambling thoughts fled as the skies opened up, offering a window to paddle onward to my EOD Deal Tower Camp.

Through most of the paddle that day I could see the rainstorms across the sky all around me, yet I moved in a protective bubble of sunlight. Feeling like I had hit the weather lottery, I pushed on until I saw the old fire tower around the bend. My day was coming to an end, but just to remind me who the boss was, the pounding rain hit with a mile left to paddle. I was caught in a sea of drops coming down as thick as the peanut butter I snacked on. With my head down, the brim of my hat saving what little eyesight I had, I paddled into the blankets of rain. Arriving at the shore, I saw the camp had a long cement dock that gave me a place to hide from the rain. The tide was low enough, allowing me to paddle through the floating sea grass and wait for the storm to pass.

After a solid hour of hiding, the rain stopped. I went to dry land, set camp and explored. A sandy road led to a gazebo, compost toilet and a highway. The highway led to a sandwich shop a mile from the camp. Google had me at "sandwich shop." Off I went to the Scallop Cove, where the employees let me charge my electronics, indulge in their tasty sandwiches and enjoy the beers I had purchased at the one-stop shop.

By then it was dusk, so I walked back to my camp with a couple road sodas to retire for the evening. I enjoyed the dark, starry sky on the dock until the stars disappeared behind storm clouds. The lightning gave me a one-of-a-kind light show until the rain forced me to retreat back to the tent. The storms lasted far into the morning hours, which usually made the next day's paddle a fun-packed day of fighting the angry water left behind.

Surprised to see the bay as calm as it was the next morning, I approached the day with positive vibes and smiles. After a mile, I'd have to exit the bay at Stump's Hole, where a small portage over the peninsula would be required to reenter the Gulf. Crossing the road, I looked at the Gulf, saw the hazard red flags, signifying dangerous currents being whipped around by the wind, and thought, "There is *no* way in hell I'm going to be able to paddle in that."

I had paddled in yellow flags, indicating moderate surf or currents, and we all know how that had gone. Today was not a single red flag, but a double red flag. Not knowing what the double flag meant at the time, I went for it. I wheeled Lola down to the surf and spent the next hour getting the shit beat out of me by the break. I've since learned the double red flag indicates the water is closed to public use. The surf had been deemed too rough and the currents life-threatening. But, there I was, getting dumped over and over again. Completely gassed, I had to come up with a new approach. I looked at the maps and came up with Plan B.

Plan B entailed walking Lola along the small two-lane highway to Salinas Park (3.5 miles), then reentering the Gulf, hoping the slight bend would shield the wind enough for me to paddle. There was plenty of daylight left and I was no stranger to walking miles, so it seemed like a solid plan. The road cut through another Air Force base property, where I was approached by drivers in their cars asking if I needed any help. Drenched in sweat, forearms tightened and quads filled with lactic acid, I respectfully declined as the drivers shook their heads and drove off slightly confused. Mile after mile, I started to regret the decision, but what else was I going to do? I finally arrived at the park and was relieved to find a screened-in shelter with electricity and restrooms.

Salinas Park is a double-sided park split by the road. The bay side was more enticing with a shelter, playground, beautiful fire ring and volleyball net, whereas the Gulf side was run-down, but adequate for a day at the beach. After working as hard as I had to get there, I enjoyed a much-needed, calorie-packed lunch, then took a walk along the grounds. I found a raised wooden dock behind the park leading into Money Bayou, which was not indicated on the maps. I was a little pissed now knowing I could've paddled to the park through the bay, but the lack of research was my fault. The kicker was that, to exit the water at the park, I would have had to heave my kayak up a skinny staircase to get her to the Gulf.

Once my phone was charged, I approached the Gulf, facing another hour or so of torture. Completely winded, I turned my frustration into determination and Plan C was born. Plan C involved another 3-mile walk along the road to Indian Lagoon, where I could bushwhack into the guarded lagoon and paddle to Indian Pass Campground. Come hell or high water, I was going to make this campsite even if it cost me my appendages.

Passing house after house along the small shouldered highway, the rest breaks became more frequent as my body wore down. The drivers of the passing cars often honked, waved or gave me a thumbs up. These drivers wouldn't have known it at the time, but they were what kept me chugging along. I finally made it to the lagoon, finding a spot to slide in the water, but the day was behind me and the sun was shining -- in the other hemisphere. After the day's events, there was no reason to take any chances on the water. I continued to walk into the night, adding another couple of miles. I was committed to getting to the Indian Pass Campground.

With less than a mile to get to the camp, a lady in a pick-up truck pulled over and asked where I was headed. I told her about my day and said I was going to the camp. She was headed there as well, and offered me a ride. Completely exhausted and with an empty stomach, I accepted the offer. We laid Lola horizontally on top of the truck bed, then I jumped in the back, holding onto her with all my might. Once in the bed of the truck, the half-mile felt like a hundred. Lola sticking out across the other lane, in the middle of the night, didn't play well in my mind. Laura, as I learned later, was being cautious by driving in the middle of the road to warn any possible oncoming traffic. At that hour, we fortunately encountered no other cars before turning into the campground.

Laura drove me to the camp owner's house. She got out of the truck, knocked on the door and introduced me to her mom, Betty. Betty, the grandma-type, invited me into her home and made me two sandwiches while we talked about procuring a site. She had a site next to the water for me and trusted me enough to take care of the payment in the morning. Laura hung around, drove me to my site and later brought over some dry firewood, so I could warm up next to a fire.

After a shower, I built a fire and sat by it, collecting my thoughts and processing the events of the day. My ideas didn't always pan out the way I would like them to, but somehow I pulled through those days with a smile on my face. These two ladies were the reason for my smile that day. I felt blessed to have met them and thanked them repetitively for their genuine Southern hospitality.

Waiting out the rain at Deal Tower

34

The Palm is Mightier than the Boar

Waking up in a place you've only seen in the dark is a pleasantry more often than not. I crawled out of the tent to a beautiful sun-lit sky. The first thing I wanted to do was square up with Betty, so I walked a short distance to the registration. The store didn't have a lot of options for resupply, but it had coffee, Mountain Dew and candy bars -- you know, the necessities. The $25 the campsite cost me was well worth it. There was no way I could put a value on the way Betty and Laura had so graciously treated a stranger. I thanked the ladies again before returning to camp.

There was an option of two different routes for the paddle around St. Vincent Island. The choice was either to go inside through Apalachicola Aquatic Preserve or paddle outside along the Gulf. Even though it added a few miles to the paddle, I chose the bay with the hope of seeing more of Florida's astonishing wildlife. St. Vincent Island is a wildlife refuge and Laura had highly recommended I take the bay route. I took her word to heart, which proved to be the right decision.

I pushed off into the still waters of the bay. Beat up from the long walk the day before, I enjoyed the gentle breezes and calm water. Within the first couple of miles, the refuge gave me a glimpse of what it had to offer. A bald eagle flew overhead, heading to its nest in a towering pine. Dolphins were playing in the distance, searching for a midday snack. A hog was splashing in the water off the sandy bank. I even slowed down to witness a shark playing tag with a crab. I felt like I was a bug on the water with the surrounding wildlife accepting me for what I was, a part of their environment.

When I reached the point of St. Vincent, where I decided to take a lunch break, I saw hundreds of jellies along the beach. It looked like a jelly mass suicide. I learned later they were Cannonball jellyfish, which do not sting, but secrete toxins. They are a translucent pink, vary in sizes up to seven inches and have small bubble-like tentacles to host spider crabs for transport. Still, I took in the beauty as they rested before the tide would rise and return them to the bay.

From the point, I took a direct cut across to Government Dock primitive camp. The small site on Little St. George Island was marked by a public dock extending into the bay. When I stepped out to the primitive campsite marked with a state park fire ring, I was instantly attacked by the hundreds, nay thousands, of sandspurs. The tiny, prickly burrs hiding in the sand clung to everything. I literally raked the sand with a palm frond just enough to set my tent in front of the water.

Once camp was set, I had to eat, but my stove wouldn't start. I was fortunate enough to find two empty beer cans. I had one shot -- and no room for error. Cutting into the aluminum cans with my knife, I was able to make my first-ever functioning alcohol stove. I'm not going to say it was the prettiest one around, but damn, it worked.

As I lay in my tent believing the day was over and planning the next day's paddle, I enjoyed the slight sweeping of the waves over the shore. The soothing sounds were interrupted by the sound of rustling palms behind me. Seconds after I heard the palms rustling, my tent was struck. Something had ripped the guideline from the tent fly, pushing hard enough to take the tent and thump the back of my head. Whatever it was retreated and rushed by me, splashing its way into the water. I heard the shrill just as it hit me -- it was a wild hog.

My head was ringing from the thunderous strike. Afraid the hog would return, I rustled around for my knife -- a Swiss Army knife with a three-inch blade. While the hog splashed its way through the water not eight feet from my tent, I sat up using his splashes as a distraction to unzip my tent. I shut my headlamp off, allowing my eyes to adapt to the darkness. When the time was right (like I knew when that would be!) I would dash out of the tent and hide behind the neighboring palm.

The splashes continued and I jumped into the sandspurs, holding my screams for another time. I sat watching the beast attack the water over and over again. It was a magnificent, yet aggressive, creature.

Hog attacks are not uncommon in Florida and I had faced one before, so I was aware of what they can do. I had enough of waiting around, so I picked up a palm frond to make myself look bigger, while I held my knife in the other hand. I jumped out, yelling at the top of my lungs and charged after the hog. The hog looked back at me, staring me down. I paused, raised the palm, waved it back and forth in the air, and cursed the animal. Then the hog made his move. He ran from the shore and darted back into the woods, away from my camp. I drew my card, showed my hand and was lucky to have pulled from the non-confrontational boar pile.

My adrenaline was pumping. I turned my headlamp back on to find my guide line and assess the damage. I was fortunate the hog had not ripped my tent. While sitting on the log next to the fire ring, I pulled the sandspurs from my body before entering my tent. During the 20 minutes I was doing it, I looked up at every little noise I heard in the brush behind me. On guard, I did one more perimeter check, then returned to my sleeping bag. The hog returned a couple hours later, waking me from my slumber. This time, he did not run through my site, but I heard him splashing in the flats again a little farther away. He was no threat to me, so I lay peacefully, hoping he was getting what he was looking for.

With quite a headache from the night before, I mustered up enough strength in the morning to pull myself out of the tent to greet the day. The night before I had set up a few options where to end the day, depending on how I would feel. A Boy Scout Camp, Nick's Hole Camp was eight miles away. With the way I felt, and the way the wind was blasting, that quickly became my goal.

Unfriendly winds kept the wildlife at bay and there were no sightings until I reached the inlet to the campsite. I came across a few five- or six-foot black tip sharks feeding in the bay and thought, "If I only had bait." I love fishing for shark and black tips are really good eating. But, I did not, so I searched for the Hobl Cat sailboats that marked the camp. I saw the masts sticking up behind the brush and found a spot to pull Lola to shore.

The camp is home to Boy Scouts of America Troop 22, out of St. George. It was empty when I arrived and had all the amenities needed to run a Scout outing. The most important were running water and shelter. With plenty of daylight left, I took a cold hose shower, collected firewood for later and took the time to fix my stove. Toward dusk, a father and his son drove up and walked in to go fishing. I didn't want to be that homeless guy over in the corner, so I greeted them while we talked fish. They left after an hour, leaving me to the sunset. The evening was short and sweet -- I had a brief fire then hit the sack.

Sunset before the boar attack

A jelly mass suicide

A Small World After All

The new day brought high winds sustaining 18 mph throughout the morning. The first thing on my list was a resupply at a grocery store in the town of St. George. Fighting the headwinds, I arrived at the St. George Island Bridge, soaked by having the saltwater whipped back in my face with every stroke. The walk to town was brief and a grocery store employee watched my food while I walked around town.

The Cape St. George lighthouse, across the street from the grocery, has quite an extensive history. It originally dates from 1833 and was placed at the inlet, marking the cotton trade route to Apalachicola between St. Vincent and St. George. Over the years, hurricanes have pummeled it to where they have to continue to relocate it. It was moved to its present location in 2008 after the foundation collapsed in 2005 into the Gulf. For historical value, the restoration crew used as many of the original bricks as it could. There were plenty of shops and eateries around the town, making it a must-see destination.

The winds were becoming fierce, so I cut the trip in town short. I returned to the water to play in the wind. In order to keep my composure, I created a game -- at times I had to stop paddling to remain upright, so I paddled in a zig-zag fashion to break up the shifty rollers. Before I reached St. George Island State Park, I had to call the park services to reserve a campsite. Along the bay, there are three sites before crossing the sound or East Pass. The young lady on the phone advised me to paddle to Gap Point PC #2, which was located at the northern tip of the island. She said the sunsets there were wonderful. I took her advice and booked the site.

A grueling 10 miles later, through the face-burning wind, I arrived at my site to set camp along the point. The game must've worked because I had daylight to spare and explore the park. The official RV camp was 2.5 miles from the PC along a sandy path. The park had a couple hiking trails I took advantage of while looking for geocaches along the way. I wandered into the RV camp and talked to the host, who was wondering where I was camping and why I was there. He was a friendly guy, but also told me if I wanted a shower, I would have to pay $10. The thought had crossed my mind, but I couldn't bring myself to pay $10 for a shower. To avoid suspicion, I high-tailed it out of there and returned to camp for the sunset view I was promised.

I could see the rain clouds spitting down in the distance. The sun began to set and, for a moment, the clouds dispersed, allowing the sun to break free of the suffocating grays and shine in all its glory. The young lady hadn't lied -- it was quite a view, leaving silhouetted trees standing tall among the vibrant variations of yellow and orange as the sun disappeared beyond the water.

Off-shore winds left me staring across the water, yearning to return, but much like a deserted castaway, I remained wind-blocked and land-locked for the day. The wind held me captive, unable to cross the open-water stretch back to the mainland. On the bright side, I got to explore the park even further and tack on a zero day.

St. George has a beach park on the other side of the island. The beach access has restrooms, fresh water, soda machines and electricity to charge my devices. I made the long, 5-mile hike across to take a beach day and make some calls back home. While sitting on the beach, I heard a voice call out, "Hey, Jeff". Confused, I looked around and didn't see anyone. I heard it again, "Hey, Jeff." OK, someone is messing with me, right? I looked up and saw the father and son I had met back at the Boy Scout camp walking toward me. The dad's name was Justin and the son was Titus. Not long after the pleasant greeting, I met his wife and daughter. The family was on vacation. We had a great conversation covering the basis of the trip and the recent hog encounter. They wished me all the luck in the world and said goodbye. "What a small world," I thought as they got in their car and left the beach behind.

It was time to return to camp to catch the sunset. I arrived just in time to have my sunset celebration while eating a hot bowl of noodles. Sitting at the picnic table, constructing alcohol stove 2.0, I heard female voices and the clash of aluminum coming from the shore. Two college girls, from out of nowhere, were beaching their canoe. They were surprised to see me and it looked like they were here for the night. To cut the awkwardness, I introduced myself after they set camp.

They made a fire and invited me over while they cooked up their meals. Nikki and Sara, from Birmingham Ala., were easy on the eyes and had adventurous spirits. I shared some whiskey; they shared their greenery before we all turned in for the night.

The girls were still sleeping when I left the island the next morning. I left a thank-you note and some gifts behind for them. I crossed East Pass and landed at the sandy beach of Dog Island. It was a Sunday and the boaters were out enjoying the beautiful weather. I met an older couple fishing off the point, who pointed me in the direction toward Carrabelle. The tide was not on my side, turning the crossing into a four-hour nightmare.

When I arrived back on the mainland, I learned I had overshot the channel and had to paddle back a couple miles. That explained why it had taken me four hours. Overshooting waypoints had recently become a theme and every time I was left with a feeling of disgust churning in my stomach. Disgusted, pissed, and lonesome, there was nothing I could do now but paddle back to the channel markers leading into the Carrabelle River.

During my zero day, I had booked a room at Mooring's Marina, just past the public boat ramp on the river of Carrabelle. The marina had floating docks included with the room and a fairly reasonable rate.

This was a must-stop resupply before heading into the more desolate areas of St. Marks Refuge. I walked to the grocery store and post office, which were a quarter-mile from the marina. I sent home gear I hadn't used to lighten my load, then filled Lola back up with more food for the longer stretch. After the chores were done, I walked to the local cantina, Fathoms, to enjoy a well-deserved burger and the live entertainment before calling it an evening.

Air conditioning and soft beds had become extremely difficult to leave the longer I was on the water. The late-morning start had me a little worried about reaching my camp before sundown, but the river route had shorter options along the way. When I left the marina, I paddled up the river to find myself along the mud-covered banks of Tate Hall Forest. I lost sight of the coast and followed the winding river north. The lashing on the seat came loose along the way, causing the seat to slide up and down, irritating my lower back. I wasn't able to pull off until I reached Sunday Rollaway camp because the banks of the river were too soft and muddy.

Up to that point, I had been disappointed with the mundane paddle. Usually when you paddle a Florida river, you see an abundant amount of wildlife, but not that day. I was able to fix the seat while I was at the well-manicured Sunday camp. While eating lunch, I was visited by a large yellow corn snake that slithered past the picnic table. I stood up and followed him to a rotted log, where I inquired about his woodland friends. For the moment, I was happy to have a friend to talk to.

For the next eight miles, I cut the banks tight around the bends, trying to escape the midday sun. The river continued to wind its way through the forest all the way to the Crooked River Camp. A gravel boat ramp on the right bank was laid out like a welcome mat, inviting me to its doorstep. I slid Lola up on the bank and explored the large campsite that included a picnic table and fire ring.

Insects were the highlight of the camp. Praying mantises crawled along the picnic table, butterflies fluttered through the air and a scorpion crawled next to me while I was pitching my tent among the high grass. The lonely hours passed. I hadn't seen a soul on the water that day and silence filled the air. It took me a while, but I finally figured out what was missing -- I was away from the crashing waves of the Gulf for the first time in over two weeks. The sound of the breaking waves had become part of my everyday life and here at the Crooked River Camp I did not hear them. I genuinely missed the comforting sounds I had left behind.

Cape St. George Light

Footprints in the sand

Getting dangerous out here on the
Crooked River

41

Atop the Oysters

There was another 18 miles of river to paddle before returning to the bay. That day, I would knock out 15 of them before stopping at Ochlockonee State Park. The paddle was long and boring -- no wildlife and no humans to talk to. To break up the monotony, I listened to music, often singing just to exercise my vocal chords.

The 15 miles flew by. I arrived at the state park ramp and left Lola to take a walk. I met Steve the Ranger, who was very informative about the surrounding areas. An older gentleman with a white scruffy beard, cheerful attitude and calm demeanor, he made me feel right at home. He set me up with a site and told me about some geocaches around the property. I set camp, then went for a hike. The wildlife was everywhere.

Within the 100 yards from my site to the shower house, I saw four deer grazing on the grass. They were unafraid and paid me no attention. The unsung heroes of the camp are the white squirrels that leap among the oaks. A genetic mutation of the common gray squirrel, they are just smart enough to evade predators to keep their species alive. The park is not the only spot to see them in Florida, but numbers prove them to be increasing across that sanctuary. My closest friends know my distaste for squirrels, but these were a pleasant and unique sight.

Another wildlife gem found in the park is the endangered red-cockaded woodpecker. The area provides an exact habitat for the breed, a rare woodpecker that can be found nesting in the living pine trees throughout the ecosystem just south of Sopchoppy, Fla. Utilizing the open, natural flatwoods to forage for their survival needs, they are found in only one other park in the state of Florida.

At sunset, I found a park bench by the river. While I was sitting there, Steve the Ranger walked up and asked if he could join me. As he lit his half-bent Dublin pipe, he asked about Lola. He went on to tell me about his 80-year-old mother, who frequently runs rapids in Georgia. I was taken aback to say the least -- 80 years young and still doing her thing. He left to do his rounds after giving me information for the next day's paddle. I returned to my tent, looked at my maps and found the quicker alternate route he had told me about before I fell asleep.

Thanks to Steve the Ranger's input, I wouldn't have to paddle back to the Crooked River. Instead, I could paddle out on the Dead River to the Sopchoppy and regain access to the Ochlockonee Bay. I planned an easy nine-mile paddle, so I took my time to break camp and enjoy the wildlife. Lola had had visitors the night before, who had frequently woken me from my slumber. For the first time on this journey, I had to deal with the masked bandits of the night. The raccoons were relentless and would not give up. They were after my food bag that I had secured in the front hatch of my kayak overnight. The straps over the hatch weren't totally tight, which allowed the raccoons to reach their dirty paws underneath, lift it up and then the hatch would quickly slam, causing me to yell from the tent.

It was another calm paddle all the way to the bay. The river spat me out along the banks of the town of Panacea and into Ochlockonee Bay. I was able to see Holiday Campground shortly after entering the bay. When I arrived there, I met Matt and Ryan, two local 20-year-old guys fishing from the bank. They told me about meeting another paddler, Mary, who had come through a week before, attempting the same paddle. They claimed she was doing way more miles a day than me. That piqued my interest; maybe I would meet her before the journey was over, but for now, I would secure a site and take care of business.

Holiday Campground is built for RVs, but is very paddler-friendly. There is a common room with air conditioning, hot showers and a dock to catch the sunset. A convenience store across the street had sandwiches and cold beer. I grabbed lunch and a six-pack and sat down to figure out my permit situation for the Big Bend section.

Supposedly, the next section along the "Big Bend" of Florida requires a permit to paddle. When I made the phone call to Florida Fish and Wildlife (FWC), it knew nothing about requiring permits. After an hour, and many transfers later, I talked to Tom, who told me not to worry about a permit. He wanted a float plan, for safety reasons. I told him I wanted to paddle it in seven days and I would call him again when I completed the section. We agreed on the terms and the plan was set.

When the evening hours approached, I sat on the bench enjoying a beer and watching the sunset. I looked over at the other campers starting their marshmallow fires. A deep feeling of loneliness came over me. The RV campers were predominantly couples, wrapped up in their blankets, enjoying each other's company. When I find myself feeling this way I try to put things into perspective, often recalling a line from one of my favorite movies, "The Beach." I travel alone a lot and to paraphrase the quote: "As for travelling alone ... fuck it. If that's the way it has to be, then that's how it is."

After leaving the campground the next morning, I was introduced to a few more "firsts" for the trip. I rounded Marshes Sand

Park along Ochlockonee Point and stopped at the ramp before the long stretch to Spring Creek. I must've stayed there a little longer than I thought because when I returned to Lola, the tide had disappeared. The ramp now led to exposed mud. I had to put my Vibram Five Finger toe shoes on in order to walk her out to the water before reentering the cockpit. Even then, the bottom of the kayak was in less than six inches of water, causing me to paddle farther out to turn the bend.

According to the depths listed on the maps, I was supposed to have 12 feet of water through the inside of the next island, Piney Island. I took the inside route into Oyster Bay, which was a big mistake. Oyster Bay is called that for a reason. The tide continued to recede, leaving me in a minefield of oyster beds and a foot of water. Up to this point, I had paddled barefoot for comfort. From then on, that would no longer be the case. Upon getting stuck on one of these beds, I had to gingerly step into the water and dig my toe shoes out of the back hull. My toe shoes are slip-on, hard-soled shoes that are made for water sports and they proved to be a necessity for stepping onto the oyster beds. Across the four-mile stretch I would routinely get out of Lola and walk her along the shallow waters and over the hidden oyster beds. Every once in a while, I would find a large pocket of deeper water with smaller sharks thrashing about feeding on the baitfish left behind.

Finding the inlet to Spring Creek, I made the cut to get to the RV camp. The Spring Creek RV camp was a rustic, Old Florida type. The proprietor lived on the property in a rundown building and I'm pretty sure the other "campers" lived there as well. The lady who showed me where I could set my tent was friendly, but was also surprised I knew the camp was there. The highlight of the camp was the restaurant across the street. Spring Creek Restaurant is one of Florida's treasures, serving up seafood caught from the local fishermen and handmade pies. The coastal gem was a walk back in time -- from the waitress who called me "hun" or "sweetie" to the soft-shell crabs with collard greens, sweet Southern tea and the rocking chairs that sat in the waiting room.

Twilight was approaching, so I walked around the barren camp and sat on the dock looking up the inlet. While sitting, a friendly manatee decided to hang out with me. I was happy to have someone to talk to. The locals across the park were hooting and hollering while the sounds of Lynyrd Skynard filled the air. My new buddy, Matty the Manatee, and I thought it would be a bad idea if I went to join them, so I said good night and returned to my tent.

What in the Hell was That?

St. Marks Refuge is the precursor to the desolate paddle through the Big Bend of Florida. The day before, I had entered the refuge when I left Marshes Park, learning I had to direct my attention to tide tables, so I downloaded a free app to my phone. I took time in the morning to plan the route according to low tide. When I was preparing Lola for the paddle, a couple of local fishermen pulled up in their crab boat and started a conversation. I asked about the tide. To my surprise, they told me it was low tide. I was looking at the wrong day on the app. Well, I couldn't wait until the tide came in, so I put on my shoes and took my chances on the water.

The first two miles the water ran deep until turning the launch at Shell Point. I made a cut to the outside, following the submerged crab traps across the bay, then beelined it straight to the St. Marks Lighthouse. The launch was back in the shallows, so I beached at an undesignated spot along the bank. Stepping out, I looked over the high grass and saw a parking lot swarming with another Florida jewel -- the love bug. If you haven't had the pleasure of meeting the sex-crazed flies, they love the idea of over population. During, and after, mating, they let everyone know how much they love their partners by remaining connected butt-to-butt. They are nuisances with no natural predators, thus leading to swarms during the months of May and September. The one plus-side to the invasive flies is that no matter how annoying the swarms can get, they do not bite.

These red-and-black bugs attached themselves to everything. They were clinging to everything I owned and entangling their tentacle-like legs in my hair, beard and clothing. I took a walk through the swarms across the parking lot and down the road to the lighthouse. A few hundred yards later, I was approached by a county sheriff, who asked me what I was doing there. Taken aback, I told him I had paddled there and I wanted to check out the lighthouse. He then asked about a permit. I asked, "What permit?" My snarky tone triggered him to get out of the vehicle. He asked for my identification, which I had left in my blue box clipped to Lola. He insisted he had to see it and I had to retrieve it from Lola.

I couldn't believe it! What right did he have to ask for my ID? I wasn't doing anything wrong, I stated my purpose and I told him I would be leaving soon. To ensure the situation did not escalate, I retrieved my ID and waited while he ran it for active warrants. Even when I handed over my passport, he was not satisfied. The officer asked why I did not have a state ID. Trying not to sound like too much of a smart-ass, I replied with a smirk, "You guys took it from me and apparently the state of Florida does not deem me fit to own one." Obviously, he did not appreciate my humor, but once he ran my name his tone changed as he granted me my freedom. He did appreciate my cooperation and offered me cold water once he knew I wasn't a vagrant. I took two, and he wished me good luck and safe journeys.

Now that I was officially safe to go to the lighthouse, I walked down the road with a few snacks and my newly acquired water, fighting off the love bugs. The lighthouse dates back to the 1820s and aided the agricultural trade through the southeast. Keepers maintained the light until 1960, when it became automated. The 88-foot tower continued to serve as an active navigation aid to the Apalachee Bay from the Civil War until its 2016 restoration. Now unlit, it serves as an inoperable historical landmark.

The love bugs finally got to me, so I walked back to Lola, washed off the hundreds of bugs that had hitched a ride, and returned to the water.

Paddling the next six miles became a little scary, thanks to my next curious visitors. Throughout the preserve, I had been seeing a lot of three- to five-foot sharks. Black tip sharks, sand sharks and the real curious hammerhead sharks. I was paddling along, looking for the next crab trap ball to weave between, when I saw a thrash and felt a bump on Lola's nose. At the time, I thought I had run aground or hit a hidden oyster bed. It happened again and, this time, I got a good look at the perpetrator as he swam by me. My brain did not register what was happening. It took a moment to process the situation and I couldn't understand until I saw a tail take a big whack at Lola again. I was being attacked by the tails of hammerhead sharks!

Once I caught on, I paddled farther inland, where the water was a little shallower. Closer to shore, the sharks left me alone, but now I had to pay close attention to the depth of the water. The tide began to roll in, and I focused on the maps, looking for Deep Creek. To get to my camp that night, I had to paddle up Deep Creek to Ring Dike campsite, along the Florida trail. I soon came to the creek and looked for the large oak tree the data book claimed was the marker. Off in the distance I saw the silhouette as the sun began to fall.

When I saw the sign marked "Ring Dike," I tried to find a beach, but it was now high tide and I had to bushwhack through the high grasses to land. The site serves as an official Florida Circumnavigational Paddling Trail and the Florida National Scenic Trail campsite to be shared during hiking season. I set camp under the oak tree and discovered another problem. Anything I set down, and I mean anything, was overrun by fire ants. They infested the campsite, but I was not moving. I ate away from camp, walked a little bit of the trail and called it a day.

Two more sections were now behind me. The following day I will be entering the Big Bend Paddling section. Tom from FWC and the locals I talked to had warned me about the isolation, but I welcomed it. I was beginning to get in a groove and with the lack of fancy beach hotels to pamper me, I was starting to feel like I had entered the world that is dreamed about, yet forgotten.

Sunset over St. Marks Refuge

Ring Dike CT/FT Campsite

Segment 6
Ring Dike Camp - Ft. Island Boat Ramp
170ish miles

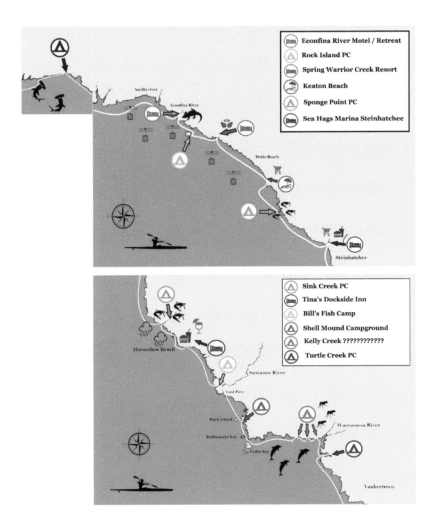

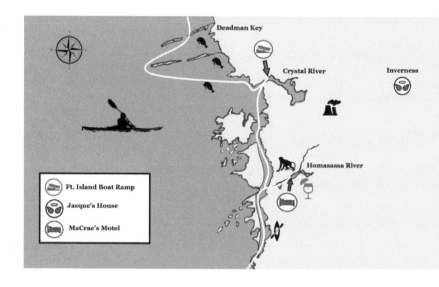

All maps were hand drawn and created by the author Jeffrey "Treehouse" Buncie

Not Enough Marys

Why start in the Gulf? The next section will answer one of the recurring questions asked. If it hasn't popped in your head yet, through all the rookie mistakes, weather turmoil and experiences, don't feel bad, I'll answer it now.

Back in 2014 , I read about the Big Bend Saltwater Paddling Trail. The experts claimed you had to paddle this section west to east; you wouldn't be able to acquire a permit if you wanted to paddle east to west. For these logistical reasons, it made sense to start on the west coast. I could've gone completely rogue and bypassed the permitting process, but I didn't want to ruin the chances of not completing the thru paddle. Therefore, by following these recommendations the next 105 miles, I would be a law-abiding citizen and paddle from the west.

The remote, unspoiled shoreline and expansive marshes through the state's largest aquatic preserve proved trying at times. Longer stretches, scarce resupply options and extreme tidal changes added to the challenges. The section that started the turn of my thinking threw some curveballs my way, but with help from the locals I was able to overcome the hurdles.

Warm-hearted individuals gave what they could when they saw a paddler in peril. I feel lucky to have shared my experiences with so many wonderful people, who happened to be around when I needed them the most. I dedicate this chapter to the sympathetic locals of the secluded towns and fish camps of the Big Bend Paddling Trail.

The next 175 miles are technically broken into three subsections. The initial is the Big Bend Saltwater Paddling Trail, headed by the FWC, covering 105 miles from the Aucilla River to the Suwannee River. The free permit required to paddle and camp at the six campsites is supposedly available online, but for me, as stated earlier, was a verbal agreement with Tom from FWC. I had seven days to make it through and keep my word to call him when I was finished. It all started a few miles before the mouth of the Aucilla River at a campsite called Ring Dike ...

Immediately after paddling out of the tapered Pinhook River away from the camp, I knew it was going to be a long day. I had cross winds that cocked Lola sideways and I was not timing the tide correctly. I was paddling in less than six inches of water, often bottoming out. I would look across the bay and scout the depth of the water according to the crab traps. If the trap was visible, which was often the case, I'd have to paddle sometimes over a mile out to find such depths. Disappointed in myself, I played my zig-zag crab trap game, which always put a smile on my face. The miles flew by as I stopped on the oyster bars for snack and stretch breaks. I felt bad for Lola grinding up against the razor-sharp edges, but this was the only way I could catch a break. The barren landscape of muddy banks would stand tall, sometimes three feet from the water's edge. The soft banks couldn't support my weight, which forced me to stand atop the oysters.

Three breaks and multiple protein bars later, I arrived at the mouth of the Econfina River. The boat ramp was another two and a half miles up the river, from which I could walk to a small motel or paddle another half-mile to a PC. Once I left the open water and paddled up the quiet river, I was surprised by a 10-foot gator that slid off the bank and into the river right in front of me. Wondering if he would pop up and try tipping me over, I paddled very gingerly, keeping my eyes fixed on the rippled water as I made my way to the boat ramp. I stopped at the boat ramp and took a walk to see what the motel and small store were like. Along the walk, I came across a pygmy rattler slivering across the road, abruptly kicking out the sand left in his tracks. They are beautiful snakes, known to the area, with an almost purplish body overlaid with black stripes and a very poisonous punch. You really don't want to get too close, so after taking some photos I kept my distance.

Up the road from the motel, in a separate building, was the store/registration desk. Joanne, the friendly caretaker, set me up with a room. I bought some refreshments and walked back to the relaxing atmosphere of the two-story retreat. I use the word "retreat" because the rooms were set up for just that. With all the distractions, such as a TV, out of the equation, I was able to enjoy the peaceful river atmosphere and take care of the necessary chores.

I was not bothered by anyone to checkout the next morning, so I stayed in the room until noon before turning in my key. The store was closed, which became a huge factor in the following days' paddle. I had planned to use this store for a resupply, but they didn't have any substantial food on the shelves during my previous day's visit. I would have to ration the next two and a half days on an already hungry stomach. The paddle, itself, was pretty boring -- a straight shot out to

51

Rock Island. When you exit the river, it's visible from the moment you hit the bay. My mind was playing tricks on me again -- I stared at the body of land the whole day, yet it never seemed to get closer. Over and over again, I had to remind myself that with every paddle stroke I was making progress.

The campsite was located on the north end. I paddled around the island until I saw the sign upon the secluded rocky cove. When I pulled Lola ashore, the site looked like it had been recently mowed, keeping the bugs to a minimum. The site had a fire ring and lots of tree cover for shade. I set camp and explored. The island seemed to be a retreat for many different species of birds. Over the remaining hours of daylight and into the evening, birds were coming and going, singing their songs and keeping me awake. Evening storms rolled in and the soothing sound of rain lulled me to sleep.

The storms continued into the morning, bringing fear into my heart. The fear was not caused by the strength or magnitude of the storms -- I was more fearful about the lack of food in my bag and that I might be stuck on the island for another day. The storms pounded the coast all morning. I was able to find a window of opportunity when the storms broke in the afternoon. The original plan was to put in the 22 miles to Sponge Point, but when I began paddling, my body hit a wall. I didn't have the food to provide the energy my body required. Nausea kicked in and my arms did not cooperate, causing me to cut the day short and stop at Spring Warrior Fish Camp, off the Spring Warrior Creek.

After a short paddle up the river, I saw a welcome sign that also stated the camp sold cold beverages. If they had beverages, would they have food as well? I thought my problems were solved. Optimistically pushing through to the fish camp, I was met at the dock by Mary, the proprietor of the camp, who quickly broke my heart. She told me the camp had gotten in trouble for selling beverages, due to licensing, so she could not sell me any and there was no food or store around for at least 10 miles.

Fortunately, she picked up on the quiver in my voice and the disappointed expression upon my face. Her warm heart and Southern hospitality wouldn't let that stand and she offered me what she could give. At that point, I hadn't inquired about a room or said I planned on staying. Out of the goodness of her heart, she gave me a couple cans of soup, a banana, crackers and an ice-cold Coke. I couldn't refuse; I needed the food, and Mary became my savior. Once she came to the rescue, I thought there was no way I couldn't stay at her establishment. How could I refuse a room when she had treated me so kindly? I buckled down, got a room and immediately ate what I could, allowing for rationing. I cannot think of a time in my life I have enjoyed a can of cold soup to the extent I did that one.

Later in the evening, there was a knock on my door. Mary had returned with a plate of pulled pork with all the fixings and some breakfast sandwiches. Her husband brought it back when he returned from work. With a tear in my eye. I thanked her with a sincere hug before saying good night. This was exactly what my body needed. It was the best damn pulled pork I've ever eaten. I slept that night not listening to the growls coming from within, but with a smile knowing there are still Marys in the world.

The sign says it all   **Big Bend camping**

In the Shallows

Up early with the morning mist, I was land-locked until the dense fog lifted. While I was packing up, a couple of locals visited Mary and brought me some homemade sausages. The two local gentlemen were baffled by my journey and wanted to hear more. They filled the time as the fog lifted. I said my farewells before paddling into the river.

The rancid smell of a nearby paper mill filled the air until I reached the boat ramp of the unimpressive Dekle Beach. The more populated Keaton Beach was another couple of miles away, so I pushed through to the beach park.

Visible from the water, the large beach at Keaton Park was a sight for sore eyes. The beach park had showers, a playground and a nearby hot dog stand. Unfortunately, the hot dog stand was closed, but there was a convenience store a mile up the road. I grabbed my bag and off I went. A few blocks up the road, a pickup truck pulled over and offered me a ride. I accepted and jumped in the bed of the truck. A hitch in Florida was something I would never have expected.

The convenience store had everything I needed to get me to my next resupply and then some. They sold fried chicken, which was a win for my calorie count. After the box of chicken, I grabbed a fountain drink, resupplied, and started walking back to Lola. The roads were empty and eerily quiet. Not one car passed me the entire mile, which I found weird for a beach-type town.

Upon my arrival back at the beach, I could not believe what I was watching. There was an overweight, shirtless guy in his late 40s sitting in Lola on the water. He was the first to speak. "Is this your kayak?" he asked. I nodded my head and as politely as I could, said, "Yes." Quick to apologize with some sort of reasoning, he said he had never been in a kayak and it was his 45th birthday. In his twisted mind, he figured he would give it a try. My response was uncharacteristically forgiving and I complimented him, saying I was surprised he was able to get in without it tipping over.

Put yourself in my toe shoes. Lola and her entourage was my entire lifeline. It was basically like walking into my home and eating out of my fridge without asking. After the response, he paddled back in, got out and then wanted to talk further. His wife and mom were nearby, walking along the beach. I dropped my guard after seeing his elderly mother. Although it was a weird situation, instincts led me to conclude he wasn't trying to run off with Lola. His name was Bo and he lived farther down the road at Steinhatchee. I was going to be there the next day and he invited me to dinner at his house. He gave me his number, I wished him Happy Birthday, then they left the beach.

After searching Lola and reassuring myself Bo hadn't run off with any of my belongings, I packed the food in my bag and paddled into the bay. Before I reached my next campsite I had another visitor. Within the two miles, I paddled alongside a manatee for a bit and ran into a couple more curious hammerheads. I tried to get this anomaly on film -- they would swim by the kayak, thrash their tails at the side of the boat and swim off to circle back and do it again -- but by the time I got my camera out, the sharks had come, whipped and gone. I am still intrigued about these sharks and their actions. Did I spook them by paddling into their feeding hole or were they seeking me out to say hello?

As I approached the camp at Sponge Point, I had to pull up to the high grass along the bank. The sign leading me to the campsite among the sea oaks was visible from the water. Low tide had brought out the thousands of fiddler crabs inhabiting the point. They retreated in waves as I approached the elevated grassy site.

Once a fire was built and my tent was set, I took a moment and reflected on the day's thoughts. I was starting to see the humanitarian spirit people not only talk about, but act upon. I found it quite amazing that people genuinely want to help. It was either that or they felt pity toward a poor soul in way over his head. The last statement became a lingering thought throughout the paddle. I didn't care to know the answer, but it did give me much to think about when I paddled the longer stretches.

The paddle toward Steinhatchee was one of those stretches. The oyster beds disappeared, forcing me to take knee-deep breaks along the muddy banks. Here, I became enemies with a new type of pest. I was familiar with the mosquitoes; the no-see-ums and now I was haunted by the biting yellow flies. The flies would swarm to my stench, which drew them nearer. I combated their attacks by wearing long sleeves, but that only drew them toward Lola. Once they found Lola's open cockpit, it became a torture session out on the water. They would hide in the shadows, waiting for the opportune time to use their stinging bites like that endless drip from the faucet you haven't fixed yet. At one point, there were two flies slowly eating away at my sanity, causing me to go to such lengths as rolling into the waist-deep water and intentionally flooding Lola.

After an hour in the water draining the brackish water from my rollover, I was back to the shallows, paddling toward Steinhatchee. Two miles up the Steinhatchee River was the Sea Hags Marina. On the dock, I met a couple of longtime fishing buddies tying off their boat. Lou and Kerry were intrigued by my get-up. Once we got through the formalities, they invited me to their cabin for more stories and cold beer. After tying off, I secured a one-bedroom fishing cabin. I think the young girl at the bait shop was playing a joke on me -- she gave me a bright pink room after she commented on my pink Oakley sunglasses. We laughed together and then I was off to get cleaned up.

The fishing cabin featured air conditioning, spacious living space and a front porch to hang out on. I made my way over to Lou and Kerry's, where they followed through on their promise of cold beer. As the stories progressed, Kerry told me there was a grocery store a little over a mile up the road and added he would give me a ride if needed. I accepted and, after we finished our beers, I jumped in his truck to resupply. The grocery also had a Subway next door, so I had a two-for. A quick resupply and a purchase of three foot-longs later, we were headed back to the fish camp. Upon arriving, I had one thing on my mind -- demolishing two out of three foot-longs. Kerry wanted me to hang out a bit longer, so he invited me back any time for free beer. I revisited after the meal, but they were in for the evening. I grabbed a couple night-time beverages and left a thank-you note in case I did not see them before leaving.

Sea Hags Marina in Steinhatchee

56

All Types of Rain

Steinhatchee and the Sea Hags had such a welcoming atmosphere I did not want to leave. The only thing that kept me going was the promise I had made to Tom from FWC. I found a pizza joint that provided the perfect send-off meal, then returned to the river. All the luxuries of town made me forget about timing the tide. Leaving at low tide, yet again, I was faced with seven miles of paddling in less than a foot of water. Tired and frustrated from mudding through the preserve, I finally had enough. I stepped out and walked Lola through the ankle deep water, sloshing through the muck and vegetation as I made my way to the channel markers. What should have been an easy 10-mile day quickly became a slow 14-mile day.

The barrier of oyster beds marked the inlet to Sink Creek. I started the long walk, yes walk, back into the cut. Poor Lola and her bottom were ripped up again over the blanket of oysters. The campsite was a half- mile up the creek, surrounded by marshes and salt flats. Mobs of fiddler crabs with their over-sized pinchers greeted me as I pulled Lola to the shore. I set up among the cedar trees and called it a day.

Throughout the evening, I was woken up by the scratching and scurrying of the fiddler crabs atop the tent. I wanted to send a message to all the crabs in the world -- and it started here. Since they had interrupted my sleep, I sat there and watched the silhouettes through the moonlight and flicked them off my tent, one by one. Hopefully, they got the point and told their compadres, after they took flight, not to mess with that bearded guy in the tent.

The late-night entertainment resulted in a later start than anticipated the next morning. Gray clouds cloaked the sky, bringing a light mist into the air. The mist turned to a drizzle before I hit the bay. I had the tide, so I took my chances, saving a 2-mile trip by cutting inward along the skinny waters of Pepperfish Key. Beyond the key, I got hit with pounding drops thumping Lola's topside. The wind blew in and turned the rain sideways, now spitting at me like poison blow darts. For the next two hours, I paddled through the stinging rain with the brim of my hat, once again, as my savior. I would look down at the bay and the water spat back up at me. All I could think about was how Forrest Gump, in the movie by the same name, explained the different kinds of rain he encountered in Vietnam. "Little bitty stingin' rain, and big ol' fat rain, rain that flew in sideways and sometimes rain even seemed to come straight up from underneath." Dealing with the same experience I began to laugh out of plain insanity. I looked for anything to motivate me to get to the green-roofed shelters of Horseshoe Beach.

Completely soaked through, I pulled Lola up to the vacant park and dashed into the picnic shelter. My paddle for the day ended there. The entire northern half of Florida was covered in green on the radar map on my phone. Refusing to return to the water, I walked to a local spot, Dixie Delights, to grab lunch and figure out where I would stay that night. The building was reminiscent of a Dairy Queen, serving reasonably priced burgers, sandwiches and ice cream. I asked the guy behind the counter about local housing options for the evening and he made a quick phone call to Tina, who owned a motel around the corner. Tina was an elderly woman who had no problem picking me up and driving me to the motel. The sleeper rooms were simple rooms for simple people, at a very reasonable rate. It sounded like exactly what I needed so I decided to hang my hat at the modestly priced Tina's.

I waited for the rain to subside before walking back to the ramp to retrieve Lola. Once I had her on wheels, I had to pull her five blocks through the neighborhood. Passing car after car, I enjoyed watching people's confused looks and smiles. In the midst of travel, the rain returned and so did my comedic outlook. I left Lola, on wheels, in the parking spot outside my room next to the other vehicles, as if I had driven her there. I tell you, it would've been priceless if the motel had had a valet. My neighbor in the adjacent room enjoyed the humor as well. We came up with joke after joke, but my favorite was when he asked how many miles per gallon I got.

Another sought-after reward is a hot shower -- sometimes just as much as the burgers and beers. Although after paddling in cold rain all day, I really don't want to stay wet, but I had to get over it in order to warm my core. Following the shower, I brought my gear inside; the room then looked like a garage after a wet camping trip. I had laundry hanging throughout the bathroom, a clothesline dividing the room to hang wet gear on and the electric outlets filled with electronic devices. It was pure madness.

To escape the madness, I ventured out to Jake's Pub for a nightcap. Desiree, the bartender from the neighboring town of Chiefland, found my story inspirational and bold. She held me hostage with her captivating smile and addictive personality. Beer after beer, she made me feel like one of the locals. She invited others to join the conversation as they walked through the door. Before too long, it was last call and I had to say goodbye to my new friends. The vacant streets brought the empty feeling of loneliness until I saw my ol' girl, Lola. I tucked her in and let her know, "it's you and me, baby girl" before saying goodnight.

Sunset from Sink Creek

Dixie Delights long distance paddler serving

What a blessing to have

Where the Hell is Kelly Creek ???

The morning brought bright blue skies inviting me to return to Horseshoe Cove. The previous day's storms had blown through, leaving high winds behind. The 20-mile-an-hour winds cursed the waters and had me floating like a bobber in a whirlpool. Unfortunately, I was introduced to the effects of the yearly red tide that day. The stench of rotten fish filled the air, water and beaches. It was the saddest sight. The fish floated past by the thousands -- to the point I had to paddle carefully between the bloated wastes. No species was safe from the algae bloom, leaving flounder, gar, mullet, trout and blowfish up and down the coast.

On the eighth day of paddling through the Big Bend, I was now entering the second sub-section, the Lower Suwannee National Wildlife Refuge. This section includes dry islands with white sand beaches. I was finally able to stand on dry land during my rest stops. I used them to the fullest extent on my way toward the famed river of song.

Salt Creek would lead me into the Suwannee River to Bill's Fish Camp. A mile up the creek is a dock inviting passersby into a historic fish camp of Old Florida. The cash-only establishment welcomes paddlers at a very reasonable rate. There are cabins, RV sites, screened-in common areas and spots for primitive camping on the grounds.

When I was setting my tent, an older couple staying in an RV across the park thought I looked a little hungry, so they brought over a Tupperware container of leftovers. Among all the commotion, I remembered to call Tom and tell him I had made it through the Big Bend safe and sound. He remembered me and was happy to hear about my experience. I asked about the well-manicured sites and it turned out there was a FWC caretaker one day ahead of me preparing the sites. That was awfully nice of them, so I thanked Tom and let him go about his business.

The evening became interesting when I met the Georgia boys while hanging in the common room. They were three generations out fishing along the preserve. There was the feisty grandfather, sauced up and ditching out the quips; the dad in his late 50s, focusing on returning the quick wits, and then the son in his 30s, fueling the fire with the help of a fourth-party outsider. We had fun as the night went on kicking back a few cold ones. Quickly, the evening became early morning, and I left them to their cooler and witty comebacks.

One good thing about the river system is that there are options to get back to the bay. I chose my route based off mileage, but proved it wasn't the smartest. The banks of the Suwannee have hidden turns, where the boats running the river took no heed to kayakers. There should have been signs up at every bank cautioning hidden drives, like they do on the mountain roads, or at least some responsible boat captains. In fear of getting sideswiped, I listened for motor craft before I made any turn the entire way to East Pass.

When I was safe again in the bay, I saw the Georgia boys cruising in to see me off. They came by and yelled, "Good luck, kayak man!" before heading back up the pass. These few words were enough to leave the stress of the river behind and motivated me to press farther down the coast. In fact, the water smoothed out and I caught the outgoing tide, making for a swift paddle.

I took an inward route around Buck Island that led me into the path of thunderous airboats running the backwaters. High above the grass, the orange flags weaved through the marshes. Faced with another safety concern, I approached the bends with extreme caution. Before making the cut, I stuck my paddle as high as I could in the air to indicate my position, then slowly paddled to the next turn. Both of the nerve-racking situations slowed my pace and brought me to a ramp just north of Cedar Key of Shell Mound Campground at the most inopportune moment.

All the books warned me of docking at the ramp during low tide. I was losing the tide by the minute, but there seemed to be just enough water, so I went for the approach. I made it halfway and bottomed out. Determined to make the paddle, I pushed, scooted and thrust my body weight forward. That was it, I was stuck. I stepped out and my leg disappeared up to my thigh in the seemingly endless muck. Thankfully, I had not jumped out entirely. I pulled myself back onto Lola's tail and pushed off as hard as I could. It took a few tries, but I lodged myself free and paddled back to the deeper water.

Wading in the bay, I had to come up with a new plan of attack. I paddled up to the brushy bank toward the pier and bushwhacked my way to the camp. It was a success, but half my lower body was covered in the stench of sulfuric muck and the other half was cut up from bushwhacking. I found a hose to get rid of the layer of mud at the ramp, then found the host to secure a site. I had to wait for the tide later in the evening to safely secure Lola at the ramp.

The campground is known for its hiking trails along the preserve and the large Timucuan mound formed by discarded oyster shells. The Timucua natives inhabited Northeast Florida, utilizing the abundant sealife the land offered. They were known to use every piece of the animal, from the meat to the bones. Technically, the mounds, or middens, are large trash piles left behind after the tribes feasted. I found humor and a sense of history while enjoying a beautiful sunset atop a garbage pile and waiting for the tide to return.

The bay water crept in inch by inch around midnight. Sitting on the dock, singing Otis Redding's " Sittin'on The Dock of the Bay," I wasted time as the muddy bottom gradually faded away as the brackish water filled the inlet. Another hour passed and I was finally able to bring Lola around to the cement ramp. My final task had been completed and now I would be able to sleep soundly knowing Lola was out of harm's way.

Damn, if I didn't do it again the next morning. Just hours after being in the same predicament I was waiting again for the inlet to fill. By now, you'd think I would have understood the concept of timing. The late start would cause me to skip the stop at Cedar Key and the paddle out to Seahorse Key. I didn't need supplies, so the stop in town wasn't necessary, but I was upset about not going out to Seahorse. The key is about three miles south of Cedar Key and is the site of an old Confederate soldier prison. Unfortunately, you are unable to camp on the island and I wasn't spending more money on a motel, so I had to settle for taking the bypass. Once the slack tide permitted me to paddle, I booked it into the third subsection, the Cedar Key National Wildlife Refuge.

It was just about noon when I hit the water heading south to Rattlesnake Key. The key marked the channel toward the bridge launch, cutting the Cedar Key option out of the equation. I rested at the bridge and fueled up before the long stretch to Kelly Creek. Paddling through the porpoise-filled Waccasassa Bay Preserve became the highlight of the day. The acrobatic porpoises moved swiftly cutting through the water, disappeared, then blasted through the plane impersonating dives worthy of an Olympic Gold Medal diver. Their energy motivated me to remain positive through the mundane stretch.

Regrettably, I was having a little too much fun and time slipped away, placing me a mile before the inlet of Kelly Creek as the sun retreated. My GPS was being finicky and was not locating my position. During this mile, there were so many inlets I couldn't recognize a creek from a cut. I chose what I thought was Kelly Creek, but after a mile or so of paddling I did not see the camp. Desperately paddling back to the bay, I took the next cut and again chose poorly. Frustrated, fear began to cast its shadow. Where the Hell was Kelly Creek? A question that six years later, I still don't have the answer to. The sun was now below the horizon and I had no clue where I was camping. I had to make a decision.

High tide blessed me with the opportunity to gauge where the water stopped. On the bank, among the high tanned sea grass, I stepped out to find solid ground. I figured it was high tide and the water was not seeping through, so I chose this to be my camp for the evening. The mosquitoes came at me in swarms; the no-see-ums took the leftovers. In record time I had my tent set and gear secured. Within minutes my tent was covered in insects as if the eighth plague of Egypt was upon me. My stomach had to deal with eating cold bars for dinner as I was not exiting my sanctuary until the following morning.

I awoke with a cool-to-the-touch backside at 1:09 a.m. I rolled over, grabbed my phone and realized my tent footprint had become a three- to four-inch thick waterbed. I knew I wouldn't have been that lucky to have found a solid camp spot. The good news was all my gear was dry with the exception of the corners. The staked-down corners had an inch of water, but the now-raised footprint held the water. I moved all my gear to the center of the tent, then watched for a while to ensure the water was not rising any higher.

My over-active brain started to go into crisis mode after an hour of sitting cross-legged in the middle of the tent. It was as if I was 6 years old again, hiding from the monsters lurking under my bed. I reached out to my good friend, Jacque, with a text giving her my approximate coordinates and told her if she didn't hear from me by the next afternoon to send help. I was sincerely worried about floating away or Lola drifting and leaving me stranded. I mean, at this point, anything could have happened. Water began to deflate the waterbed around 3 a.m. and I knew the worst was over. Exhausted, I laid down and immediately fell asleep.

The sun brought a muggy tent and the blankets of mosquitoes. I slipped out of my damp sleeping bag and prepared for combat. For the next 15 minutes, I lived out one of my childhood dreams. Kick-ass '80s music filled the air as I reenacted montages of an '80s Schwarzenegger movie. The toe shoes went on, lacing them up like combat boots and with the appropriate sound effects. I tied shirts around my shins just below my shorts, then slung my arms into my fleece jacket, vigorously zipping it to the collar. I wrapped my head with a towel, securing it with a sick-ass, bandana-tightening scene like any montage should end.

I was the commando that was facing the predators awaiting the Running Man.

Kneeling by the door, hand on the zipper, I took three breaths then pulled open the flap. White doves flew by in slow motion, Bon Jovi's "Wanted Dead or Alive" occupied the brain waves, and I aggressively dove out, rolling among the grass. As soon as I stood up, the shirts on my legs didn't hold and the entire head wrap lay on the ground. I wasn't too worried about the legs, but the head wrap proved to be important, so I rewrapped it and broke camp as soon as I could.

To my dismay, it was low tide. There was a three-foot bank of mud between me and the water. Once Lola was loaded, I pulled her to the bank and tried to lower her slowly without tipping her over. She was unbalanced and when she started to tip, I fell over the bank, hit my head off her topside and sank knee-deep into the mud below. In disbelief I pulled her down and accepted the fact I would have to walk her to the depths of the bay.

Dredging through the mud and out to the bay, I stopped on an oyster bed to have my breakfast. My body hit a physical wall as I failed again to keep my body properly fed. Exhausted from the prior evening's events, the paddle along the oyster-ridden bay went by in a blur. Every break upon an oyster bed I ate whatever I had that didn't require cooking. The only way to describe the day's miles could be said in one word -- miserable.

I couldn't have been happier when I saw the three white poles marking the inlet to Turtle Creek. The campsite was just up the creek on the left bank. It was still early in the day, so I took advantage of the sun and dried my gear. I ate two cooked meals before realizing I had never called Jacque. Not only that, I had never turned my phone back on. Oh, was I going to be in for it! As soon as I turned it on, I had alert after alert. Thank goodness, I had service and was able to give her a call.

Jacque has been a friend of mine since my early 20s. Sharing many memories of Jimmy Buffett concerts and golf outings, we always look out for each other and call one another out on their shit. She was not happy when I finally returned her missed calls. After a severe ass-chewing, she still reached out and asked if I was going to stop and see her in Crystal River. Looking at the maps, I saw I was 24 miles from a boat ramp north of King's Bay that she was well acquainted with. She would pick me up the next day at the ramp, after she got out of work. I was to call her around 3 p.m. if I was not going to be able to make the park. I promised her I would call and we set the plan in motion.

Why did I put myself out there and say I could paddle 24 miles? Well, after the past couple of days, I had had enough of the crappy food, swarms of bugs and the malodorous mud. I needed motivation and what Jacque had waiting for me was quite enough. In 24 miles I would have a bed, a hot shower, real food and ice-cold beer. There was nothing that sounded better. To motivate me further, I doubled down and ate all my food, except two bagels and three bars. With a full stomach and a plan in motion, I called it early so I could get a good jump on the day.

Full of anticipation, as if it was Christmas morning, I opened my eyes before the sun came up. After breaking camp, I sat on a log eating a moldy bagel that tasted like old feet and watched the sun greet the day. The tide was on its way out, and the swift current propelled me beyond the flats and surrounding oyster bars. Soon enough, I was unexpectedly watching the white smoke coming from the power plant in the distance. This sight was familiar; having grown up around the area I knew I was close to the Crystal River nuclear plant. I couldn't believe I had already paddled over half the day's miles. Soon I would be coming to the Cross Florida Barge Canal spoil islands (islands created by dredging the canal). The failed project to cut shipping routes around the straits was another waypoint for the Central Florida section. The spoil islands would provide a break before heading two miles out to the jetty crossover.

Alas, I reached Deadman's Key, one of the spoil isles, and looked out to the lengthy rock jetties. Unable to pin-point the crossing indicated on the maps, I picked a spot and hoped I had estimated appropriately. My track record had not improved -- I chose poorly and ended up paddling around the outermost part of the jetties. The current made it almost impossible to land, so I continued into the warm power plant-fed waters.

By paddling around the jetties I added a couple miles to the day. Keeping a look out for manatees that call this area their home, I cut the corner of the bay and followed the channel markers to the inlet of the Crystal River. Relieved to have found the inlet, I took one last break on a small island and called Jacque.

The river was easily navigated and heavily traveled by motorized vessels. I found myself at the Fort Island boat ramp, waiting my turn to exit the water. The ramp was filled with pickup trucks waiting for their opportunity to pull their boats out of the water and onto their trailers. Patient owners worked their unspoken, but understood system. I yelled up to a guy, asking if it was OK for me to unload when he was loading his trailer. Marveled by the well-stocked

Lola he joked around, but eventually agreed. I was able to sneak in, dock and pull Lola out of harm's way before he left the ramp.

The park was equipped with restrooms, water, shade and a walking trail. I sat watching the well-oiled machine for entertainment and rehydrated while waiting for Jacque to show. Just as planned, she pulled up around 6 p.m. in her white two-door coupe. I wondered how we were going to get Lola on top of her car safely. Jacque greeted me with an attempted hug, but pulled back and said, "You smell like ass." Taking the greeting with a grain of salt, I said, "Thanks," as she handed me a full bag of McDonald's food and a cold beer.

Her car was smaller than Barry's car had been, but we weren't going six hours, we were only going 30 minutes into Inverness. The boaters watched as Jacque and I loaded Lola up and strapped her down. Once we felt good about it, we hopped in the car and headed inland.

Jacque's condo in Inverness, Fla., was my home for the next couple days. After 20-plus days without a zero, I welcomed a day off or two. Jacque supplied the provisions and I provided the stories. I was able to clean my gear, fix Lola's rudder, replace the corroded charging cables and added a brand-new GPS unit for the next section. We visited local cantinas, ate copious amounts of food and even made a trip out to see all my former bar patrons.

The Big Bend Segment was now behind me. The lessons learned weren't always the easiest, but the people of the bend made the experience bearable. I can't thank them enough for their generosity. Somehow in the midst of it all, I made up four days toward my float plan, leaving me less than a week behind. If that counts for anything, I would spend the well-deserved zero days in Inverness resting, eating and preparing for the upcoming Nature Coast.

Smoke on the water

66

Segment 7
Ft. Island Boat Ramp - Anclote Key
77 miles

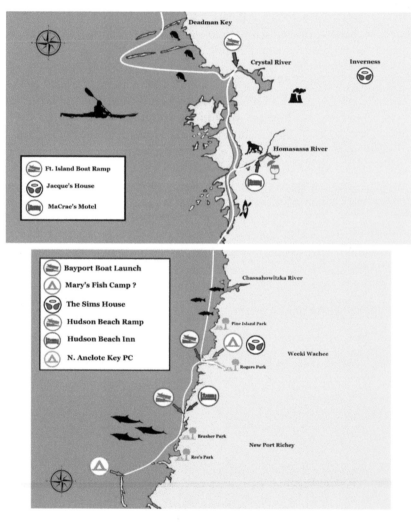

All maps were hand drawn and created by the author Jeffrey "Treehouse" Buncie

Paddle to Nowhere

You would think I would have left the long, shallow stretches behind once I cleared the Big Bend, but that was not the case. The beginning of the Nature Coast continued with the oyster-bed breaks and the shallow flats of the neighboring Chassahowitzka National Wildlife Refuge. Over the next 70 miles I found myself winding through tidal creeks, spring-fed rivers, marshes and grassy mangrove-covered islands. Throughout the segment, I encountered energetic porpoises, curious manatees and the famed monkeys of Monkey Island.
I had a full bag of food, a brand-new GPS unit and two days of rest under my belt. Although the warnings came from every angle to keep a keen eye on your navigation, I felt well-equipped and readily prepared. In my mind, there was no better way I could've approached this section, but as I'd learned thus far, no matter how well you think you have prepared, each section is quick to cast it away and leave you dead in the water.

The time came when Jacque had to return to her daily routines and bring me back to the Fort Island boat ramp. During the drive, I was fighting the urge to stay in Inverness a few more days. I wasn't ready to return to the chaos that waited along the water. Jacque made it clear that it was time, and played a huge part of basically forcing me back into my journey. When we arrived at the boat ramp, we unloaded Lola and my gear, and said our farewells. I stood at the ramp, Lola at my feet and leaning half off the ramp, as I watched Jacque and her little white car pull up dust on her way out the exit.

Motivation eluded me. I spent an hour sitting under the shade of an oak tree next to the dock. While I ate a snack, I looked over the maps and saw another ramp across the river. I talked myself into taking a baby step and paddling to the ramp for a change of scenery. I was trying to trick myself into paddling. It was the first time I had encountered this feeling and it started to worry me, so I went across the river.

When I pulled up to the cement ramp, I saw a small portable information building and a sandy road. The building was locked and unattended, but a map showed that if I followed the road for two miles, it would take me to a nature museum. It had been a chore for me to paddle here, let alone hike a couple miles, so I scratched the idea and walked back to Lola. As soon as my back was turned, I heard an older gentleman call out and ask if I was lost. As he approached, he saw Lola, which started a conversation that would help me find the motivation to continue that day.

Bill was a silver-haired fellow with a sea-worthy physique and an inquisitive smile. His worn shirt and perspiration stains -- along with his black suspenders -- indicated he was doing some sort of work. It turned out he was building a boat with the Crystal River Boat Builders (CRBB) around the corner. This educational organization works to preserve and continue living traditions, skills, lore and legends surrounding the traditional boats used along the Nature Coast. In short, they build old boats with old tools by hand, thus preserving the history and skills of the trade. He took me over to one of their shops and showed me what he was working on. The conversation quickly became more about his work than what I was doing (I had had that chat plenty of times). I was fascinated by his knowledge and teachings. Something happened while I was talking to Bill. He had steered my mind off what I had to do and gave me something to smile about before leaving the workshop. We exchanged contact information; I shook his hand and left him to his work.

After I left Bill, I paddled into the Salt River. The GPS tracked me through the narrow route surrounded by grassy banks. For once, the wind did not play as a factor and I was able to catch the tide, turning the thread-like channel into an express lane leading to the Homosassa River. At the mouth of the river, I was greeted by three curious manatees. I saw their rounded snouts breach for air, so I paddled cautiously over to get a better look. They were in the shallows, grazing on the sea grass. They looked like three baked potatoes lying in a side of greens. Not wanting to risk being dumped over if they moved or got too close, I left them to their meal and paddled up the heavily trafficked Homosassa River. About a mile or so up the river was a boat ramp, next to Macrae's Motel. I scouted the location and ended up getting a room for the night.

The weather turned for the worse soon after I booked the room. Originally, I had not wanted to stay, but the on-site bar and its happy hour lured me in, like a siren along the rocky banks of Anthemusa. While I was sitting at the bar, Jacque called to see how far I had paddled. I told her I was sitting at the Freezer. She laughed -- she had brought me to this bar the first night she picked me up. It was hard for me to imagine how different a place could look through two different points of view. I got up, walked to the parking lot and then retraced my steps. The memory came back to me almost instantly. We laughed, then she decided to join me for a few drinks.

By the time my burger arrived, Jacque and her husband, Bob, had joined me at the bar. Not 24 hours before, Bob had been in Ohio and I had been unable to meet him. I felt bad for Jacque because she had to sit through all my stories again. We kicked back a few, shared pleasantries and, after awhile, said our goodbyes. It was wonderful to see good friends again in a familiar place.

The next morning, a thin layer of fog blanketed the river as I prepared Lola for the monster 25-mile day. I stood at the ramp and finished my coffee as I looked down the river at Monkey Island. The day before, I unknowingly had passed it while I was focusing on getting up the river. The island, once an eyesore, had become somewhat of an Alcatraz for the troubled monkeys of Homosassa. Although the original inhabitants have died, the island is now home to five spider monkeys that are well cared for by the owners.

I went to get a closer look at the island. It featured a mock lighthouse, painted red and white, that sat opposite a stranded boat shell. As I neared the splotch of land, I saw the monkeys had chosen to take a lazy day. They sat on the jungle house porch, watching me circle the island. As I completed my tour, one jumped over to the empty boat shell and sat topside giving me a memorable send off.

When I returned to the tidal creek route, my GPS was not locating my position. Navigating by map, I was able to get to the Mason Creek launch four miles down the creek. I recalibrated the GPS at the launch, solving the problem and allowing me to paddle swiftly to the Chassahowitzka River.

The miles flew by as the morning concluded. I had half the day behind me when I stopped at an island just south of the Chazz. My body felt great, my GPS was working and my mind was goal-oriented. The next 10 miles were a blur until I hit Pine Island Park. The people there were a welcome sight. Since leaving the Homosassa, I hadn't seen another soul that day. There were families swimming, couples enjoying a stroll along the path and other kayakers hanging about the water. With Bayport Launch only another couple of miles downstream, I chose to watch the activities from afar and continue onward.

Bayport's fishing pier was full of hopeful anglers and photographers setting up for the sunset celebration. I took a break in the soft grass of the park before heading into the Mud River. With 24 miles down and only one to go, I took a walk around the park while eating a snack and talking to the anglers. I had at least two hours of daylight ahead of me, and I basked in the knowledge I could blast the mile if needed.

No matter how long a break you take, especially if there are more miles to go, it always seems-short lived. I was soon back on the water, paddling up the river. After being on the water as long as I had, I had gotten a feel for how far a mile is and how long it takes to paddle a mile. My gut told me I had gone a mile, but I had not seen any indication of a fish camp. I figured it was the last mile of the day, so maybe it just seemed farther. I paddled on until I arrived at a park where kids were swimming. I knew something was wrong and my gut feeling was correct. A sign read "Welcome to Rogers Park."

I was beside myself. This sign indicated I somehow had paddled down the wrong river. I didn't even remember a junction where I could've screwed up. There was no reason to pay any mind to the GPS, there was only one way I could have gone. Taking this wrong turn and backtracking was not only a mental hurdle, but would also add hours, not minutes, to the day. As I sat at the ramp of Rogers Park, I had to gather my thoughts, regroup and get over the feeling of defeat.

Time was now the enemy as I had allowed the daylight to slip away. I shoved off the ramp and headed back to Bayport with the GPS in view. The race against time began as I wove my way through the inlets populated by private docks. Frustration built as I learned my GPS was useless -- for the second time it was not picking up my location.

Lost within the rows and rows of houses, I couldn't take the frustration any longer as the docks became silhouettes. I finally snapped and yelled, "Where the fuck am I?" A homeowner happened to be on his boat and heard my cry. He asked where I was trying to get, then gave me directions I could follow, even as night fell upon me.

It turned out, way back at the Bayport ramp there was a fork, where if you stayed to the left, you were on the Mud River, but if you took a slight right, like I did, you ended up on the Weeki Wachee River. As I prepared for a night paddle, I pulled my headlamp out and followed the homeowner's directions back to the fork. Looking back at it now, I don't know why I didn't just set camp at the boat ramp, but the events that unfolded on the Mud River would influence many changes to come.

Navigating the moonlit waters of the Mud, I hugged the bank to the left. That way, I figured, would decrease my chances of straying from the route again. The GPS remained useless and the headlamp was ineffective. The river was much like any other river I've paddled along the way, which sparked my over-active brain. I couldn't get images of the big gators I'd seen sliding into the water out of my head. Every left-handed stroke was taken cautiously, hoping the potential gator didn't think it was a chicken thigh. I have to admit that, mentally, it was the longest mile I have ever paddled.

Mary's Fish Camp was said to be on the left bank, a mile from the ramp at Bayport launch. I came upon a spot that might have been an old fish camp left unattended with "For Sale" signs covering the property. The temperature had dropped, my brain was fried, and I was ready to be off the water.

Low tide had emptied the tidal river, making docking impractical. The neighboring house had a ramp and I figured if I was really quiet, I could dock there and walk Lola along the seawall. I crept over to the ramp lit from a spotlight off the corner of the house. Smoothly lifting my leg out and into the water, I took a leap of faith. My feet searched for a grip on the river bed, but traction gave out and I went under. Completely submerged, in less than 3 feet of water, I held on to Lola as the muddy water filled her cockpit. I popped up, drenched and cold, as the yapping of a dog broke the silence. My loud splashes had put the dog on alert. I had to get out of sight, so I jumped into the shadows and waited for the dog to lose interest.

Crouched behind the bushes, seeing Lola lie in the water, half off the ramp like a storm had wrecked her on the shore, I felt terrible. Where was my loyalty? I couldn't stand it any longer, so I crawled over and pulled her along the seawall next to the property. I lowered myself into the water, drained her out, got my camping gear and found a spot behind the empty building at the old fishing camp to set my tent.

Stealth camping is an adventure and an art form within itself. There are multiple choices to approach it, but one thing, for sure, is that you don't want to draw attention. This means no lights, therefore setting camp takes a little longer. Every crinkle, every crackle echoes through the dead air like you are banging on a gong. The worst is the zipper; you want to minimize the count of zipper pulls. Before entering the tent, I changed into dry clothes, ate a light snack-bar dinner, and gathered my gear for a one shot go at it. The font size can't get big enough to fill the way the long ZIP felt, but I was successfully and safely in for the evening. The morning, on the other hand, brought many unwanted surprises …

Saving the Journey

I was up and packed before the neighbors might become suspicious, conducting a damage report. My phone was in my pocket when I fell into the water, which normally wouldn't have been a big deal, but my headphone jack had a leak and my phone was waterlogged. When Lola had flooded, my brand-new GPS disappeared into the murky water below and somewhere, somehow, I had lost my food bag. Frantically searching the grounds and Lola's hulls, I was in a state of confusion. Screw the half-working GPS, how could I misplace an entire bag of food? I failed once again as I did not find the food nor the GPS after I went diving along the ramp. There were decisions to be made -- I had no food, only snacks, no navigation or communication. I didn't have a clue how I was going to pull through, but I did know the abandoned lot wasn't the place to wallow. Begrudgingly, I paddled out of the river and found myself back at the Bayport ramp.

If you took a moment to read the opening to this book, this was the park where I sat on the bench under the tree as a broken man. The man from the boat shouted over, "You OK? Do you need some help?" For some unknown reason, I said no. Determined to figure out a way out of the mess on my own, I did not allow them into my world. While they continued to go about their business, I watched as the wife backed the trailer into the water. The husband and child hit the throttle and landed the boat before the wife pulled away from the ramp. The smooth transaction impressed me.

The concerned wife walked over and introduced herself with a twang and a drawl from the back country of Florida. Her name was Michelle, and she wouldn't let me wallow in sorrow. Her Southern faith pried me to inquire about a town or stores nearby. The husband, Mike, had come over by this time, leaving the child by the truck. They saw Lola, I explained the situation, and briefly told them about the journey. To be honest, most of the conversation was a blur and I don't know why I agreed -- or they agreed -- to help, but I do remember Mike and I lifting Lola into their boat and jumping into their truck.

The town of Weeki Wachee had a Sprint store to replace my phone and a grocery store to buy food. Mike was driving, but we weren't headed to town, we were headed to their house off the Mud River. The plan was Mike would get ready for work and Michelle, with

Wayland, their son, would take me into town after he left. We spent the short time getting acquainted. Mike stayed until he felt comfortable enough to leave his family with the vagabond found at a boat ramp, then we loaded up and headed to town.

Michelle was curious, asking question after question. I mustered all the energy I had to remain positive and not stand-offish. When we arrived at the Sprint store, I was given more bad news -- the phone was on back order and it would be at least a week until I could get a replacement. I asked if they could send it to a post office farther south, but they would not budge. Incapable of problem solving or troubleshooting I invited Michelle and Wayland to lunch, so I could take my time to process the situation.

One cheeseburger and four cocktails later, I attempted to call in the cavalry. Weeki Wachee is just over an hour south of my hometown, Ocala. I planned to return to Ocala, wait until I got a new phone, then start back at Bayport. Using Michelle's phone, I reached out to Barry, but he was on his way to Las Vegas for the weekend. I called my family, but they had no way to get Lola back to Ocala, and I didn't feel comfortable leaving her behind. Finally, I called Jacque, but unfortunately she was in Ohio. The more rejection I faced, the farther I fell down the rabbit hole.

Michelle offered to put me up for the week at their house, but I didn't feel right about intruding for that length of time. She then had an ah-ha moment and made a phone call to her mom. I stepped away to use the men's room and when I came back, she had another option. Her parents owned a house down the street from their house. It was a secondary home used for weekend trips, so it was unoccupied. She had gone out on a limb and asked her mom if it was OK if I stayed there until my phone arrived. Her mom agreed and left the option up to me.

I placed my hand over the rim of my bourbon glass and spun it like a top while attempting to come up with another dumb excuse. I was having an internal argument with myself for no reason. I took a final drink, looked across the table at Michelle and said, "Sure, why the hell not?" She called Mike and her mom; I paid the bill, then went back to Sprint to order the phone.

Once we left the phone store, we went to the grocery to prepare for the week-long stay. I bought a bunch of food and replaced the food I had lost for the paddle. We returned to the house off the Mud, then walked Lola down to my new home. Michelle let me in, gave me a quick tour, then allowed me to get acquainted with my new surroundings. The house was a typical river home on stilts above the open garage. There was no cable TV, but plenty of movies, a hot shower, warm bed, coffee pot and full kitchen. I threw some frozen lasagna in the oven and took a shower. Michelle came over to make sure I was comfortable, then invited me over later to meet her mom and sister, who were visiting from Plant City, south of there.

Around 6 p.m. I walked down the road to Michelle's house for a meet-and-greet. When I arrived, the three ladies and Wayland were sitting in the den. Mom was a down-to-earth individual in her 50s. She had a laid back demeanor and was curious to meet this strange traveler who was staying in her home. Michelle's sister, Linda, was an out-spoken young lady a few years my junior. I was attracted to her smile and Southern drawl the moment I heard her speak. We shared stories and got to know one another pretty well as the evening progressed. After I passed the "mom test," the ladies left and Mike pulled into the driveway. Michelle and Wayland called it an evening, leaving us boys to our toys.

Mike and I got acquainted over cold beers in the garage. He was really into the idea of living off the grid. We talked about surviving in the wild and someday moving to Alaska to be mountain men. We shared a lot of similarities, which made the transition of becoming friends effortless. Time flew by as the empty bottles filled the recycling bins. He wanted to help me any way possible, so he gave me free range to use his tools in the garage while I stayed. The sun was playing with the idea of rising overhead, so we finished our beers and said goodnight.

During my stay with the Sims, I was teated like a family member. The weekdays were spent improving gear storage and fixing Lola's minor repairs. I took the time to make neoprene hull covers, reinforce the rudder and tighten the topside deck net. Mike supplied me with a spear gun, so I made an attachment to keep it safe and within arm's reach. I also prepared the GoPro for the open water stretches coming up. Lola was starting to look like a kayak you would use for a special ops mission. If I wasn't working on Lola, I spent time with Michelle and Wayland in the yard playing or drinking morning coffee on the porch deck.

The weekends were the time for play. Mike worked hard all week and he played even harder on the weekends. The weekends would start with the crack of a cold beer in the morning before taking the skiff out to the Chassahowitzka Bay to go Red fishing. If the fish weren't biting, we would cast our beards upon the waters and run the skinny bay. He enjoyed showing me some of his spots hidden behind the marshy islands. I enjoyed the fact I didn't have to paddle to get somewhere. It's funny how your body gets used to going a certain speed and if you end up going faster, like on a motor vessel, it feels like you are traveling through space and time. He took me to one of his honey holes and we bottomed out on an oyster bar. All I could do was laugh. I knew this feeling all too well. He eventually was able to push the boat off the oyster bar, returning us back to the water.

If we weren't fishing, we were running the waters, stopping off at bars or meeting his friends. His boating friend, Jaimee, came by with his skiff. I recall a midnight run we took. Everyone loaded up on the two boats and took off into the bay like bats out of hell. We raced to certain islands, then played a high-speed game of tag. I'd never been involved in this type of tomfoolery, but I sure as hell was enjoying it. Someone may or may not have been thrown from a boat during the game.

We ended up at a neighbor's house for a late-night fire. TA and Carla's house was across the channel. When we pulled up, Mike somehow ended up in the water, taking his wallet and phone with him. Yea, we had our fun -- and somehow I always woke back up in bed safe and sound the next morning.

After nine fun-packed days, Michelle received the call from Sprint, saying my new phone had arrived. The call couldn't have come at a better time. My thoughts were turning into the fuck-its. These thoughts are the most dangerous of them all. I started to lose track of why I was on the journey -- and all the fun I was having wasn't contributing to the idea of returning. Having the phone in hand helped me get past those thoughts and we came together one last time before I went back to the water.

Mike thought it would be fun to put Lola on the trailer and back me into the water, like he was unloading his boat. I entertained the idea, even though I thought it would be risky. We shared one more thank you and a good bye before I jumped into Lola's cockpit and prepared to be sent off. Michelle stood by recording the scene on her cellphone, I gave Mike the thumbs up, then he backed me in, nice and slow. It went surprisingly smooth and was somewhat anticlimactic. I raised my paddle, spun around to face the bay and left the sight of three angels behind.

Was it fate?

The saviors of my journey

Risk vs. Reward

I couldn't have chosen a better day to return to the water. There wasn't a cloud in the sky, the wind was almost non-existent and the water was like glass. The rudder helped me cut through the plane with precision and accuracy as the miles added up. I felt spoiled.

Even though everything was falling into place, the extended time off the water caught up to my body. I was using muscles I hadn't used in a while and my shoulders felt like they were holding up the world. I took a break at Hudson Beach ramp after 16 miles. The muscles in my forearms tightened to the point I thought they were going to burst through the skin. Across the ramp was an inn with an on-site bar. Uneasy and worried about pressing my muscles beyond their limits and getting hurt, I rented a room after having a few cocktails to rest my body. I sold myself on the idea by treating it more like an investment. Another 10 days off the water was out of the question, so I rested and relaxed.

I was excited to get back to the paddle the next morning, when I loaded Lola in at the ramp. If all went to plan, by the end of the day, I would find myself back in the open waters of the Gulf and setting camp along a sandy point of a barrier island. The day's 18-mile paddle provided strategically spaced county parks, where I could have dry snack breaks that didn't involve standing on oysters or in shallow water.

Airboats roared behind the marshes of the four-mile stretch along Werner Boyce Salt Springs of Port Richey, Fla., I stuck to the outside and pushed another couple miles to rest at the small ramp at Brasher Park. To prepare for the primitive camping site that evening, I filled my water containers at the restrooms and ate a hearty lunch before the four-mile stretch of open water.

Leaving Brasher Park, I passed Ree's Park, off the coast of New Port Richey. From the water, the park appeared to be a little more developed than Brasher. It had a swimming hole, picnic tables, restrooms, and a playground for the kids. Across the bay, I watched a pod of four or five dolphins skim through the shallows using their strength and endless energy to show off among their friends. I chose a spot just beyond the pod on the out-reaching strip of dredged land to rest before crossing the tumultuous stretch.

Forcing down another snack bar, I stood fixated, peering across the four miles of open water at the point of Anclote Key. The cyclonic wind created turmoil within the colliding waves between the two lands.

78

It had been a while since I had seen rough water like what lay ahead of me. I had goose pimples again and the hair on the back of my neck was standing at attention. This would become the classic tale of risk vs. reward.

I left the slice of sand and paddled with confidence. I constantly reminded myself I'd been here before and I'd made it through worse conditions. It took a bit to settle my nerves, but I was able to find a rhythm that the water, Lola and I shared. The wind tried to cock Lola off course, but the rudder was in full swing, allowing her to track with the utmost precision. For the first time since I began my trek, I had a one-up on the wind. Once I realized how much security the rudder provided, I was relieved and overly confident. I had a hard time believing I had made it that far without it.

Anclote Key's north point grants access to the three-mile barrier island. Primitive camping is allowed along the open sandy field. When I beached, I found myself alone. The wind whipped the fine sand over the landscape and pelted my exposed skin. There was a spot behind some brush that provided a small barrier for my tent. I set camp, then took a walk along the point as the sun fell, painting the sky with an array of deep oranges, reds and yellows.

Throughout our lives, there are few unadulterated moments we keep for ourselves. Somewhere along the way we allow people and situations to steal our joy found in the smaller things. On the point of Anclote Key, overlooking the fiery Gulf sky, I sat in the sand with a smile on my face. This moment was mine -- and mine alone. There was nobody to tell me otherwise and nobody shunning me back to Earth. The purity of the moment was exactly where it belonged, a lasting memory that lies in the depths of the heart of a wandering castaway

Anclote Key sunset moment of purity

79

Segments 8, 9 & 10
Anclote Key - Manasota Key
110 miles

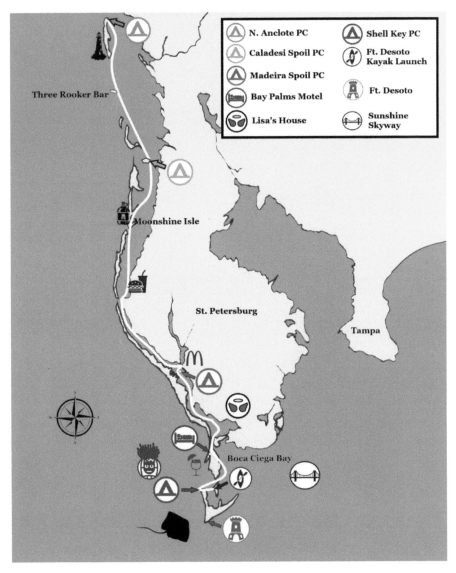

N. Anclote PC

Caladesi Spoil PC

Madeira Spoil PC

Bay Palms Motel

Lisa's House

Shell Key PC

Ft. Desoto
Kayak Launch

Ft. Desoto

Sunshine
Skyway

Three Rooker Bar

Moonshine Isle

St. Petersburg

Tampa

Boca Ciega Bay

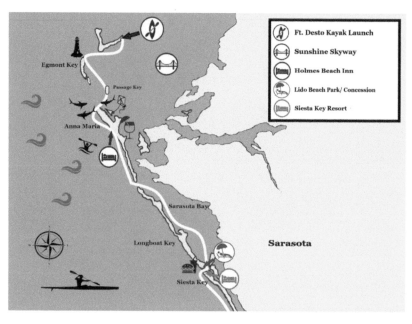

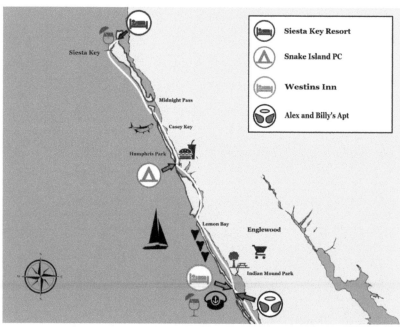

All maps were hand drawn and created by the author Jeffrey "Treehouse" Buncie

Gulf Beach Evenings

Anclote Key was a benchmark I looked forward to achieving. The island is a waypoint to the urbanized Gulf beaches of Pinellas, Hillsborough, Manatee and Sarasota counties. Each county marked a new section of my paddling adventure, as well as new challenges.

The beautiful sandy beaches of Pinellas were just a few strokes away before rounding the Gulf peninsula toward Hillsborough's Tampa Bay. The distant crossing, where the bay waters meet the symphonic waves of the Gulf, is able to turn even the most experienced paddlers' knuckles white. The reward for crossing here is it lands you on the soft sands of Anna Maria Island, where the sun plays all day.

Twenty miles through, the built-up Manatee Intercoastal Waterway leads you through a surprisingly remote paddle of the Sarasota Bay and its illustrious sea life. After paddling among the Loggerhead sea turtles, the route passes by the quaint beach town of Siesta Key. The not-so-quiet beach warms your feet by day and heart by night. If you are able to leave the island flare behind, the paddle weaves through a diverse network of mangroves and seagrass preserves, which allows you to regain your composure just in time to search the beaches of Venice for fossilized shark teeth.

I must've written that 15 times before settling on the passage above and I swear each time, I sounded more like a travel agent trying to sell a vacation. This was how much I was ready to paddle these next three sections. With a new state of mind, brought on by new experiences with the locals and beach-goers, I was open to slowing down and saying yes to different situations that brought new opportunities and possible lifetime friends.

In no way was it all unicorns and rainbows. As a matter of fact, the morning I pulled my head out of my sleeping bag on Anclote Key, I had what seemed like a blizzard rip through my tent. The wind howled all night and even though the tent fly was tight, the sand was so fine it flew through my bug netting and covered everything. That was how my day started, followed by an hour of digging out my gear and removing as much sand as I could.

Once the gear was packed, I was stoked to visit a lighthouse on the south end of the island. A brisk three-mile paddle brought me to the ferry launch, where in season, tourists arrive. I beached with the small sparrow-sized piping plovers running in and out of the lapping waves.

These sand-colored shorebirds play like children, racing the rising and falling water within the surf. The seasonal park did not have any ferries that day. It was just me and the birds. Along the path to the lighthouse, I saw two bald eagles flying overhead. The 1887 lighthouse, commissioned by President Grover Cleveland, aided ships for nearly 100 years before decommissioning in 1984. The skeletal pyramidal structure, known to the keepers as the old sentinel of the sea, was vandalized after becoming automated in 1952, but has since been deemed a heritage structure and was restored to all its glory around 2003.

Leaving the island, I chose to take a southern route across the preserve, where I encountered high winds that pushed me to a surprise sandbar, Three Rooker. I met an older couple fishing from the bar, which soon led to sharing the daring stories of the Big Bend. The two were enjoying the sun's warmth on an uncommonly cold, windy day. They had a few extra sandwiches packed away in their picnic basket, which they shared with me. As I said goodbye to the couple, I took the time to enjoy the paddle from the bar and into what seemed to be a trail system among the inlets.

Weaving between these inlets, I popped out to a bridge and saw my intended spoil isle campsite overrun by sailboats. Luckily, the Caladesi area has plenty of spoil islands and I could take my pick. I paddled just south, completing over 16 miles for the day, and landed on a cove with a beach big enough for me to have a fire and set my camp. The day seemed to disappear rather quickly. I sat by the fire and watched the silhouettes of the sail boats blend into the night.

My excitement continued upon my early rise with the sun. I took the time to cook a hot breakfast and warm my innards with some hot, sticky oatmeal. When I shoved off, I kept track of the countless number of camping possibilities among these spoils. There was a quick break on Moonshine Isle, which to my dismay, did not have any moonshine, but I made the best of it. Sitting in the sand at Moonshine Isle, I looked down the beach. My mind took me to the 20s Prohibition era. I pictured the black ships and their bootlegging captains running the inlets and imagined them leaving the payloads beyond the beach camouflaged by the scrub. Maybe, just maybe, I was sitting at a spot where William "the Real" McCoy had run some of his finest booze from the Bahamas.

I had started passing under the causeways that day, which had plenty of boat ramps to take breaks. I even found a causeway that had mobile food carts, ice cream trucks and cold beverages. Naturally, I chose to grab a hot dog and beverage before leaving the hidden oasis.

Somewhere along the way, my arms went into autopilot while listening to music, through what the maps called the narrows. The narrows I had faced thus far were much more difficult to navigate. Since I was making good time, I decided to push to Madeira Pass. Back in 2014, a lot of stores were built around the pass, which would be more beneficial for future paddlers. I was surprised to see the golden arches sitting right there off the water. I had to reassure myself, was I witnessing a mirage across the water? I remained leery until I hit the dock with Lola's bow. It was true, McDonald's was the second oasis I had found in one afternoon. This trip was becoming a little too easy.

After indulging in a thru-paddler's amount of greasy goodness, I found a rogue, unmarked island, where I was able to set camp just beyond the pass. Unfortunately, I chose a mosquito-infested island, but after the amount of food I had had, my stomach was telling my body I wasn't paddling any farther. I did what any other paddler would do -- ran around as I set my tent, avoiding the swarms, before diving into the tent to hide for the evening.

The next morning, there was another decision to be made. I would be paddling that day through the Boca Ciega Bay inland from the St. Pete Beach peninsula. St. Pete had played a key role in why my family moved to Florida from western Pennsylvania. Every year, my parents would take a two-week vacation, spending the better half of it chilling at that beach. In a way, I felt it had become a part of my upbringing. So in the great words of The Clash, "Should I stay or should I go?"

I played around with the idea as the morning paddle progressed. I rounded the cut and saw the Don Cesar Hotel towering over the silhouetted palms. The "Pink Building," as our family referred to it, has been a landmark for the sleepy Gulf Beach for as long as I can remember. Built in the Gatsby Era of the 1920s, the crown jewel of the Gulf beaches has served in the war efforts, housed the famous and even found its way to the silver screen. From that moment, I knew I would spend some time here in honor of the ol' family tradition. All it took was a hard right turn to get me to the inlet, where I had spent many hours fishing throughout my life. I recognized the Bay Palms Motel from its playful color scheme and pulled up to its grill-and-chill dock.

A quick phone call landed me a room for the next couple days. I planned on a little rest and relaxation, accompanied by some night-time predatory fishing. Once my gear was stowed and Lola was secure, I took a walk down the beach to the tackle shop before embarking on a search for burgers and beers. I remembered a spot down by the water, known as Woody's. It was a Pittsburgh-friendly bar that served ice-cold

Yuenglings and pretty decent burgers. I decided to put my left foot in front of my right foot and head that way.

The bar stools were filled with the local barflys chatting. I was able to pull one aside and squeeze in at the end of the bar before the bartender, Lisa, greeted me with a smile. She placed a frozen mug filled with beer in front of me and was curious. Being a local joint, I was pretty much the only face among the regulars she did not recognize. A whirlwind of questions and stories swept across the bar. A simple, "I kayaked here from Alabama," either confused or intrigued the staff and day-drinkers.

After a delicious burger, the stories were out in the universe and my frosted mug had become somewhat bottomless. The next couple hours flew by as the attentive, doe-eyed bartender remained intrigued. Lisa invited me out for drinks with her other bartender friends around town when her shift was over. How could I turn down beach hospitality like this? Would you?

As the sun set, we sat at a bar, Willy's, tucked away from the beach resorts, waiting for her friends to join the party. Once her friends arrived, the shots flowed. My new drinking buddies weren't feeling the vibe at Willy's, so they made their rounds and introduced me to some other establishments. We were now on a St. Pete Beach pub crawl.

I felt a draft of warm sun-lit air crawl up my leg as a beam of light punched me in the face the next morning. I opened my eyes with a blurry misunderstanding and cloudy recollection. Confused, I looked for the source of these two horrific entities. I peered across the room at a door hanging wide open. It took a few moments for me to realize I was laying bare-assed across my bed at the hotel. I rolled off the bed and crawled along the cold tile floor to stop the giggling neighbors from enjoying the show.

A hot shower and some breakfast beers brought me into the mid-afternoon hours. Wanting to know what the hell had happened, I walked down to Woody's, looking for answers. Lisa met me with a heart-warming hug. Grabbing a seat, I soon had a frosty mug of beer in front of me. A little embarrassed, I asked about the sequence of events and how I ended up in my birthday suit. With a laugh, she said she had had no idea I was that intoxicated, but after the bar crawl we went to the beach, where I ended up in the water. She assured me I had remained clothed, but after she dropped me off at the motel, she had no clue what I had done.

What a build up and such a letdown. Her friends came by the bar as I was still trying to figure it out. They were happy to see me again and we rehashed previous night's pub crawl. I guess they had enjoyed my company as they invited me out for another evening on the town.

We left the open air of Woody's and headed to a sports bar, Mac Nasty's. Tequila shots set the evening off with a bang -- which led to midnight dancing and make-shift bar stool karaoke. Obviously, a mixture of Bon Jovi and tequila is the perfect combination to entice you to stand on a bar stool and sing at the top of your lungs. Before being asked to leave, we decided to take the party back to Lisa's house.

I'm not sure what is more terrifying, waking up confused, naked on a bed, as I had the morning before, or waking to a big, strange dog licking my face on an unknown couch. I was two for two -- it seemed that as soon as I had gotten to the after-party, I sat on the couch and passed out. Lisa was running around, trying to get ready for her shift, but was running late. She said she could get me back to Woody's, but I would have to walk back to the motel from there. I had no qualms, since I had no clue where I was, so we jumped in the car and off we went.

Following my walk back to the motel from Woody's, I reserved the room for one more night in order to recoup and rehydrate. Once my chores were complete, I was going to relax in a hammock and fish from the dock. The day became what the past two days should have been. I felt quite at peace. Lisa swung by for a couple last-moment beers before I shipped off in the morning. We swapped phone numbers and said farewell one more time.

Anclote Key Light   **They see me coming**   **The Don Cesar**

The Chuck Nolan Project

Leaving the motel in the morning brought mixed emotions. I was super-stoked to paddle farther, yet saddened by the idea of leaving the beach I knew so well behind. A storm was brewing in the distance, cutting my day short, and I ended at a primitive camp on Shell Key. I found a sweet spot on the south side of the key, next to the channel, looking across at Fort DeSoto County Park of Pinellas County.

In a matter of minutes, my fishing line was baited and tossed into the depths. The tide was moving and there was no time to waste. Moments later, I landed my first catch -- a beautiful spotted sea trout that would soon become dinner. Luckily, the storm held off and I was able to find some driftwood to set the fire, so I could enjoy the trout. The chores were done and my belly was full, all before sunset. I had plenty of bait left, so I threw in the line and had some fun.

Standing, toes slightly dug into the dampened sand, I blankly stared at the porpoises playing across the channel. The sun was beginning to set, returning warm colors along the horizon. Deeply enjoying the serenity, I forgot my line was in the water. Just then, it started running. The force was incredible as the drag ran on and on. Whatever it was, it was big. I was excited, but patient. I let whatever was on the line run until it slowed and then, with a sudden jerk, I hooked it.

The weight was dead with very little fight, running, then halting. I thought it had to be a shark, but the fight wasn't as great as those I had caught before. I changed my tune and hoped it wasn't a catfish -- those are damn near useless and tend to run, then go dead. But, when I got my prize up to the surface, it was even worse than a sailfin, it was a common stingray, three- to four-feet wide. What a pain in my ass! I didn't have shoes to hold down the tail while I unhooked it, so I used my paddle as a counterweight for leverage. Once I flipped it over, I placed one blade on the tail and stepped on the other as I removed the hook and shooed it back into the water.

Once the sun fell and the fire went out, the flying teeth, also known as no-see ums, came at me with vengeance. I quickly stowed my gear and battened down the hatches before disappearing to the safety zone. Lying there, in my tent, I thought,"What a beautiful spot. Tomorrow is Halloween, why not have some fun with it? Let's take another zero."

Technically, it didn't become a zero because I paddled over to the fort to do some sightseeing and gather some firewood. The fort's kayak ramp was roughly a three-mile paddle around the island. The fort, which dates back to the 1900s, acted as a sub-fort to the neighboring Egmont Key, fortifying the Tampa Harbor. The fort never saw a battle, nor were any weapons ever fired. It was a beautiful, well-built fort, but it was soon decommissioned and became a marine hospital service that quarantined immigrants. It was later sold back to Pinellas County as public land.

Stashing firewood in the hulls to keep it dry was a mess, but it all worked out once I returned to the camp. Being Halloween, I decided to re-enact some scenes from the movie "Cast Away" and dress up like the protagonist, Chuck Nolan (Tom Hanks). I used a red Sharpie and a crab trap ball I found in the surf to create Wilson, found a staff among the drift wood and tied a bandana around the top -- and yes, created fire. I was having so much fun I even staged photos for evidence back home.

After all that hoopla, I went back to fishing, with even better luck than I had had the day before. I was pulling fish in left and right -- pin fish, grunts, drums and another sea trout. Blessed to have trout two nights in a row, life couldn't get any better.

The fire roared well into the evening, keeping the bugs at bay. The fun didn't end there -- I am sure you could hear me yell and scream, "Look what I have created!" or "I, I have created fire!" from the other shore as I danced around the wall of flames until the whiskey came to an end.

It happened again -- I awoke to a blanket of sand covering everything in my tent. The wind howled into the later morning hours. After checking the forecast and discovering the wind was not going to let up, sustaining at 28 to 32 mph the entire day, I called in the reinforcements. Before leaving Lisa behind, she had told me to give her a call if I needed anything. Today, I needed to get off that island.

Lisa had the day off work and said she would meet me by the kayak ramp in an hour. As I broke camp, I battled with the wind. Constantly getting hit by the stinging sand, I danced around like a boxer in the ring. Usually I had a certain, careful way to stow my gear, but the wind was too much. I crumpled, squeezed and threw my gear into any opening Lola had, just to get off that island.

What I thought would be an easy two-mile paddle turned into another hour bout with the wind. Three paddles forward moved me one paddle back. If I stopped moving my arms, the wind pushed me back and to the left. Refusing to give up, I pushed harder, leaning forward and using my entire body to power stroke my way to the bridge.

Lisa was watching as I battled my way to the ramp. She greeted me with a hug and a few laughs. Warning me of the high winds across the bridge, she was concerned about Lola sitting snugly on top of her Honda. While tightening down the ratchet straps, I assured her I had done it before, calming her nerves just enough to get her back behind the wheel.

White-knuckle driving ensued as the car got bullied by the high winds across the Tierra Verde Bridge. Lola shifted a few times, causing us to pull over and adjust the straps. This happening early in the drive did not make Lisa feel any better about the situation, but with our fingers crossed, and a few adjustments, we somehow made it happen.

Back at the house along Blind Pass, the day was going to be a grill-and-chill situation. After a few beers to calm our nerves, we built a fire in the pit out back. The lazy afternoon put us in a lazy haze; grilling became a phone call to the pizza delivery man. Pizza, beer and a fire -- nothing better.

The fire burned until everything burnable in sight was tossed into the ring. We had to call it an early evening in order for Lisa to get me back to the ramp before her 9 a.m. shift. I found myself back on the couch with a warm, snuggly blanket, hoping for calmer winds in the morning.

Chuck Nolan, now who is he?

Creating fire

Not for the Faint of Heart

The morning was going according to plan. We were up and out by 8 a.m. with a quick stop at the Subway for a breakfast sandwich. I dashed through the door to see a very confused employee standing behind the counter. The Subway was closed, but Tim, the super-cool employee, offered to make me a sausage, egg and cheese sandwich before I headed out. So this is for you, Tim from Subway in 2014, my awesome sandwich-making friend. That wonderful breakfast helped me get through the toughest day paddling thus far on my journey.

Lisa dropped me at the ramp and after we said good-bye, I once again was on my own. Ahead of me was a two-mile, open-water paddle across the shipping channel to the home of Fort Dade and one of the first three lighthouses in Florida.

Egmont Key, now primarily a wildlife refuge accessible only by boat, has a history dating back to the Spanish conquistadors. The lighthouse, built in 1848, was damaged in its inaugural year during the Great Hurricane. It was rebuilt in 1958 to be able to "withstand any storm." Fort Dade sits on the northern tip that protected the key's channel from the start of the Spanish-American War to 1923. In its day, it housed 300 residents with amenities, such as electricity, telephones, movie theater, tennis courts and even a bowling alley. After the military closed the fort, the Tampa Bay Pilots Association took it over in 1926. Ships entering and leaving were required to have a pilot aboard to navigate them through the harbor safely. Upon arriving on the shore, I took the time to explore and appreciate the island's rich history.

The wind really started to pick up while I was walking the red-lined brick roads of Egmont. I hurried back to Lola and prepared for the remaining three-mile paddle across Tampa Bay. I was soon in the middle of an out-flowing tide, where two bodies of water met. The rollers turned into three to four-foot swells, causing stability issues and panic. I was saved by a sandbar, Passage Key, that sits a mile north of Anna Maria Island. The bar was big enough to break the out-going tide and calm the water. I was able to step out and take a standing break in the shallows. Surrounded by water for miles around, I took a moment -- as anyone should -- to admire the situation. Roughly six miles to the east was the infamous Sunshine Skyway Bridge, towering above the bay, and with a quick head turn west was the endless perfection of the Gulf of Mexico. How many people in their lifetime can say they found themselves in that type of circumstance? The question was exactly what I needed to work up the audacity to get back out in the chaos.

The last mile from Passage Key to Anna Maria Island can only be described as completely insane paddling. No less than four-foot breakers approached Lola and me in four-second intervals. Yes, I timed them. Every approaching wave cresting just before it sucked us into the next. Fear of the white-capped water upending us before we reached the shore was enough to turn my beard hair gray. Easily disappearing behind the passing swells, I aimed Lola toward the shelter of the northern tip. Hoping to escape the raging sea waters, I leaned forward and really put my back into it. Some 300 yards from the shore, we successfully entered calmer, shallow water. We were no longer battling the water, but now we were in the middle of the largest school of black-tip sharks I have ever encountered -- hundreds of sharks sitting just off the island. Reaching for the rudder cord, I pulled the shiny silver rudder out of the water and slowly paddled through the shark frenzy.

Upon reaching the shore, I was greeted by another Jeff, who was using the high winds to his advantage while flying a very expensive-looking kite. Pumped full of adrenaline, I approached him. I had hoped someone had witnessed what the hell I had just gone through to see if it looked just as crazy from the shore as it did from the water. In agreement, he asked what I was doing out there on a day like that day. We shared stories, information and tips, including a phone app called Windfinder. As an avid kiter, he led me onto this app that sailors, kite surfers and boarders use to plan their outings, according to wind speed and direction.

After a while, a lady walked down the beach and said she had watched me crossing from the point and made me feel like a real badass by saying, "You must be a real warrior, out there on the water today." With a chuckle and a smile, I looked over at Jeff and replied, "you have no idea ..."

Like a real professional, or at least a seasoned veteran, I returned to the water from the shelter of the island rather than chance the beating the breaking waves would have put me through. Off I went, disappearing behind the swells like a ghost in the mist. I still had four miles of rough water to get through before I could call it a day.

Holmes Beach and the Anna Maria Inn were my home for that evening. Timing it as well as I could, I took an educated guess which building was the Inn, turned Lola's nose toward the shore and rode the break onto shore. Success! I wasn't upended as the bystanders watched the attempt. I surfed that wave in, stayed upright and stepped out before having the next wave roll Lola to shore. Just a little bad news -- I was two buildings from the inn. Nothing new to me, so I drained Lola out and pulled her through the sand to her home for the night.

Another day was in the books. The Inn was near a Circle K, which had a solid resupply, and a bar named Sharkey's. Over a burger and beer, I mulled over the eventful day. It all came down to one conclusion -- big sharks and big surf are not made for the faint of heart.

A big day started with a solid breakfast from the Circle K the next morning. I planned a 20-mile day through Bradenton and into Siesta Key. Morning waters were calm and I made it to the pass after Coquina Beach in record time. I found myself in Sarasota Bay battling the non-rhythmic waves and seawall returns throughout the morning.

The long paddle down Longboat Key left me restless and unable to find John Durante Park for lunch. My back was tapped out and my ass fell numb. I had to take a stand-up break while hanging in the sea of mangroves. Private land and high seawalls made these recurring standing breaks the norm in the Sarasota Bay. A grueling 16 miles later, I was finally able to eat a late lunch and take a substantial break at Lido Beach with its over-priced concessions.

An uneventful four miles along the Sarasota beaches put me in a trance induced from boredom. The thought of paddling to a key named after a midday nap seemed to be fitting. When I arrived at Siesta Key, the story became otherwise. The beach was lined with red Solo cups and young, tanned bodies. After pulling Lola ashore, the sight of Wilson, who had become my mascot, brought over some curious beach goers. Wilson instantly earned me a beer from a younger threesome -- Tom, Chad and Rachael. They listened to my tales and helped me carry Lola up the long beach to the parking lot. They had an evening out on the town planned, so we swapped phone numbers and went our separate ways.

The hand cart came in handy again as I walked Lola across the road to the Siesta Key Resort. I was able to secure a room and got cleaned up for the planned festivities. I gave the young'uns a call, but they never picked up. Trying to be a responsible adult and actually have an early evening, I decided to take a walk through the nightlife of Siesta Key. The village reminded me of a scaled-down Key West. There were free shuttles and bars filled with island music lining the cobblestone strip. I still hadn't heard from the kids, so I headed back to my room to rest my eyes.

It was unfortunate I wasn't able to hook up with the college kids. Then again, I would've spent another day on the key trying to recoup, so at least that was an advantage. Getting Lola back to the water without help was a long, drawn-out process. It literally was a pain in my ass -- my hamstrings were not up to it that early in the morning. Eventually, Lola and I returned to the calm morning waters, happy to have escaped the party potential of Siesta Key.

Along the way I became lost in my thoughts and overshot Midnight Pass, which was my cut back into the bay. Snapping out of my daze, I felt the timing didn't seem right. Beaching on a tapering strip of sand, I found a path to the other side of the bushy dune and followed it to the bay. The well-travelled path led to a cove, where boats were anchored. I returned to Lola and took her on another portage across the sand.

Back on the bay, along the spoil isles of Casey Key, I found the honey holes of the local fishermen. Tarpon were breaching the surface, feeding on the greenbacks, and redfish left muddy trails behind as I sneaked up on them in true ninja fashion. If only I had had some bait, I could've had a field day pulling these monsters out of the water. Unfortunately, I didn't, so I kept pressing south to a camp off the Venice inlet.

Snake Island is a camp well-known by fishermen in the area. When I pulled up, it almost looked like people regularly lived on the small island. There were obvious cutting boards built for cleaning fish, a noticeable fire ring and a 360-degree view of the surrounding areas. I claimed a spot for my tent, ate some takeout I had grabbed from Pop's Restaurant at Humphris Park and watched the sun set over the Gulf.

The evening became quite interesting after that. A boat with three drunk locals pulled up to the shore where I was sitting. I politely asked how they were doing, and waited for them to tell me I was not supposed to be there. Well, it was exactly the opposite. They welcomed me to the island and claimed they were the official Snake Island government. There was Keith, the mayor, and Scott and Bruce, his lackeys. Keith opened a cooler and threw me a beer. I chose to play along with their "government" scheme. Their stories topped a lot of mine... and wouldn't you know, their government was legit. The locals actually do vote them in. After a few beers, they went on their way before "the wives got too angry," leaving me with a nightcap and telling me to enjoy the island.

Over a Bottle of Rum

My body hurt so badly the next morning I swear the Snake island government came by and beat me up in my sleep. Between the long, open stretches, strong winds and battling the bay, my body just about had had enough. The route that day would lead me out of the Gulf and into the Intercoastal Waterway, around Venice to Manasota Beach. I thought that, with this change, I might have an easier day, but we all know how that had usually gone.

The boat traffic through the corridor had me working my hip flexors and putting my balancing act to work. Thankfully, there were plenty of beach parks around for taking sanity breaks. Exhausted, I stopped off at Indian Mound Park, where I met an interesting character named Captain Kelly Shelton. An older gentleman with a dark, tanned complexion, lack of hearing and a sweater full of sand spurs, he claimed he had been sleeping in the restroom at the park for a week. He pointed me in the direction of the corner store, then gave me $20 to pick up cigarettes and beer.

I walked into the town of Englewood, where the store was, bought some grub and picked up his supplies. When I returned, he was surprised to see I was a man of my word. Over a couple of beers, he told me about his boat anchored in Lemon Bay and offered me a deckhand job. He was a little bummed I turned his offer down. To assure I did not outstay my welcome, I bid him farewell and returned to Lola.

From Indian Mound I had roughly 2 miles until I arrived at the hotel on Manasota Beach. The bayside of Westin's Hotel had a ramp next to the office, but only had Gulf-side rooms available for the evening. The desk clerk Tiffany was super chill and helped me secure a room. When I loaded Lola on the handcart to cross the road, I discovered one of the tires was flat. I had to walk just under a mile to the Circle K for some Fix-A-Flat, which fortunately it had.

On my journey to the gas station, I saw a number of bars and restaurants that I planned on returning to after cleaning up a bit. I chose to swing into a joint, Flounder's, where I had a very tasty Tiki burger, topped with jalapenos and pineapple. My belly was full and I was ass-whipped. I returned to the air-conditioned room to enjoy a comfy bed and trash TV.

Calling the evening short, brought an early rise and a daybreak walk along the beach, which I used to look for fossilized shark teeth for my niece, Kelsey. I dug in the sand and pulled the gems out, one by one. My success motivated me even more to hit the water.

Approaching the hotel I was greeted by two older guys, hanging out under a tiki hut and drinking rum. One asked about my "rig" over by the bayside ramp. He was referring to Lola and I claimed her as mine. Mark, a tanned sailor resembling an older version of British actor Clive Owen, offered me a drink. My first thought was, "It's 8 a.m."; the second was, "Absolutely!" Mark, Rick and I sat under that tiki hut from 8 a.m. to 3 p.m., sharing traveler tales and a bottle of rum.

Mark was the talkative one with a new positive outlook on life. He was preparing his sailboat, anchored in Pompano, Fla., to become self-sustaining and capable of removing from the grid. He spoke of his walk up the Florida coast a few years prior and gave pointers for stealth camping on the beaches. Rick presented himself as more of the Captain Morgan-type scallywag. He loved his rum and drank it like water. Although he was the quiet one he tried to follow the storyline until the rum took over and drove him to his room.

We were rudely interrupted by the hotel manager just before 3 p.m., when she came over and told me it was time for me to leave. By this time, I was too intoxicated to return to the water, so I asked about renting a room for the night. She told me they were sold out and I had to leave the property -- even though the parking lot was empty. Mark invited me to sleep on the floor of their room, and I sat back down and continued the conversation. Not 15 minutes later, the manager came back with a big security guard, explaining again that if I did not leave the property, the police would be called and I would be charged with trespassing. Mark had my back again. He said he could load Lola on his truck and drop her off at a friend's house around the block. The idea sounded a lot better than pressing. We drove across the street, loaded her up and dropped her at his friend's house.

Once we dropped Lola off, Mark and I agreed to stay out of sight of the hotel. We went to catch some live music and dinner at Flounder's. As we sat there eating our burgers, Mark received a call from the groom of the wedding he was to attend the next day. The whole story had gotten blown out of proportion and the bride was worried about me causing a scene. I told Mark not to worry about anything and I would find a spot away from the hotel to sleep.

Mark was a trooper. He hung out and drank at the bars with me until the early morning. We had our own little pub crawl along Manasota Key. Just before last call, and four bars later, we swung through Flounder's again for one final drink. While I was ordering the round, a stunning young lady, Alex, came over and stood next to me.

She tapped me on my arm and said she really liked my ocean sleeve tattoo. Excited to show off her half-sleeve, she invited me to join her and her friends.

I returned to Mark with our round and told him I just met Alex and she seemed really into me. I might have found a home for the night. Mark gave me a wink and a smile as we joined her friends.

While I was playing it cool, telling some tales, Alex's captivating smile and tanned surfer body was giving off all the right signals. It wasn't too long before I was introduced to her tall, fit husband, Billy. Immediately I thought, "Fuck, guess it just isn't my night." But still, they were super-friendly and welcoming. Mark stood by and mentioned I needed a spot to crash. After they heard about the bitchy manager, they invited me to stay at their apartment.

The party moved a block down the road to a one-bedroom apartment. Mark and I set a time for me to pick Lola up and we parted ways. Alex and Billy showed me to a very comfortable papasan chair. The couple welcomed me into their lives that evening with support of the journey. They were excited to see people were still out there living outside the norms of the societal world. As the evening progressed, the chair swallowed me up and put me to sleep.

Egmont Key Light

Showing off

Manasota living
Photo credit: Mark Reinhardt

Sunset over the causeway

96

Segments 11 & 12
Manasota Key - Bowtie Island
76 miles

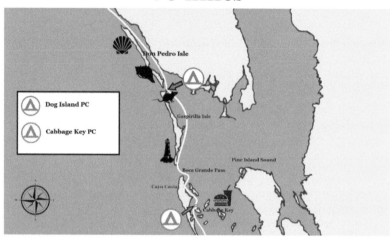

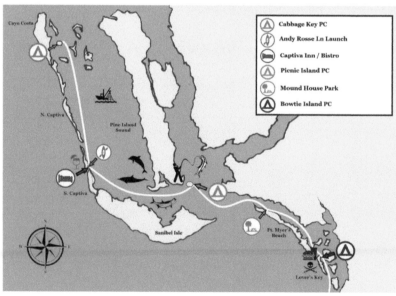

All maps were hand drawn and created by the author Jeffrey "Treehouse" Buncie

Return to the Blueway

8:30 a.m.

Drunk, alone and in a strange apartment in Manasota Key. What a hell of a way to bring in the new segment! Manasota Key was the last stop before rolling into the Charlotte Harbor. A short 22-mile journey would lead me through five aquatic preserves, spanning over 150,000 acres. The pristine barrier islands and surrounding estuaries are home to valuable nurseries for fish, crab and shrimp. Harboring over 86 different endangered species, paddling through this hidden gem is an opportunity of a lifetime.

After saying farewell to some beautiful people, I was on my way. Charlotte Harbor, just south, led me through condos and mangroves before heading into the segment that started it all -- the Estero Bay. Earlier, I mentioned a very special island overlooking the Sanibel causeway. Picnic Island, which is nestled along the Great Calusa Blueway, is where I found myself wanting to do, see and encounter more. The Estero Bay segment covers another 55 miles through the shallow waters of Pine island Sound, protected by the highly praised island life of Captiva and Sanibel islands. With all this in mind, why are we wasting any more time? Let's get back to that strange apartment.

There I was, stumbling through an apartment to find that Billy had left three choices of beverages on the counter. Next to them was a note explaining he was walking their dog, Marley. Coffee, orange juice and coconut water all waited. The only thing better would have been some Pedialyte -- the perfect hangover cure.

Billy showed up soon after and accompanied me on the walk to meet Mark where we had secured Lola. We spent some time talking over the gear and how I stowed it. Mark and Billy carried her to the water's edge behind his friend's house. Just like that, I was on the water again waving good-bye to a couple rad-ass dudes who had helped this paddler more than they'd ever know.

Feeling like death, I managed to paddle a mile before taking my first break at Stump's Pass. The foul stench of sour booze oozed from my pores as the midday heat assaulted my body. I was able to find a bit of shade along the palms, just before making my way through the rip tide-infested pass.

It was a day of many breaks along the length of Don Pedro Island. The shells and solitude of the island were surprising.

Somewhere between picking from the shell gardens and slowing the pace, my body slowly recovered.

Re-energized, I continued south toward Dog Island. Maintained by the Florida Paddling Trails Association (FPTA), the island is one of the only permissible camping spots among the bird sanctuaries. The inviting site became a solace for my desiccated body.

Throughout the evening, I was ransacked by the local inhabitants of the island. The mice and rats scurried over the tent and among the camp. Slowly becoming more and more pissed off, I lay there waiting for the shadows to shine through the moonlight. Patiently I waited, reached up and punched the sons of bitches clear off the tent. I made a game of it and cursed them while watching them fly into the darkness.

Lack of sleep pushed the morning start later than anticipated. I ended up leaving the island on a negative tide. The shallow water slowed my progression on the way to the Port Boca Grande Lighthouse. To rest, I took a moment to enjoy the free air conditioning and free museum before crossing the populated Boca Grande Pass. In the museum you learn how the light aided early cattle ships from Port Charlotte to Cuba in the late 1800s, then progressed to aid more than 30 ships a day during World War II protecting a safe harbor for shipping into the Gulf. As with many lights along the Florida coast, they run their course and become deteriorated. It was no different for this one once it was abandoned by the Coast Guard in 1969. These slices in history should never be left behind and that is where the National Register of Historic places and the county of Lee came to its rescue. In 1986, the light was refurbished and recommissioned before being handed over to the State Parks in 1988. By 1999, the light and museum was open to the public and once again under Coast Guard control.

My prior two trips across the pass, known for the best tarpon fishing in the world, was quite dangerous. Although it is not a far crossing, it holds records for large amounts of boat traffic. This time was no different. The walkarounds and sport-fishing yachts turned the already ripping pass into a nightmare for my non-motorized vessel. But, once I was able to reach the other side, a paradise awaited on Cayo Costa.

With the hope of staying in one of its state park campsites, I docked and visited the registration building. As usual, they were booked, so instead of calling it a day, I had to push farther into a brewing storm. At that point, the route enters the Estero Bay section and can either swoop westward over the north end of Pine Island or continue south toward Captiva. I chose to take the latter with a stop at the notable Cabbage Key. Before that could happen, my lagging GPS on my phone failed me again, adding a two-mile side trip around Useppa Island and landing at Part Island, just off the mark.

Facing the waves of rain, I hustled to get to the Cabbage Key Inn and Restaurant. On the way, just north of Cabbage, is a small island with a pocket beach. I popped ashore and found a spot for my tent. There was a break in the rain, so I took the time to set camp, then paddle on to Cabbage Key.

In the past, on prior ventures, I had stopped at the inn to hide from the sun and visit the famous Dollar Bill Bar. The bar is known for its thousands of signed dollar bills taped wall-to-wall and hanging from the rafters. The burgers have been said to be the original "cheeseburger in paradise," but that story has been proven to be local lore. The lure of this little slice of paradise has brought notable people, such as Ernest Hemingway, Jimmy Buffett, Katherine Hepburn and now, for the third time, long-distance paddler Jeff Buncie.

My cheeseburger disappeared rather quickly, so I ordered another for the journey back to the camp. I sat and enjoyed a few ice-cold longnecks before heading back toward my island retreat. The rain returned for the remainder of the evening, confining me to the tent. No complaints though, I had a lovely dinner with Lola, while listening to the sweet sounds of the rain.

Restless legs and a really wicked heel spur drew me out of my bag around sunrise. I gingerly stepped out of the tent to an overcast sky. That's what the day was going to throw at me? OK. I bucked up, fashioned my newly acquired rain gear and headed south to Captiva Island.

My optimism about the day was shut down in less than a mile before I pulled over and returned to my usual paddling clothes. The thickness of the neon-orange rain suit caused me to overheat and become quite nauseous. One thing I had going for me was familiar territory. I knew of a kayak ramp off Andy Rosse Lane in Captiva that would lead me right to the Captiva Inn.

The dismal weather kept the pleasure craft to a minimum. Over the 12 miles, I only saw one fishing boat. While passing, the three commercial fishermen rubber-necked as if they were about to watch a train wreck. I suppose they were thinking what I was thinking -- What the hell was I doing out on the water on a day like that? What they didn't know was how much a warm, dry spot and a burger can motivate a long-distance paddler.

A quick Google search led me to the Calusa Blueway sign at the end of Andy Rosse Lane. Lola was put on the hand cart and

100

escorted a quick two-tenths of a mile to the island cottages of the Captiva Inn. The kayak-friendly Inn booked me in the exact same cottage as they had in the past. For a meager $100, I had a one-bedroom cottage, a fence and free breakfast at the Key Lime Bistro.

Every piece of my gear was soaked. The first step was to get into dry clothes. After changing, I turned the room into a spider web of laundry lines to dry everything out. I had to escape the ensuing thick, musky air.

I spent the remaining hours of daylight around the island, sampling the local fare. Margaritas led me to the Mucky Duck to celebrate the Gulf-side sunset and a stroll along the beach. The day came to a close when I returned to my pungent, air-conditioned room.

Boca Grande Lighthouse Museum

Cabbage Key rain gear   **Andy Rosse Lane, Captiva**

Islands of Inspiration

Free breakfast is always a great incentive to wake up. The bistro set me up with a protein-packed feast before I dragged Lola back to the water. I had pep in my step -- it wasn't raining, I was returning to Picnic Island and I had an adventurous route through the spoils planned.

I was headed due east, across the flats of the Pine Island Sound. Breaching the outstretched plane, the springing tarpon caught their midday lunch, while the dolphins jetted through the inlets. The spoils were within reach when I had a spooked tarpon jump over Lola's bow as if he was clearing the high jump. Why? Why is it every time I witness an awesome spectacle, my GoPro is not running? Amazed, I stored the phenomenon in the memory bank etched in my brain.

Once I reached the cuts between the unlandable spoils, the paddle became less exhilarating. Rounding the south end of the cut, the island I knew so well appeared on the horizon. The inviting banks of the shore drew me closer with its gravitational pull. Autopilot ensued, landing me on the white crystals within moments. I had the island to myself.

I set camp in the shade of the mangrove trees and began the hunt for ripe coconuts. The island was surrounded by the fruit brought by the tides. I set a few good ones aside for later. Walking between the shallow mangrove roots, I also found some greenbacks in a tidal pool waiting to be baited and hooked. Foreseeing a fishing excursion, I used my water scoop to trap a few and ran to get my rod.

Slowly wading knee-deep to the drop-off, radiating positivity, I was stoked to have fresh bait. Ever play that game in economics where you have to start with an eraser and see how far you can barter? That was my idea with the greenbacks. I was hoping to catch a small pinfish and work my way up, using cut bait, to land a tarpon. I had the right idea. Moments later, I was able to land the next size baitfish, switch my tackle and try for a game fish. My plan was in full swing when a tarpon latched onto the rig and ran a record 100-yard dash. I had successfully reached my goal! Ecstatic, I got a little too aggressive, allowing the fish to break free on his second jump. He shook free and took my tackle with him. And that was that. He got away with my last steel leader.

Resorting to fishing with lighter tackle, I hoped for a speckled trout or a decent-sized red fish to cook up with the coconut water. The fish stopped biting, leaving me unsatisfied. Instead of wallowing in my sadness, I hit the mangroves with the spear. The mangrove snappers were schooled between the murky roots. The waves lapped, moving my body in and out of the mangroves. Gripping the slippery roots, using one arm to steady myself, I aimed into the school, eyeing the bigger of the snaps and pulled the trigger. It was a direct hit! I reeled him in and headed back to camp with another fresh fish to cook on an open fire.

There was just enough firewood around the island to get the fire hot enough to cook. While the coals were accumulating, I cleaned the fish, cracked and shucked the coconut, then put it on the fire. For a tasty treat, I shucked another coconut and prepared some wild rice. The spread was fit for a king and, tonight, that king was me. I enjoyed my feast sitting on a sun-bleached log and watching the sunset behind the Sanibel Causeway.

The evening brought swarms of mosquitoes and no-see-ums. The fire gave way as I retired to my tent. The air was hot and stale. It was the beginning of a sticky, sleepless night.

The next morning, as I left Picnic Island behind, there was so much to look forward to. I was paddling onto the waters of Lover's Key, where legends of pirates fill the backs of the local bar menus. That day I would cross over the 700-mile mark in my journey and make my home on Bowtie Island, finishing another section. But, before all that happened, I found myself exploring another hidden gem on Fort Myers.

Mound House Park invites visitors into the world of the Calusa Indians. The shell mounds left behind by the natives are visited year-round in this tropical paradise. The park was intimidating from the water's edge. The well-manicured property features a museum built on top of one of these mounds. Unfortunately, when I paddled through, the indoor exhibits were being refurbished. I had to enjoy the property from the outside, looking in.

Following the fishing boats toward the pass, I found a waterway restaurant, Flipper's. It was just about lunchtime, so I stopped in for a burger and a beer. The open-air deck allowed me to escape the sun and learn more of the local pirate, Calico Jack. As with most islands, a legend came with the name. Some say Lover's Key was named as such because a local couple would escape the mainland for some sexy time on the then-secluded island. I prefer the story of how Calico Jack and his sweetheart, Anne Bonny, got swept up on the Gulf coast during a storm and named it after their romantic relationship.

Head in the clouds and heart with the ocean, I paid my tab and headed south to Bowtie Island. The GPS failed me again; this time I was using the coordinates given for the actual camp. It led me to a large mangrove forest, where I saw no way to set camp. I circled the island until I found what looked like a campsite. I was unsure of the definite location, but it was roomy enough to celebrate the milestones and look onward to what the 13th leg of the trip had in store for me.

Celebrating Picnic Island with a fresh coconut

Mound House property   **Calusa Blueway marker**

Segment 13
Bowtie Island - Everglades City
70 miles

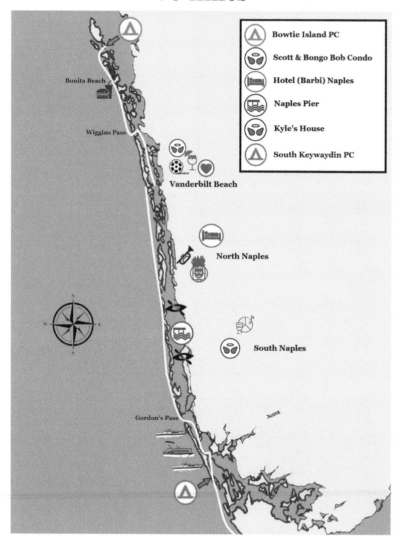

Bowtie Island PC	
Scott & Bongo Bob Condo	
Hotel (Barbi) Naples	
Naples Pier	
Kyle's House	
South Keywaydin PC	

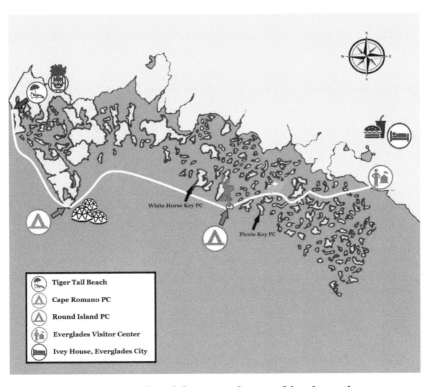

Legend:

- Tiger Tail Beach
- Cape Romano PC
- Round Island PC
- Everglades Visitor Center
- Ivey House, Everglades City

White Horse Key PC

Picnic Key PC

All maps were hand drawn and created by the author
Jeffrey "Treehouse" Buncie

No Reservations

If you guessed more mangrove protected keys, you guessed appropriately. To be more accurate, there are over 10,000 of these islands surrounded by mangroves. The mangroves protect these islands from being washed away and the root system stops storm surges. However, before I encountered these uniquely formed habitats, the cabana-lined beaches of the Gulf lay in wait.

Bowtie Island continued to be a mess well into the morning. The thick blanket of biting bastards shielded out the sun. Precautionary measures were taken, but I was dancing around trying to shake the infestation to the rhythm of "The Scatman" playing in my head.

Ten miles of Gulf-side beach parks provided rests and concessions. Breakfast was put on hold until I reached Bonita and Barefoot beaches, four miles south of Bowtie. Doc's on the Beach was a blessing with its over-priced menu items and to-go adult beverages. While eating, I reserved a room at the Lighthouse Inn on Vanderbilt Beach. With an easy 5 to 6 miles to go, I cut inside at Wiggins Pass to cruise into the inn.

The high seawall wasn't the only challenge the Lighthouse made me overcome. Upon my arrival, they claimed to have never received the reservation. Even after I showed them the online confirmation, they did nothing. Thinking of my last hotel fiasco, back in Manasota Beach, I politely asked for a room, but it was sold-out for the Veterans Day holiday weekend. That was the last straw.

Before I became hangry, I sought out a burger bar and decided to do some drinking thinking. Every, I mean *every* hotel on or around the water, was no less than $250 per night with a two-night minimum, which I couldn't afford. Beer after beer, I began to think about how Mark would approach the situation on his walk up the beaches. Sure, I could paddle south, but in order to get to a non-privatized beach, I would have to paddle another 10 miles. It was already four in the afternoon, so that idea was plumb out. I searched for a late-night bar, but Google had no answer. I did, however, find a movie theater with the latest showing at 8:30 p.m., putting me out on the street again around midnight. Maybe, by that time, I could nestle into a dark corner of the beach.

The progressions and thought processes are funny at times, but it sounded like a solid plan. If only I had gotten a few hours of sleep during the movie, it would've been. The movie, "The Equalizer," with Denzel Washington, was so good I *had* to stay awake.

Exiting the theater, I saw an older fellow on a bicycle, who yelled out, "Hey Rick!" Naturally I looked up, but said nothing. The next strip mall over, I heard music coming from what appeared to be a bar. I strolled over to a bar that was open until 2 a.m. A new plan came to mind. I was now staying until the bar closed, drinking only beer, and then finding a spot on the beach until sunup.

While I was at the bar, ordering my first beer, I heard "Hey Rick!"again. It was the guy from the parking lot. Bored, I turned and walked over to his table, asking "So, who the hell is Rick?" He was embarrassed when he realized I was not his friend, Rick. He was polite enough to continue the conversation as his buddy joined him at the table.

The two characters were Bongo Bob and Scott the skier. Bob was a portly, jolly fellow in his early 50s, enjoying his visit from Wisconsin. Scott, the slightly older of the two, claimed to be an ex-U.S. Pro skier turned lyric writer, who had a condo a few blocks away. You know by now how I started my conversation. They were happy to hear my tales and had plenty of follow-up questions, mostly about how I could afford such a journey.

I joined them outside for a change of scenery and we continued our conversation. A young brunette in her mid-20s was out there also, gallivanting around. She walked over and introduced herself. Her four-inch, seafoam-green heels clicked on the concrete distinctly over the patio music. She introduced herself as Ashley and wanted to join our fun. The guys jumped at the chance to brag about my journey, which led to a private conversation between Ashley and I.

The mutual views of leaving the societal world behind had been a wet dream of hers. She said she realized how locked down in her mind-dulling routine she had become. Of course, I romanticized the idea and embellished, just a little, how awesome it has been. It kept her interested and me somewhat of a mystery. Her entourage of yes-men and do-boys began to get worried and we were interrupted by one, who was obviously picking up the tab. She said she had to get back and leaned in for a hug and a peck, which grew into a tender farewell lip-lock.

I returned to Scott and Bob for another round. From that point on, I was distracted, in and out of the conversation, and peering out of my peripheral vision at the skinny-jeaned, halter-topped Ashley. I could tell she wanted to escape the norm and I started to plot how I was going to get to talk to her again. There was no need. We locked eyes from across the bar, smiled at each other and she moved back over to our table.

With no hesitation, she placed her hand on my thigh and said, "Let's go talk." I excused myself from the guys and followed her through the back of the bar. We found ourselves in a deserted parking lot away from any distractions. Breaking the silence, I asked, "So, what's up?" "You know what's up," she replied in a seductive voice.

Before I said anything stupid, we intertwined our bodies. Within moments, our shirts lay on the blacktop, while our bodies shared one another's heat. She paused, held me tighter and whispered in my ear, "I love the way you smell." It took every ounce of focus I had not to break up the heat, but I couldn't contain my thoughts and laughter. I hadn't showered in four or five days and I was covered in sea salt and sweat. At that point, I couldn't believe she was able to stand in the same space I was in, let alone moving into second base, but it all seemed to be working.

The movements remained effortless until those pesky skinny jeans caught her heels, tripping her and the momentum. "My shoes! Get my fucking shoes!" She kicked them off as a car pulled in, catching us in the glare of its headlights. We moved into the shadows of the building for leverage and discretion. Beading sweat accumulated and energy built as our bare backs became raw from the brick-layered building. She removed her grip from my shoulders, grabbed my face -- and then abruptly halted, saying, "I have to stop. I have a kid."

I am no saint, but once this mutual understanding became a little less mutual, I had to stop. I pulled her off and set her on the ground to talk through the situation. Her child must've been a fleeting thought because she went right back to getting intimate. Moments later, she pulled the same shit again. After I set her back on the ground, she stated she could not go any further. Before we got caught red-handed, sort of having relations, I picked up her clothes and helped her get dressed. Re-entering the bar was our next challenge. Her do-boys were looking for her, so we went in as every couple would re-enter a room after having a quickie in the bathroom -- one at a time, with a few moments in between. We parted ways and never said another word to each other.

Bob and Scott had a field day with me after that whole debacle. They wanted to continue the party and invited me back to the condo for a few beers. Along the way, Scott said if I needed a place to crash, I could do so on their couch. Another problem solved. We stayed up until early morning pounding Fireball shots and ice-cold beer.

When I woke up the next morning, the condo was silent. Pulling myself off the couch was a task in itself. When I finally did get up, I realized I was in another empty home. The clock read 11 and I was still tipsy from the night before. A few moments after I had grabbed a cup of coffee, Bongo Bob walked through the door telling me Scott had had to work for a few hours. Bob relayed a message from Scott to make myself at home and "mi casa es su casa."

The afternoon progressed; we reminisced about the evening's activities and shared a few laughs. Bob and I made plans for the evening over a burger and a beer, then split ways so I could check on Lola.

Lola remained at the condo wet dock, a little over 2 miles away. The excruciating walk was two miles of unshielded concrete pathways. When I arrived at the dock, I jumped in the swimming pool at the condo to cool my core. She was there, untouched and unbothered. I gathered a new shirt and my charging cables and headed back to Scott's condo.

When I returned, Scott and Bob were sitting on the couch, kicking back a few drinks. Scott was down for the plan for the evening, so we hit the Village, as he called it, to continue the pub crawl. Unfortunately, that evening was a little less interesting than the night before, but we had a great time before returning to the condo.

A Man with a Cornet

I had behaved the previous night. Partaking in the festivities, enjoying only beer, in turn, I woke earlier than my two new friends. Fearful I could end up in a new routine, I left a thank-you note and began the walk back to Lola.

The seawall was not playing nice -- it was low tide, and the wind was pushing water against it, also I had to lift Lola four feet over the wall. To continue my journey, I had to unload all the gear, jump down into the water, and lift Lola up and over the seawall to prepare her for another portage. While repacking my gear into Lola on the manicured lawn of the condo, the manager came by and asked what room I was in. Hungover and not feeling like playing nice, I replied, "I'm not and I was just leaving." The befuddled look on his face seemed to indicate he was considering bringing in some reinforcements. I was now in a bit of a hurry, so I loaded Lola up and escorted her across the highway to the Gulf.

I was definitely off my game. The three-foot rollers got the best of me. Not four miles into the day's journey, we were side-swiped and up ended. Dragging Lola to the shore, I found my phone on the bottom of the break. Again with the phone! What the hell? When I dove underwater to retrieve it another wave came by and Lola smacked me in the head. It was time to go ashore.

Sitting just beyond the break, Wilson did his job again. An older lady, strolling by on her morning walk, asked about Wilson. She got the full scoop about him and my frustration. She wished me the best before continuing her exercise. Then along came the free-spirited Lee -- with his white tee and rolled-up capri-style khakis -- who approached me. His scruffy beard and the cornet in his hand interested me. I gave him the rundown, then he told me a few of his stories.

While we were talking about his sailing adventures, Marggie, the walker I had met a little while before, returned with some friends and fresh fruit, cashews, Snickers and had collected $20 to put toward a new phone. I fought to hold back the tears as I jumped up and gave each one of them hugs. The ladies saw their work had been done and left Lee and I to our conversation.

Lee, a Naples native, saw the bewilderment still on my face. He invited me to grab lunch at the Publix down the road, saying food would get my thoughts going in the right direction. We shared a rotisserie chicken and some potato salad on the picnic tables while getting to know one another. He had had a rough month, which had forced him to the streets of Naples. He let me use his phone to connect with a friend of mine, who lived in Ocala. Barbi, my former teaching mentor, happened to be in Naples and was happy to help. We set a time to meet for dinner and went from there.

Lee and I killed a few hours walking around Naples. He had his cornet and people were not too shy to ask him to play a tune. I found it hilarious that he would oblige, but would always choose to play taps. We met Barbi at a mall parking lot and we drove to a restaurant. I told her about Lee and she was happy to have him along.

Barbi has supported my ideas since the days when I served her drinks from behind the bar. She motivated me to become a teacher and was always a phone call away when I had any doubts. That night she was there to put a good meal in my stomach and paid for a hotel room to get me out of the streets. She even offered to take me into town the next day to get a new phone.

After a wonderful meal, Barbi dropped Lee and me off at the hotel and said good-bye until the morning. My roomie for the evening seemed a little hesitant, but appreciative. He was probably in the same boat as I was, not having a shower in a few days and a soft bed to crash on. We talked and watched mind-numbing TV until the early hours of the morning.

Barbi was right on time the next morning. She took me to the Apple store that couldn't help us, then to the Sprint store, which also had no answers. After taking up most of her morning, I told her to forget it and take me to get a cheap burner phone. Before parting ways, I gathered all the thank yous in the world and sent them her way. I met Lee back on the beach, where Lola was stashed in the bushes. We formed a plan to kayak to Marco Island together, but he couldn't get his kayak, which was being stored at a friend's house, until the following day, so today was going to be an easy six miles to the Naples pier. Easy my ass -- the surge kicked up beyond four feet of shore, making those six miles a nightmare. To add to my nightmare, before going ashore I got tangled in a fisherman's line at the pier. As I broke free, I saw Lee walking down the boardwalk, sporting a shit-eating grin. After getting untangled from the fishing line, I paddled ashore, where Lee sat waiting.

Lola seemed to be OK left behind the hedges, so I pulled her up again and gathered a day bag. A food and wine festival downtown was kicking off in a few hours, and Lee and I planned to enjoy the

112

festivities. Everywhere I turned, Naples embraced the bohemianism from more of a boujee scale of things. The boutiques and cafes pushed local artists, from bands to painters. My brain had a very eclectic afternoon processing the fusion of the two.

As the sun fell, we headed to the square, where the streets were popping with people in cocktail dresses and fancy dinner jackets. I felt completely under-dressed in my Captain Morgan swim trunks and sweat stained T-shirt; Lee was as comfortable as they came. The festival was free, but to sample the fine wine you paid for a glass. Somehow Lee was able to procure a glass, which turned heads as we approached the sampling booths. Slowly making our way through the herds, following the sounds of steel drums, we found the real party.

Live music, dancing, and smiles elevated the positive energy to new heights. The band, Inner Circle, a reggae band famous for its song, "Bad Boys," was on point with covers of the Marleys and reggaeton. I joined the dance floor and had a few go-arounds with the single ladies enjoying the vibes. I became parched, so I stepped away to quench my thirst with a Stoop beer. When I returned, Lee introduced me to an old high school buddy, Kyle, who was on a new journey in life trying to better himself for his daughter.

The band played its final set and Kyle invited us to come back to his pad to crash. At first I turned him down, but he wasn't having any of that. He reassured me by promising my return to the water's edge early in the morning. Lee and I agreed, so we hopped in his car and headed to a neighboring town of Naples.

Kyle was a fantastic host. He supplied us with a few nightcaps and blueberry yum-yum pies. His conversation dove deeper into discussing crystals and energies. He asked if I would spread certain crystals throughout the Everglades. I was happy to oblige since he was being so accommodating. Time began to creep up on us, so we called it an evening.

The Domes of the Cape

As he had promised, Kyle was up super early and found the time to get me a hot coffee and bagel. We were back at the water in no time. Unfortunately, Lee had not been able to get his kayak, so I was riding solo. Kyle and Lee gave me a proper send off -- I got in on the shore and they gave me a heave into the oncoming waves.

The Gulf was forgiving in the early hours, allowing me to push quickly to Gordon's Pass. From there I had smooth sailing through Dollar Bay. The weekend had come around, bringing a plethora of boats to the local island parties, Keywaydin Island being one of them. Boats lined the sandy banked bay from the north camp to the south camp. The party atmosphere played a mind game with my head. I saw everyone relaxing and having fun, then wondered why I was working so hard. I was able to make it 11 miles to the south camp, where the party was at its best. I pulled over and decided it was as far as I was going for the day.

Sitting alone on the Gulf-side bank, I watched families and friends soak and have fun. Just over the dune was a beach lined with some of the most exotic seashells I'd ever seen. While scouting the location, I collected a few gems before returning to Lola. Waiting for the boaters to call it a day, I took the opportunity to re-band my spear gun and give Wilson a new makeover. As the party was nearing an end, a lady came over and gave me a fish she had caught so I could have a solid meal. I thanked her and watched the boats pull out one by one.

The last boat backed out, leaving me alone on the island with only the sounds of the Gulf. I paddled over to the bayside bank, where I scouted out the best camping option. Before it got too dark, I set the tent and cooked up the fish with a side of rice. I greeted the evening and the cool breeze with a full belly. I sat in the moonlight, listening to the waves and watching meteors flash through the sky.

Eerie stories I had heard about the abandoned Cape Romano Dome Homes had me up and out early. Before I got to these locally known structures, I had to make my way through the exclusive beaches of Tigertail and Marco. Stopping at Tigertail to replenish my water supply, Wilson's new makeover drew the attention of a family from Ohio, who pointed me in the direction of a water spigot. By the time I had returned with full platypus bags of water, they had two stacked deli sandwiches ready for me. I was overwhelmed with glee. My body required fuel and on this island of $15 burgers, they saved me some money. Best wishes and safe travels were exchanged, then they watched as I continued south toward the point.

Gray clouds gathered in the sky just before seeing the four odd domes in the distance. The clouds decided to hang around, but ended up only threatening to wreak havoc. Local lore has it this cluster of domes on stilts was once a commune and has some sort of Stonehenge quality to it.

Truth be told, after a little research I found they were actually sustainable living quarters for the Lee family back in the 1980s. Even back then, the home was the subject of many stories from the locals. Bob Lee designed and built the home to withstand gale-force winds, while providing solar energy and collecting water for household uses. Its downfall came from Hurricane Andrew in August 1992. The structure survived, but the windows were blown out, demolishing the interior. Hurricane Andrew and the erosion from the constant storm surges over the years have pushed the structures into the waters of the Gulf. Since they became inhabitable there have been plenty of debates on what to do with the property, from artificial reefs to tourist destinations. That night it would be a backdrop for my campsite.

Camp was set beyond the first dune. Shortly after I was set up, a boat captain brought by a bride and groom taking photographs of their big day. When they beached, the captain came over and told me a nasty storm was heading my way. He informed me about a structure farther inland, if I needed stronger cover. At that time I believe he was referring to the Pyramid Home built by the Innes family in the 1980s. Neighboring the Dome Homes was a cedar-framed pyramid topped with golden mirrors allowing views for all of Marco Island. In its heyday the property had a zoo-like atmosphere with aviaries, horses, emus and even a couple skunks. The Innes made this their home through the '80s until erosion took the shoreline, making it unsafe for them to stay. The final straw was when a tornado demolished the home shortly after being sold in 1988. I thanked him, but paid no attention. I knew what my tent was capable of and I wasn't worried.

My tent held up just fine, but my location was not at all adequate. In the middle of the storm, just about midnight, I had to move out of a puddle to higher ground. It was a rude awakening, but it definitely could've been worse. Did I ever mention how awesome it is to leave a dry sleeping bag to return to it completely soaking wet? Let's put it this way, you leave a dry environment with a warm and cozy sleeping bag containing hours of concealed body heat to go into a cold, misted rain. You spend about 15 minutes out in the elements, if you are lucky, losing most of your remaining body heat and then you bring back into the tent dripping wet clothes. Tents are confined spaces -- seriously, let's face it, a two-person tent is really only made for one -- so now most of your dry gear becomes just as wet as the ones you brought back inside. With cold, wet feet you now slide them back to the footbox of your sleeping bag hoping to regain the warmth you left before. Simply stated, it sucks and it makes it very difficult to get a decent night of sleep afterward. I was eventually able to return to slumber with some confidence.

The rain petered out in the morning, allowing me to break camp and make a run for it. I was headed through the blunt of the Ten Thousand Islands. High winds kept me close to the bank, reminding me to keep land to the left at all times. I arrived at White Horse Key, the first designated campsite, a little early in the day so I pushed farther. I believed I could make it another six miles to Picnic Key, but got caught in a nasty, cold rain storm around Gomez's Point. The rain froze my core and I became borderline hypothermic. I was saved by a small undesignated site, Round Island. There was just enough room for my tent to stay above water. Seizing the opportunity, I beached, got my rain gear on and set a semi-dry camp.

Temperatures dropped to the low 50s and the rain resumed. I embraced the suck, became slightly delirious and began dancing a jig on the point of the small island. Who the hell was going to tell me otherwise? I don't know what came over me, but I felt a sense of acceptance. I guess I lost my shit positively rather than hating what life was throwing at me. After the brief lapse of sanity, I regained my composure and began to batten down the hatches. Round Island was tall enough to lie on dry land, but I wasn't sure about Lola's safety. I pulled her as far up as the island allowed and tied her off to the overhanging branches. Still weary, I also tied her to my tent -- if she went, I was going down, too. It was the only way I was going to get any sleep.

That sound night of sleep never materialized. Waves crashed closer and closer as the tide rose. Sleeping with one ear open, the sound of the tide receding granted me some peace of mind. My feet were another issue. With the temperature dropping, my toes did not retain heat and I had to get out my "thick socks." Of course, they were soaked. Unable to preserve what little warmth I did possess, the sleepless hours dragged on turning the late hours into a very rough evening.

Cold temperatures continued into the morning hours. For the second time, I had to prepare for paddling with my cold-weather gear. Facing 53 degrees and 20 mph winds, I needed to navigate my way through the Ten Thousand Islands to get to the Everglades Visitor Center. If that wasn't enough, after I rounded Picnic Key, I was stopped by a NPS ranger, who asked me where I had camped. I knew better than to tell him I didn't stay at a designated spot, so I chose one and pointed it out. He then asked to see my whistle. I told him I had four of them somewhere, but I couldn't locate a single one. He flipped a lid at that point and told me to stop at the visitor center, stating that if I couldn't produce one, I would be ticketed. I said, "Yes, sir. I'll see ya there."

This normally wouldn't have been a big deal, but along the way on my journey a good friend had given me a few Altoids dripped with a psychedelic. The NPS ranger not only said I would be ticketed, he said he would be waiting to search my vessel. I figured I'd better pull over on the next bend and ditch the minty felonies. A little bummed out, I watched those puppies dissolve into nothing, then searched for a whistle. Once I had located one, I threw it around my neck and paddled to the yellow visitor center building across the bay.

At the Everglades National Park Visitor Center, kayakers are required to give a detailed itinerary before paddling into the swamp. I was met there by the ranger, who saw the whistle around my neck. He gave me a quick thumbs-up and I immediately regretted the decision to send the mints into the deep.

When I went inside to apply for my permit, the ranger asked for my itinerary, but I could not supply one. Honestly, the idea overwhelmed me, so I inquired about staying at the Ivey House in Everglades City. Thankfully, the ranger called a shuttle driver and within 20 minutes Lola and I were on our way to town.

The Ivey House is reminiscent of a hiker hostel/ B&B. For $90, I got a shuttle to and from the visitor center, a private room, breakfast and a common room to engage other travelers in conversation. Unfortunately, there were no other travelers, but I enjoyed it nonetheless.

Everglades City allowed me to resupply before I headed into the treacheries of the swamp. I grabbed a solid dinner at the Island Café and went back to the room to plan my trip accordingly. This would be the first time since the Big Bend I would have to stick to a strict itinerary. I was not happy about that aspect of the paddle, but felt rejuvenated and ready for the challenges of the Everglades.

The Dome Homes of Cape Romano

Landing at the Everglades Visitor Center

Segment 14
Everglades City - Long Key
100 miles

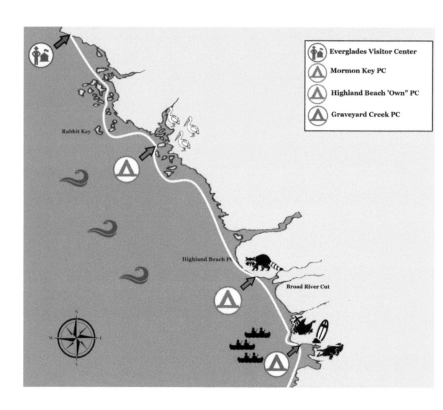

Everglades Visitor Center

Mormon Key PC

Highland Beach 'Own" PC

Graveyard Creek PC

Rabbit Key

Highland Beach Pt.

Broad River Cut

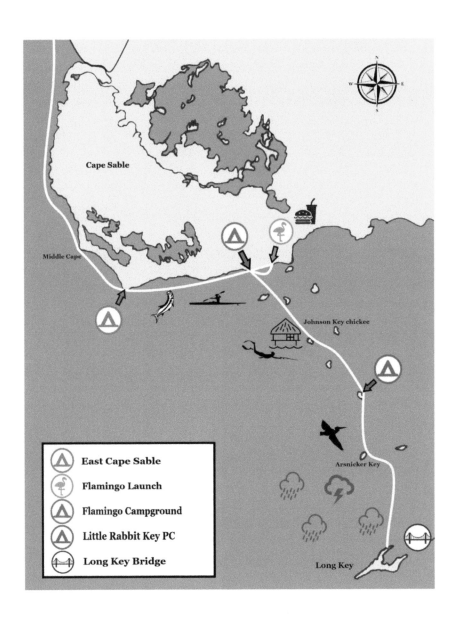

All maps were hand drawn and created by the author Jeffrey "Treehouse" Buncie

Treasures of the Glades

It's the fucking Everglades! There's no other way I could
express it. The Glades continuously test mental stability, wildlife and
survival knowledge, and navigation skills. Possible crocodile
encounters, definite alligator sightings, ravenous raccoons and Zika-
ridden mosquitoes waited to challenge my abilities. On a good day, the
trials can be difficult, let alone on the cold, windy days that lay ahead.
Just under 100 miles kept me from the beautiful Florida Keys and as
they say, sometimes you have to go through the darkness to see the
light.

The European-style continental breakfast at the Ivey House
filled my stomach, while excitement coursed through my body. The
night before I racked my brain and laid out a float plan for the rangers
at the visitor center. Jon, the shuttle driver, had Lola loaded and ready
to go. We headed back to the visitor center, where I purchased a back-
country permit and secured my campsites. For a meager $20, ($10 for
the permit and $2 per campsite), I had the next seven days to myself in
the heart of Florida's National Park.

I was ready to rise to the challenge, but I hadn't felt this
nervous since I shipped off back on Sept. 1. While filling up my water,
I caught myself talking out loud, reassuring and psyching myself up. As
I double-checked supplies and ran inventory, I became confident I was
prepared.

After leaving the visitors center I had 17 miles to navigate the
back-water passes to get to Mormon Key. Attention to detail and spatial
awareness was imperative to navigate through the skinny passes of
Rabbit Key. Using the GPS, I followed the route through the winding
maze of mangrove inlets. Riding an endorphin high, I continued south
to Mormon Key campsite. A mile south of Rabbit, there was no longer
land to my right. The Florida Bay went on for miles beyond the
horizon. It became a little easier for me from this point; all I had to do
was keep land to my left.

Mormon Key sat three miles south, welcoming campers with
the run-of-the-mill government sign sitting beyond the sea grapes.
Bearing witness to the large, white pelicans hanging off the bank, I
paddled up to the sand spur-ridden site. I thought I had experienced
sand spurs before, but this was on a whole new level. Thank God, there
was a palm frond around. I used the frond as a rake to collect the spiny-

covered burrs to clear a spot for my tent. A pat on the back and a smirk led to a fleeting thought of "Survivor," here I come!

The first day through the Everglades was a success. I achieved my goal with daylight to spare and few to no issues. The weather was beautiful and I was already looking forward to the next day's paddle. After dinner, I secured my food and water in Lola's hulls to keep the thirsty raccoons out and retired to my tent.

I really wish I could say the second day went as awesome as the first. Aeolus, the Greek god of wind, did not play well. He threw 20 mph crosswinds my way all day. The water was as angry as a wildfire supplied by waves of fresh oxygen. Set after set rolled across the bow, being fed by the next gust of wind. Rudder fully cocked against the grain, I became a one-armed bandit paddling only with my left, hoping to stay on track. Lola was still being pushed around by the merciless force even with the rudder fully engaged. Weary and blinded by the piercing rain, I surpassed the daily goal and somehow went beyond my planned stop at the Highland Beach Campsite.

The Everglades had thrust its fear upon my thinking, so at the next approachable spot I beached Lola. The dainty patch of sand was just enough, although there was one problem -- the grade of the land was not in my favor. I had to fashion a bed out of sand using a large piece of driftwood to anchor the foundation. The rain had finally let up. A shimmer of sun shone through the breaking storm clouds, which allowed me to escape the tent and check on any damage to my newly fashioned bed. Impressed at the positive results, I buckled Lola down and watched the tide retreat with the sun.

Are you ready for it? I'm going to throw another "Castaway" reference your way that summed up the evening. Over and over, I was awakened by strange plops. When you are in unfamiliar surroundings, you're not accustomed to the usual sounds that environment creates -- exactly like the protagonist, Chuck Nolan, when he was faced with those noises the first few nights on his island. It turned out to be coconuts falling and hitting the ground, but unaware of what was causing the sound, he was very frightened. My "plops" were not coconuts. As I yelled into the darkness, the sounds would recede, allowing myself to get a few winks, but they would always return. I finally had enough and grabbed my flashlight to face the unknown.

Upon exiting my tent, I saw beady little eyes shining from atop Lola. I ran at the trash panda, flailing my hands and yelling obscenities. He stood up, looked at me, snarled, and I swear he growled before running off into the scrub. I searched Lola for missing food, realizing I had not tightened down the hull straps 100 percent. Just then, I heard

122

rustling in the front hull. Could there be another raccoon left behind and now trapped? There *was* another masked bandit! The lid lifted up, then plopped. The case of the mystery sound was solved -- the hull lid was being lifted, but the straps were tight enough to slam the lid, causing the sounds to echo through the silence.

The squirrely little bastards had infiltrated Lola. While watching the raccoon's tricky paws frantically try to escape, I picked up a palm, created a half-assed spear, and prepared myself for battle. I decided to give him a little help, so I unbuckled a strap, stood back and waited for him to pounce. Shortly after, his snout appeared, edging slowly out, and then he bolted into the scrub to catch up with his accomplice.

It was time to assess the damage. The sneaky bastard didn't get any food, but he did tear into my 3-liter platypus bag, thus cutting my fresh water supply almost in half. That wasn't the worst part -- he had decided to leave his "calling card" and had shit all over everything left in the hull. The stench hovered throughout the hull as it seeped into my gear, but I was not ready to tackle such a feat. A little bummed, and still very tired, I decided to put that problem on the next day's checklist and go back to bed, after tightening down the straps, of course.

The tide monster caught me again. Thinking I was done with the extreme tides, I was land-locked, thanks to the morning's tide. Thankfully, I only had nine miles to paddle that day to get to Graveyard Creek Campsite. The kicker was I didn't have water around to clean out the "presents" left behind by the midnight bandits. So I sat and waited for the water to return.

Leaving my improvised sand bed behind, I was able to paddle around to the Broad River Cut before the wind smacked me like a right hook from Mike Tyson. The open water cut brought cold winds, ensued by harder stinging rain. With the afternoon hours already upon me, I had to face whatever the Glades would throw my way. I dug deep, accepted the situation, and muscled my way through the blinding storm.

The storm dissipated as I landed at Shark Point. A battered boat, left abandoned along the beach, piqued my curiosity. After beaching, I took a stroll toward the boat to explore the wreckage. As I got closer, I realized what I stumbled upon in the back waters. I inched closer until a voice in my head told me to turn around and leave it alone. Three packages had been cast ashore. In the '80s, we learned of the famous squared groupers, secured bales of floating drugs, spread along drop points in such secluded locations. Seeing enough drug lord movies, I knew what these smugglers would do to people who came across their misplaced drugs. It never turns out good for anyone, so I listened to the Jiminy Cricket voice in my ear and retraced my steps back to Lola.

Returning to the water, I came to a cove, where I saw a long board lapped up on the shore. My conscience may have stopped me from exploring the boat, but it was reconciled with looking into the stranded surfboard. It wasn't in too bad shape, so I tied a tow rope to Lola's stern and lugged it behind her to Graveyard Creek.

Wouldn't you know, Graveyard Creek seemed exactly how it sounds? At the mouth of the creek lay a plot of land, hidden behind the trees, large enough for group camping. Even in the daylight, the setting had an eerie excitability lingering about. This was the first site where I truly felt Lola and I had disappeared into the nothingness of the Everglades.

Before the rain returned, I set camp, cooked up a meal and finally cleaned out the raccoon scat. The chores were done and it was time to have a little fun. The surfboard turned out to be worse off than I expected, but it didn't stop me from imagining Wilson and I surfing Oahu's pipeline. When the notion grew old, I moved on to another craft to fill the time. I was challenged on the FaceySpace [Facebook] to create a conch necklace, so I rose to the challenge. It seemed pretty petty at the time, but I had a few hours to kill before sunset. In the making of the trinket, I took a chunk out of my finger large enough to warrant worry, but nonetheless I got 'er done. The fresh blood brought out mobs of blood-thirsty mosquitoes. Early rain had soaked the island's wood supply, so I couldn't even smoke them out. Before too long came the no-see-ums, of which my body had had quite enough. I conceded and escaped once again to the tent, and got an early night's rest.

If the sounds of the Glades were a soundtrack, I'm not sure anyone would get a good night's rest. The witching hour woke me to some of the craziest sounds I have ever heard in the wilderness and I've even spent evenings in the jungles of Costa Rica. My back teeth were floating, so I got to see first-hand the best of the creepy and the crawlies of the Glades. When I stepped out of the tent, the fog was dense, but oddly, never rose any higher than my waist. The multi-layering of insects and frogs grew almost deafening as I stepped farther away from the camp. A scent I could not place, but was very similar to the older lady sitting next to you in church, lingered. In search of the wildlife the weather was hiding from me, I took a stroll to the bank. At last, sitting idle in the mud, I saw an American crocodile.

I sat on a soggy log in the mist and darkness, watching a prehistoric animal and embracing an evening in the Glades. The narrow snout pointed inward to the water, the shy and reclusive species kept a close eye on the hidden fish of the brackish water. Known for feeding at night I was captivated by the stillness of the reptilian while anticipating his kill. I imagined what would happen if those pesky raccoons crossed paths with him or, even better, drifted into another scenario, including a battle between the crocodilian and one of those invading Burmese pythons known to the Glades since Hurricane Andrew came through in 1992. But unfortunately, there was no kill as the urge to relieve myself crept up again. I had almost forgotten why I had left the tent. Once relieved, I double-checked the hatches on Lola and returned to the tent.

A few hours later, I was abruptly woken by voices coming from the water. I laid still and waited as the voices grew closer. It was not yet sunrise and I swore I was hearing a youth group paddling through the early morning. I sat up and listened closer while a group of teenagers, led by their leader, started gathering offshore, hoping for a spot to camp. Camp? It was nearing 6 a.m. What the hell was going on?

The soft spot in my heart led me out of the tent to show the leaders I was occupying the site. The leaders saw my headlamp and gave the bad news to the others. See, most groups aren't allowed to mingle with other travelers while on these treks -- especially in the middle of nowhere, like the Everglades. I went over to the bank and welcomed the leaders ashore to talk civilly.

They paddled over, introduced themselves and told me they were an Outward Bound group from Miami and had been lost most of the evening. The group was on day four of its 14-day trip and the leaders said it has been quite a learning experience for the kids who had never spent a night in the woods. All this being said, I had a tender spot for the leaders and told them that once I packed up, I would leave the site, so they could get some rest. They thanked me for the kind gesture, then returned to the group with the good news.

My day may have begun a little earlier than expected, but it was happening for a good reason. I'd been exhausted before and I felt the kids' pain all too well. I wasted no time and was on the water, waving them over, within minutes.

The weather was completely shitty. Headwinds turned to crosswinds and drizzle turned to heavy rain throughout the day. I was lucky the group had woken me as early as it did. The wind was so problematic, large blisters formed on my hands despite wearing my gloves. Being in the exposed shoreline south of Graveyard Creek and around Cape Sable granted the wind full entitlement to kick my ass.

The goal was Middle Cape, which since has been washed away from storm surge. I came ashore to feel waves of stinging sand whip across the open landscape. Refusing to be a part of another in-house sand storm I needed to reassess the camping situation. The next site was five miles away at East Cape Sable. I had ample daylight, the rain had subsided and, even though it was another beach camp, it displayed possible hiding spots out of the wind. Everything was pointing to pressing on and so I did.

East Cape, upon arriving, proved to be the right decision. Closer to the heavily used Flamingo Campground and launch, the site was well-maintained. Tucked around a bend, the site was out of the wind, allowing me to have a calm fire to dry out my gear and cook a hearty meal. Even though the day became longer than expected and I earned every stroke through the wind, I was pleased with the decision to continue. I retired early, thinking how I was now only 10 miles away from my next cheeseburger.

Making my first camp in The Everglades

Surfing the pipeline of The Everglades

126

The Crossing

Excited for a solid meal, the tent zipper couldn't open soon enough for me the next morning. When it did, I saw that the morning had brought with it a thick blanket of fog. I had no choice other than to sit and wait for the fog to lift. The wait was well worth it in the long run. When I finally did get on the water, it was as smooth as silk. The sun decided to make an appearance and, I can't say this often enough, a cheeseburger was within my reach.

Along the way, I crossed paths with another sea kayaker. His rig was decked out, which led to all sorts of questions. I shared my insights on the campsites along the cape. He was only going out for a couple nights, but nonetheless, I was stoked to see another kayaker. After passing him, I found myself in the calm flats, sneaking up on more tarpon. Lola met one face-to-face as we stealthily paddled through, causing the tarpon to jump and land square on top of her bow. It was a big fish, too. It took everything I had not to lose my balance and roll over. All in all, we had fun cruising into the Flamingo launch.

The launch was beyond the campground, but that's where the visitor center, restaurant and marina store were located. While docking at the marina, we were greeted by two manatees feeding in the seagrass. I secured Lola to the floating dock and beelined it to the restaurant. The food was a bit pricey, but at that point, I seriously doubt there wasn't a price I wouldn't have paid. Hell, I even got a pizza to go. Once my belly was full, I scoped out the store for possible resupply. The store had the usual camping snacks, protein bars and candy, but not much else. I bought a few snacks for insurance, then went to secure a camp for the night.

Craving a hot shower, I returned to the water for a quick paddle back to the campground. The sites were located in an open field and I had my pick. I found a spot nestled under a small tree that was somewhat shaded and set camp. Unfortunately, the only open shower was across the field and out of sight of the water. I didn't want to be too far away from Lola, and I debated the long journey versus her safety. Talk about worth it. The showers were hot and clean.

While I charged my electronics at the bathhouse, I met some of the other campers and shared stories. It was short-lived because let's be real, we were still in the Glades and as soon as the sun began to fall, the ruthless mosquitoes treated us as their personal blood banks. We said our farewells and retreated from the attacks to seek shelter. The night continued with me hiding in the stale, muggy tent, hoping the Sandman would whisk me away.

The much-welcome sun provided a great morning to begin crossing Florida Bay. The journey began as a straight shot past Murray and Clive keys to one of the Everglades' unique camping options -- a covered, sturdy wooden platform (known as a chickee), located in the shoals of Johnson Key. Throughout the Glades, these structures sit three feet above the water allowing paddlers to stay the night above the swamp and out of harm's way.

Upon the initial docking, I really would've enjoyed staying, but without any type of sleeping pad, I could see it being quite uncomfortable. The roof provided shade and, since I had some time to spare, I figured I would try to spear some dinner. The notion of spear fishing in the Everglades sounded like another grand adventure, so I got my mask and prepared for the experience.

Gently lowering myself into the murky water, I began to imagine what was lying beneath. Images of large saltwater crocs and sharks circling the pylons hit my mind like hundreds of pop-up ads. I took a deep breath and sank below. As I allowed my sight to readjust, I gripped that spear as if rigor mortis had set in. The tide was shuffling in and out of the structure, sucking me in and pushing me out. A few moments later, my mind eased as I realized there were no monster crocodiles and man-eating sharks, but there was an ecosystem created around the structure, in which every critter had its place.

A calming presence came over me. I was no longer interested in finding dinner, but rather in exploring this unique environment. The longer I stayed under the water, the more sea life began to show. Crabs were hanging to the barnacles, snatching some lunch. The schools of snapper became unafraid of their new intruder and inched closer. The sea urchins lurked along the seafloor, searching for some grub, and I was even blessed with swimming with a feisty barracuda. Whenever he appeared, the schools of fish began to disappear -- I had lost my spear-fishing opportunity. I lost interest and returned topside.

All alone now, I wanted to check another "to do" off the list. Although it was not the summer solstice, which is known, among other things, as Hike Naked Day, I wanted to take the opportunity to paddle the rest of the day in my birthday suit. My trunks came off and my tan lines began to disappear as I paddled au naturel. The smooth paddle to Little Rabbit Key had become a little more freeing.

Rabbit Key was my last campsite in the Everglades. When I arrived at the north shore, I saw a dock with six pallet- sized boardwalks in disarray. The soft ground grabbed my feet, sucking them into the coastal muck. To get to higher, drier land I straightened the pallets and walked beyond the scrub. A clearing in the middle of the island was waiting for me to enjoy.

Doing my chores, setting camp and settling in, I decided to treat myself to a hearty serving of campfire-style burritos. I had a big day of open water paddling the next day. Eight burritos later, a food baby had grown in my tummy. The breeze was pushing in a storm system, but also keeping the mosquitoes away. I lay on the picnic table looking up at the stars and thought back on my latest experiences until the wee hours of the morning.

Restlessness kept me tossing throughout the night. The day I had been dreading since I had planned the journey was finally there -- the open water paddle ... no escape route.). There was no way around it; I was already a third of the way there to the keys). I was facing an over-10-mile open water paddle to land in the Florida Keys. With no time to waste, I had to get to it.

Due to an early high tide and head winds, the day was not off to a great start. Before the growing storm hit, I stopped by Arsnicker Key to collect my bearings. The island was covered in bird droppings and smelled like an unclean bird cage. The stale smell was unbearable; I couldn't imagine hanging out there a second longer. Overcome with fear, I pushed off into the storm clouds along the horizon. The system was sweeping in from the south -- and I was heading right for it.

Halfway to the landing spot on Long Key, the skies turned from blue to gray, shielding out the sunlight. The tides began to shift. The winds picked up and the rollers turned wildly angry. I had Lola's rudder fully cocked and still the gusts were sending me back into the bay. One after another, the oncoming waves began to lap over and fill the cockpit. Sheets of stinging rain came in droves, impairing my vision.
I was four miles from any land. It was time to nut up or shut up. Although I was firmly pressing on the rudder pedals, the wind fought back, kick after kick. Perfectly balanced, I leaned hard to the left, using a lower center of gravity and power stroked on the right. I was winning; I had found a rhythm. Every five strokes I stopped and bailed out three scoops of water using my Gatorade bottle. It continued this way until I reached the embankment of the keys. There was no time to think of the "what ifs?" there was only time for action. I had not gone that far to be upended and carried away by the tides of the bay.

The rocks of the Long Key Bridge bounced me back and forth upon arrival. Approaching the dry land with care, I was able to step out and brutally drag Lola to safety. I welcomed the rocks with bended knees and, as cliché as it was, a kiss or two, grateful to be on dry land. The overhung trees sheltered me until the storm passed and as I reflected and processed what had ensued. I remember my moment of realization to this day -- I was no longer in the Everglades, but in one of the most beautiful destinations in the world, The Florida Keys.

Sunset from the last camp before stepping in the Keys

Spear fishing from the chickee

Lola, welcome to the Keys

Segment 15 (South)
Long Key - Key West Dinghy Dock
95 miles

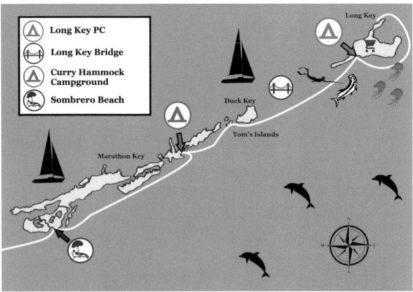

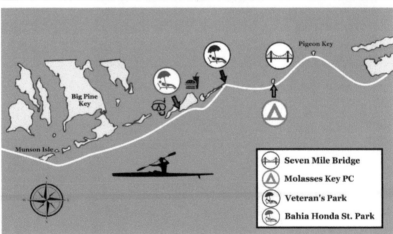

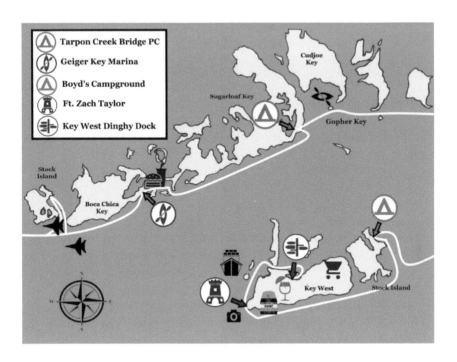

Tarpon Creek Bridge PC

Geiger Key Marina

Boyd's Campground

Ft. Zach Taylor

Key West Dinghy Dock

All maps were hand drawn and created by the author
Jeffrey "Treehouse" Buncie

A Keys Thanksgiving

I am choosing to split the next segment, The Overseas Paddling Trail, into three different sections. When in the Florida Keys, one tends to end up on island time, therefore falling into a vortex-like atmosphere. If I tried to include everything that happened during these next months, it would entice you to skim. So, with no further ado, the first part of three begins on the rip-rap rocks of the Long Key Bridge.

With the rain letting up, the skies returned to blue and the sun welcomed me to the isles. It was as if the keys knew I had arrived. Since the wind had blown me off course, I had to paddle a bit farther to cross under the bridge and into the Atlantic. This was the first time I had entered the Atlantic Ocean, thus motivating me even further. I rounded the key and explored the coves with excitement.

There were hundreds of poisonous jellyfish floating everywhere. The Man-O-Wars must've been blown in by the recent storms. I had never seen these creatures, so naturally I investigated them. The mixture of pinks, blues and purples resembled a deadly bag of cotton candy. Their tentacles stretched well beyond the surface, snatching up the passing bait fish with ease. Luring you in, entrancing and captivating you almost like you were being hypnotized, I could see why they had no problem catching prey. I paddled the rest of the way between the floating bubbles carefully, trying not to get the paddle wrapped in their tentacles.

Long Key was my camp for the evening. I landed at the beach next to its rental kayaks and walked to the ranger station. Along the way, I met a guy crabbing from the bridge. He had a long string hung over the edge of the wooden boardwalk, pulling blue crabs up one after another.

JB told me about the cheaper primitive campsites available that were away from the commercial campground. For $8, you got a covered platform with cold water showers. Rather than pay the $42 for an uncovered site sleeping on crushed shell, I was sold. The primitive sites were labeled A-F and were on a first-come, first-served basis. I secured a site and shared a beer with my new friend.

JB and I hit it off. We were like-minded and enjoyed the outdoor life. He had a waterside site and allowed me to stash Lola there so I wouldn't have to drag her down the boardwalk. We shared a few beers and travel stories before he offered to drive me the mile to the convenience store for food.

The store was a little overpriced, but it is the keys and I had to suck it up. We got more beer and headed back to the camp. We made a fire in the grill and stared at it like cavemen while we shot some bullshit and drank our beer. The word of my arrival must've spread because the camp host came down in his golf cart to give me a tray of leftovers from the campground Thanksgiving dinner. I felt welcome and was thankful for the free meal. I offered to share it with JB, but he refused, saying "it's your gift, not mine."

Thanksgiving was the next day and JB suggested we share a Florida Keys meal together. He promised some more blue crabs and I promised to catch a fish or two for the main course. For our side dishes, we could pull together our camp food and fix up some rice and mashed potatoes. I was sold -- it sounded a lot better than pushing onward and spending the day alone on the water. Before finding our way to our respective tents I agreed to the plan and said good night.

The day of the festivities I did some chores before getting wrapped up with the fun and games. I wanted to send my decrepit iPhone back to Barry, who would have it repaired for my journey back north. I figured if I sent it to Long Key, I could swing by and pick it up on my way around Key West. On my way to the post office, I saw JB up early already fishing for our crab feast. I gave him a nod and a shit-eating grin when I saw him guzzling down a morning beer.

It didn't sink in that the post office would be closed for the holiday until it was too late. After the wasted trip, I returned to camp, and JB and I searched for coconuts among the mangroves. We were able to find plenty of ripe ones. After stashing them at the camp, I gave the fishing a try. I gave up after little to no luck and explored the coves with my spear. The inlets and coves were full of mangrove snappers, but nothing really warranting the prep work to cook them up. I would have to return when the tides were on the move.

The rest of the day, JB and I walked around the main campground, kicking back a few beverages and reminiscing about our Boy Scout days. Both of us had been Eagle Scouts and we shared our hazing stories and favorite camp games. When we passed the host's camp, we saw a pirate flag flying above his RV and both of us had the same thought. The game, Flag Wars, was often played between rival troops at jamborees. Each troop would try to commandeer each other's flag for bragging rights. We decided to attempt this feat later that night.

The sun and tides were on the move, so I returned to the fishing. Still no luck and time was a-wasting. I was damned if I was not going to follow through on my promise. I grabbed the spear and returned to the coves. The water had become murky, but I dove in for a try. I saw a few worthy specimens and shot into the school of fish. Bingo, a direct hit! I couldn't tell what I had hit, but it began flailing and running toward the roots of the mangroves. I held on with all my might and sank my feet into the muck for leverage. As I reached for the retrieval wire, the fish made its last effort to escape before giving in. As I was pulling my catch in, I realized I had just committed a crime. Unknowingly, I had just taken the last breath of a tarpon.

The tarpon is a protected game fish in the state of Florida. Not only had I speared one, I had done it in a state park, which the rangers don't take too lightly. I hid the tarpon under a boardwalk and ran to get JB to help me get rid of the body. I felt as if I had just shot someone and was trying to dispose of the evidence. Wrapping the dead fish in a towel, we returned to the camp to hide the body until nightfall.

When the time was right, we bushwhacked into the scrub to descale and bury the evidence. The hole was dug and I sent JB back to the campsites to be the lookout. We had the worst timing ever -- the ranger walked up to check on us right as JB returned. JB spoke loudly to give me a warning. I immediately dropped the knife and returned to the campsite, acting as if I had just gone into the bush to take a piss. Thankfully, the ranger was quick and to the point, wishing us a happy Thanksgiving before continuing his rounds. I retrieved the fish and automatically wrapped it in tinfoil.

The fire was set and ready for cooking. The tarpon was seasoned with coconut water, lime and sea salt. The crabs were wrapped and covered in Old Bay. While the seafood was cooking, we got the rice steamed and the mashed potatoes rolling. To satisfy our sweet tooth, we shucked and cracked open some coconuts, preparing our palates for a tasty meal.

Once the food was plated, we ate our catch with gratification and contentment. The tarpon was seasoned and cooked to perfection with the flaky meat peeling off the spine. I have to say tarpon is one of my favorite fish I have eaten. I would feel like a dick if I didn't give JB his props on the crabs -- well done, good buddy, well done.

Now that the tarpon was stripped clean, leaving only its carcass, we took great care to dispose of the last bit of evidence. We made sure to dig deep into the trash and hide the foil body bag well beneath some nasty trash. The crime was complete and our tracks covered. It was time to retrieve that pirate flag.

Darkness was upon us. We tiptoed into the host's camp and up to the RV. The flag was on a pole, but secured with knots we couldn't reach without a ladder. JB gave it a go, but in fear of getting caught -- or shot -- he backed out of the stunt after sizing up the situation. I was not going to give up so easily. I gathered a bucket and a chair laying around, stacking them for extra height. Stepping up on the Jenga pile, the flag was still out of my reach. The bucket gave out, making a noise that echoed throughout the camp. JB and I ran away, giggling like a couple of school girls.

Although we were unsuccessful at our endeavor, we were satisfied with the attempt. We returned to camp to enjoy a few more adult beverages and laugh about our day's adventures. Pleased with my decision to stay, I thanked JB for the child-like Thanksgiving and for his company. We retired in the early morning hours with full bellies and wonderful memories.

Long Key primitive art

Thanksgiving main course

**Portuguese
man o' war
or**

**floating
cotton
candy?**

Open Water

JB met me in the morning for breakfast burritos and coffee. He was sad to see me go, but I had many more miles ahead of me -- 13 miles south was another state park, Curry Hammock, on Crawl Key. We exchanged our contact information and said our farewells before he watched me paddle off to the open waters of the Atlantic.

High head winds attacked me from the moment I left the primitive site. Along the way, I stopped for a break after the long four miles south across the bridge. Tom's Island, next to Duck Key, was a welcomed stop. After fueling up, I headed inside to the cutout beach of Curry Hammock State Park. It was a little bit of a walk to reserve a campsite, but was well worth it.

Curry Hammock is one of the largest uninhabited parcels of land in the keys. Marketing itself as "uninhabited, untouched and unrivaled," this was a stop I could not pass up. The 1,000 acres of protected mangrove swamps, rockland hammocks and seagrass beds were waiting to be explored, which I planned to do once I secured a spot for the night.

The crushed shell sites were ideal for RV camping, but I needed a spot to lay my head and I shelled out the $48 needed for an RV site. On the walk back from the reservation desk, I saw a get-together at one of the sites. I made myself known with a tip of the hat and a smile before retrieving my gear. When the folks saw me again, I was invited over for a beer. There were two older couples vacationing from Canada and one couple from Panama City Beach. Curious, they wanted to hear a story or two, which I did happily as they threw more cold beverages my way. We chatted until suppertime, when they happily fed a hungry traveler eggplant parmesan and fresh string beans. After the meal, the gentleman broke out the Scotch whiskey and cigars. It felt like I was back in the '20s waiting for the ladies to disappear while the guys talked stocks and bonds.

The sun began to fall and I said good night, and walked to my site. I was able to set camp rather quickly and didn't have to worry about cooking dinner, thanks to the shared meal. With the shower house directly across from my site, I was able to grab a hot shower before the temperature dropped. By dark-30 I was in my cozy, warm sleeping bag and planning the next day's paddle.

It was tough to pull my tattered body off the ground the next morning. My triceps felt like they were going to burst from my body and the blisters on my hands had progressed to becoming permanent cuts. I can assure you salt water on open wounds is not a comfortable feeling. The open water forced me to double up my meal plans and still my stomach would speak to me in the middle of the night. Even though I had foregone the expedition and exploration of the island, I was stubborn and chose to push forward. I would not let these irritants dictate my paddle.

South along Marathon Key, I found a pocket beach, Sombrero Beach. Electing to take a snack break upon the public beach I paddled into the swimming area. While sitting there, I heard a call. The couples I shared time with on Curry Hammock had just pulled up in their vehicle. The coincidence threw me for a loop, but I was not feeling up to being quite so chummy this time, although I forced myself to have a short conversation. To escape more chatter, I returned to Lola and gave a wave before leaving them behind.

My next snack break came at Pigeon Key. This small island, located two miles into the north end of the famous Seven Mile Bridge, played a significant role in the building of the once-known eighth Wonder of the World. Stretching seven miles over open water, the newer automobile bridge (1982) mirrors the older Overseas Railroad bridge from the early 1900s. Engineered by Figg and Mueller Engineers (who also engineered the Sunshine Skyway in St. Petersburg) once it was completed it was one of the longest bridges in existence. When the Flagler Railroad was being extended to Key West, the 11 buildings on Pigeon Key housed the workers taking on the feat of connecting the Middle Keys to the Lower Keys. These pioneers made commerce that much easier for goods and services to reach the mainland. I would join this historic district for my last stop before crossing the open waters.

Parallel from mile marker 42, five miles into the crossing, is a primitive camp on Molasses Key. When I stopped by the island, there was already a family of four that had scored the prime real estate on the isle. Forced to either paddle a strong seven miles to Bahia Honda or circle the island and find a spot behind the mangroves, I jumped on the opportunity to camp across from this wonder. I was delighted to find a spot on the west end of the key, solidifying my choice to take another look at the bridge. My new slice of heaven left me with a postcard view overlooking the magnificent man-made structure.

Exhausted and probably the hungriest I have ever been I set camp and dove into the food bag. Ravaging my food inventory like a bear out of hibernation, I ended up eating half of my supply. Satisfied

138

for the time being, I sat watching a remarkable sunset bring out a silhouetted testament to architectural achievement.

The family staying across the isle made sure I was up nice and early. Between their Latin music and kids whining, there was no sleep to be had. Forgiveness came rather easily -- I did have 23 miles planned for the day. In the data book, it stated there was an abandoned bridge campsite a little way up Tarpon Creek. It sounded like a cool spot, so I made my way south to Sugarloaf Key.

Veterans Park and its facilities were waiting after a smooth two-mile paddle. At the southern end of the Seven Mile Bridge, the park's clean restrooms and tiki huts steered me off the water. It was a perfect spot to drop a few pounds and watch the roadside coco frio hustler.

One of the world's renowned beaches, Bahia Honda, was just five miles from the park. I had heard there was a concession serving hot food and that was enough for me. Wailing away at the watery path ahead, I landed on the western beach in no time. Sunbathers lined the popular destination tempting any paddler to go ashore. A brief jaunt over the boardwalk led me to the concessions, showers and flushable toilets. Thanks to the short-order snack shop, my apprehensions about gorging the night before were ironed out.

Bahia Honda has more to offer than just pristine beaches. The picturesque railroad bridge provides panoramic views; a butterfly garden trail enchants the young to old, and the nature center educates the unfamiliar. More lavish travelers can spend some time renting bikes and kayaks or take a snorkeling trip out to the nearby reef. I hung out in the shade, ate generously and explored the trails.

The afternoon winds elevated, so I returned to the day's journey. Lengthy open stretches and congested mangrove keys hindered any opportunity for breaks. When I rounded Gopher Key, my ass actually fell asleep. A downed limb became my savior --I ran Lola aground, atop the limb and crawled out of the cockpit with numb legs and tried to stand. Failing miserably, I succumbed to hugging the limb while floating my legs in the water below. It was, by far, the most uncomfortable paddling break up to then.

The entry to Tarpon Creek is hidden between the mangroves of Sugarloaf Key. A southwest route from Gopher Key is identified by a white PVC pipe marking the inlet. Mangrove tunnels made the paddle to the abandoned bridge feel like I was lost in another time. Expecting to see an actual bridge, I continued to make my way up the creek. There was no bridge, but I did locate where there might have once been a bridge.

High sand banks and swiftly moving water marked the primitive camping site. Unable to drag Lola up the banks, I resorted to hiding her among the mangroves. When I opened the hulls to retrieve my gear, they were filled with saltwater. Everything was drenched. This scenario had become a recurrence of late. I examined the hull lid seals and found they were victims of dry rot. That could be a problem over the remainder of the trip and I still had a shit-ton of open water to navigate.

It was already late in the day and rain clouds were on the horizon. Time was dwindling, so I climbed the bank and collected wood for a fire. I needed to dry my sleeping gear before the rain came. Like a bartender on coke, I was everywhere. Yep, I was a master of multi-tasking. The fire burned hot, cans of ravioli were cooked, the sleeping bag hung, the tent was drying and Lola was draining. It was a well-written routine and a sight to see.

The rains came after dinner. Thankfully, the tent was dry and set. My sleeping bag, on the other hand, was still damp. The weather may have forced me to spend the night in a soggy bag, but there was no way I was going to allow it to get me down. I was one day from partying in Key West.

Landing

on

Bahia Honda

State Park

Paddling 7 Mile Bridge   **A break on Tarpon Creek**

The Conch Republic

Eighteen miles stood between me and Boyd's Campground. The morning rains forced me to pack up and get out of there. Driven by thoughts of burgers and beers kept my arms moving around the southern keys in the misty, cold rain. Rounding Pelican Key, I cut inside to the Geiger Key Marina Restaurant.

Docking along the RV camp, I walked to a restaurant that had just opened. Before I sat down, Todd, my waiter, took my beverage order and brought me a menu. I built my own burger and enjoyed the cold beverages. I had intended it to be a quick stop for fuel, but Todd wanted to hear more about my journey. Once I had eaten, he came over and sat with me. The Minnesotan was enthralled with my recent Everglades adventures. When he opened up about where and what he was doing down here -- he wintered in the keys and went back to Minnesota in the summer -- I told him about my plans for paddling the Mississippi River. He told me to look him up on the interwebs and exchange info for later on down the line.

It was time to say goodbye to Todd and Geiger Key. I scurried back to Lola and headed south past the military airfield. The fighter jets were out and about, flying overhead just above the water line. Turns out Boyd's Campground isn't on Key West, but on the key just east of there, Stock Island. I saw the RVs standing tall above the water and followed the markers into the boat ramp.

Boyd's tourist-trap atmosphere was reminiscent of every KOA I have ever visited. The grounds included a pool, game room, common area with TV, laundry services and a camp gift shop. The cheaper of the two sites wasn't exactly cheap -- $70 for a non-electric site, where you had the pleasure of sleeping on crushed rocks. I really didn't have a choice at the time, so I secured a site for the evening and set camp.

The day was still young and I was already bored with the scenery of the campground. Searching on Google, I found a Publix grocery mart three miles from the camp and decided to hike there. The walk took me down US 1, along the water, where you run into all sorts of characters. The random leathery-skinned locals scooted by on their bikes; the paler out-of-towners walked in groves often stopping for photos and enjoying their vacation, and the homebums lay in the shade, trying to catch a nap before the evening festivities. No matter what type of journey they were on, the island surrounded them with a friendly disposition. Something about the sun shining and the salt in the air brings out the best in people.

Publix was right across from Garrison Bight of Key West. (A bight is a term for places to harbor.) I escaped the heat and cooled down by walking around the store's frozen food section. While doing it, I returned to Google and searched for Duval Street. The famous strip of downtown Key West was another two-mile walk. I was feeling good and wasn't quite ready to return to camp, so I continued my journey.

Ahh, Duval Street. What can I say? The street was alive with day drinkers, buskers and hustlers. I had been to Key West a few times previously and had the skinny on where to enjoy a good meal and frosty beverage. I stopped by some of the staples, such as Willy T's and Sloppy Joe's, then ventured over to Margaritaville. Time began to slip away, but I remained focused on my chores. Returning to Publix before closing was imperative for my resupply. I left the street's carnival-like atmosphere for another day and headed back to camp.

The day had been a success story. While sitting on the picnic table next to my tent, I reflected on the accomplishments of the day. I was able to paddle 18 miles through the water, met a Minnesota connection, secured a spot for the evening, resupplied and walked over 10 miles visiting Key West. I couldn't wait to see what the next day would bring.

I was excited when I awoke with the sun. I got on the phone early to scout the opportunity to visit the Dry Tortugas. Visiting the National Park 68 miles west of Key West had been a dream of mine since learning about the islands. The catch is, these islands are only accessible by boat or seaplane. I had to figure out some logistics for Lola. I called the ferry and inquired about tickets -- and that's when it became even more interesting. The lady told me there was camping at Fort Jefferson -- and she had a cancelation. How stoked was I? Giddy as a school boy. The ferry would take Lola for an extra $20 and, if I waited that day and the next, I could camp on the island for three nights. A plan was forming. I reserved the ticket and the three nights before hanging up and moving onto the next problem.

The ferry left at 630 a.m., but I was 10 miles away from the loading dock. There was no way in hell I was going to wake up and paddle 10 miles before 6:30 a.m. I had to find somewhere I could leave Lola overnight. I called around and found a dinghy dock at the Key West Bight that would watch Lola for a $6 docking fee. I was sold. All of the new information led me to spending two more nights at Boyd's campground, but it would be well worth the extra days in the Tortugas.

I went to the office and secured my site for another two days and went from there.

The whole day was ahead of me. What should I do? I returned to the hustle of Key West in order to scout the ferry location and dinghy dock. Surprisingly enough, the two were right next to each other and my chores were complete. It was time to have some fun.

Since I had hit up Duval Street the day before, I ventured out to see some of the establishments where the locals hung around. Whitehead Street was one block over and was home to the Green Parrot. The open-air bar has been a staple since the early days of Key West, a place where the locals gather and live bands flourish. I stayed a while, laughed with the local fishermen and exchanged playful banter with the bartenders. From the Parrot, I followed the music to the more quaint experience of The Porch. It had more of a gastro pub flare with local brews and tasty treats. Spending $8 a beer got old real quick, so I wandered into the unique three-storied bar, The Bull and Whistle.

What an experience that establishment was! The bottom floor, The Bull, had a live band playing classic rock covers and tearing up the joint. Curious to see what was on the next floor, I followed some patrons up the stairs to The Whistle. At this time, the sun was setting and I walked to the balcony to enjoy the breeze and watch the people below. Duval Street was now a scene right out of the Vegas strip. The crazies began to hoot and holler as they stumbled in and out of the bars. The flood gates were open -- and I had a front-row seat. Not to say I wasn't doing a little of damage myself; I, too, got lost in the on-going party Key West was turning into.

Night was now upon us and my drink was empty. I left the balcony and ordered another round at the rustic second-story bar. As I turned, I saw a few people walk down a small flight of stairs to my right. Turning to the bartender, I asked if there was another bar on the roof. She giggled and said I should check it out. In a stupor, I took the flight of stairs passing warning signs along the way -- the type of warning signs you would see if you were about to enter a strip club. The type of signs stating no cell phone use and you must be 18 years old to enter. "Where am I going?," I wondered. When I got to the top of the stairs, a sign on the door read "The Garden of Eden," a clothing-optional bar. Thinking this could be a fun experience, I reached for the door and gave it a go.

This was the fantasy life Key West grants to the beatniks and the hippies. The rooftop bar screamed free love. I was drawn to it. I mean, I wasn't going around all willy-nilly, but I enjoyed the smiles and freedom of the bohemian spirit. I sat at the bar for a bit and reveled in the aura surrounding the place. Up to this point, I had pretty much stayed to myself, but then I caught sight of a beautiful tanned lady dancing and eye-fucking me from across the floor. Wearing only her black stilettos and swaying her firm body to the rhythm of the music, she made her way to the bar. I felt a hand turn my shoulder and brush through my beard. As I stared at her newly purchased breasts, she pulled me onto the dance floor to show me her moves. My shirt was stripped from my body as she pressed against my special purpose. This went on for a few songs until a huge gigantor sum bitch came over and pulled her away. Apparently, she had a husband. I wasn't going to get involved with that. Before leaving she thanked me for the dances, grabbed my goods and threw her tongue down my throat. I was beside myself. In fear of the behemoth whooping my ass, I chugged my drink and got the hell out of there.

It was all her fault. I had a head full of liquor and she had gotten the blood flowing elsewhere. I continued down Duval Street and into Willy T's. The bar was hopping and the entertainer was playing my type of music. I bought a drink and stood by the rail, cat-calling the pretty women as they walked past. I got a bite; I reeled her in and got the pretty lady a drink. Her friends weren't too happy about it, but she was all about the bearded-Jesus look. The entertainer was even impressed with my spontaneity and "no-fucks-given" approach. He was so impressed, he bought me a beer. In a way, I was bringing more people into the bar to hear him play. Then, he played Bon Jovi and damn if I didn't get up on stage and sing with him. He was a good sport about it and so was everyone else in the bar. The ladies grew tired and wanted to go where half-naked dudes were dancing on the bar. Why not?

The story changed abruptly when we got to The Bourbon Street Bar. There was a $5 cover charge and the friends expected me to pay their covers. Well, that was a No! I bid them good night and walked away. While I was on my way back to the camp, I ran into my server, Todd, in the middle of Duval Street. We did a double-take as he was being dragged one way and I another. We said hello and a super quick goodbye. Who would've thunk it? By this time, I was petered out and it was 3 a.m. I had a long five-mile walk ahead of me to get back to Boyds.

It was 5 a.m. -- and I was drunk. Before taking the final steps to my tent, I stopped at a gas station for some food. Three mega burritos later, it was time to stumble home. Exhausted to all ends, I crawled into my sleeping bag and finally got some rest.

My Cape Horn

Rightfully hung over, I pulled myself out of the tent sometime in the afternoon. I didn't care what time it was; I only had to get Lola to the dinghy dock today. Preparing for the trip, I downed a few Gatorades to get me over the hump and separated my gear into two piles. I kept all my expensive equipment with me and put everything, except my tent and bag, with Lola.

We were on the water early the next day and rounding Stock Island. That day I was going to finish the 1,000 miles of the Gulf of Mexico. The sun was shining, gulls were culling and the wind was soothing. It couldn't have been a more perfect day.

I saw the Southernmost Point Monument from the water. This cement buoy-shaped pillar marks the southernmost point in the continental United States. The rip-rap rocks do not allow boaters to safely dock there and I had to settle with taking a photo from the water. Although it marks the southernmost point on land, it did not mean I was through with the Gulf. Fort Zachary Taylor Beach is the jumping off point to claim such a feat. The data book stated you had to have permission to land at Fort Zachary Taylor Beach, but I said who cares? I was going for it.

The beach was within reach and the waves pushed me in. It was obvious the waves would submerge Lola and me, so I planned for the side-straddle dismount. Bystanders watched as I approached the break and, with one fell swoop, I took the leap. Unknowingly, I continued to sink, searching for the bottom. After what felt like an eternity, I finally touched bottom and pushed up to swim Lola ashore. I lay in the sand celebrating my success with a smile upon my face. It was wiped off when I realized I had lost my camera to the break.

The camera held all the photos from the start of my journey and now lay in the sandy bottom of the cloudy break. Frantically, I grabbed my mask and snorkel to search the depths. The waves beat down, swirling me around. A whirlwind of sand blew by like a sandstorm through the desert. It was impossible to see. I had to resort to searching the sand blindly with my feet. As time lapsed, I became more afraid I had lost the camera. I made a pact with myself that I would not leave that beach until that camera was in my possession.

A solid 20 minutes had passed. I had stubbed my toes five times on rock formations, picked up a half-dozen shells and swallowed enough salt water to fill an aquarium. Then I had a glimmer of hope. I felt a smooth surface just below the sand with my toes. I had found the needle in the haystack. Gripping the camera with my monkey-like toes, I retrieved it successfully and returned to the shore.

Leaving the beach would be my next challenge. If you've made it this far into the book, you know that's the more difficult task. After all the commotion, I couldn't let my fanfare down. I chose to use the ass-first straddle method, using my legs as outriggers. I sat holding Lola just after the break, timing the sets. I had the count and thrust her into the water. Slick as goose shit, I timed the actions just right and paddled off like a real O.G.

There were more challenges to come once I left the Gulf waters behind. Right out of the gate, I had to get through the cruise ship and shipping lanes, where the channels are dredged, therefore causing the water to react differently to the depth. Luckily, I was there at the right time and there was no traffic coming in or out of the port. I had a smooth sail into the dinghy dock.

The dock master showed me where to tie Lola up and recommended I take what I could with me, so nobody could steal anything. The docks did have cameras, but lack security. When I pulled up, I met a salty live-aboard sailor Caleb. He was hanging in his dinghy, already drunk as a skunk. I tried having a meaningful conversation with him, but he was way too gone. He reminded me of a drunken pirate shown on the Pirates of the Caribbean ride at Walt Disney World. I almost expected him to start singing "The Pirate's Life For Me."

I went to Margaritaville for a specialty margarita and a Volcano Burger to properly celebrate completing the Gulf. After eating, I walked around and enjoyed some of the free sites of Key West. I enjoyed the air conditioning of the Little White House, where notable presidents Taft, Truman and Kennedy had spent time. If you have the opportunity while in Key West, I recommend swinging through. From there, I went to the world-famous Mallory Square Sunset Celebration. Here street performers, artists and musicians all partake in celebrating the ending of another sublime day.

That night I had to forgo gallivanting around town. I had an early wake-up call set in place to get me to the ferry. After the celebration, I started the five-mile walk to Boyd's Campground. As I sauntered back, I took the time to look back at the goals I had met so far. The thought of actually paddling the length of the Gulf was still all surreal. I felt like I was floating and couldn't wait to see what was ahead. As for the next day, and the next few days, I would reward myself with the true feeling of being stranded off the coast of the Florida Keys.

Late night stroll back to Boyd's

Key West Lighthouse

Southernmost point by water

Celebrating the completion of the Gulf of Mexico

Segment : Vacation
The Dry Tortugas

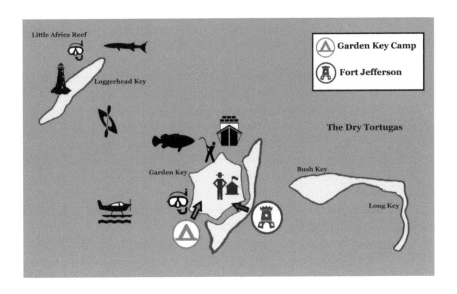

All maps were hand drawn and created by the author
Jeffrey "Treehouse" Buncie

Tortuga Celebration

Sixty-eight nautical miles west Key West sits seven small islands, remotely accessible by seaplane or ferry. These islands, The Dry Tortugas, present a unique opportunity to explore the magnificent sea life surrounding the nearby reefs and shipwrecks. Garden Key, home to the historic Fort Jefferson, houses one of the largest brick structures in the Western Hemisphere. Between the rich history and turquoise blue waters, the national park draws hundreds of visitors daily.

During my travel to the islands, I was one of the lucky few able to secure a campsite on Garden Key. For the next three days, I would call that picturesque background home. Well, at least that was the idea. Let me tell you a tale of 15 castaways stranded on an island paradise ...

Pattie, Boyd's Campground security guard, was generous enough to act as my alarm. I broke camp and was in a taxi by 530 a.m. When I returned to the dinghy dock, Lola was submerged, lying just below the surface. I was forced to jump into the darkened water. The clock was ticking and I had decisions to make. I threw my gear onto the dock, scooped out as much water as I could, then flipped Lola over my head, returning the remaining water to its rightful place.

Once I was able to lift her from her watery grave, Lola sat on the docks awaiting transport. I fastened her half-assed to the cart and swung her to the loading bay of the ferry, The Yankee Freedom. The crew met me with astonishment. Out of professional courtesy, I unloaded what I could, allowing them to lift Lola over the guardrails and onto the boat. After all, I knew their struggle all too well.

Breakfast and coffee awaited me in the briefing room. The $220 ticket included breakfast, lunch, the return trip and cost for transporting my kayak. The two-hour ferry ride put me in a catatonic haze. Before I knew it, we were docking. The captain came over the intercom, asking the campers to remain on board for another briefing. When I sat with the group left behind, I had an odd feeling, certain I knew one of them. We were briefed on how to select a site and what to do from there. After the instruction, we were free to exit the vessel.

I knew I was right about that déjà-vu feeling. The older guy I thought I knew, in fact, knew who I was. He was the kayaker I had met briefly a week or so ago in the Everglades and gave pointers to about the Sable camps. Roger, a Canadian retiree, remembered the morning we had met, and approached and introduced himself. He claimed that through my recommendations he had had a great camp spot and enjoyed himself thoroughly. We made plans to meet later, then went about our business.

As the crew members were unloading Lola, I met a couple other campers waiting for their kayaks. Brothers Joe and Ryan were on vacation with their dad. Joe was super-approachable and had many questions. He invited me on a fishing trip planned for the next day. I was worried I didn't have any bait, but Ryan assured me they had it covered if I cared to go. The conversation was cut short for the race to the prime campsites. I was in no hurry, though. Sometimes you have to embrace island time and take what's given to ya.

The only site left was in the middle of the grounds. The sun beat down as I set camp. I felt like I was on stage giving a performance -- all the ferry goers were staring as they walked by with their snorkels and masks. I placed that thought in the back of my mind and planted camp among the hermit crabs of Garden Key.

Hungry, I returned to the ferry to pamper myself with air conditioning and its wicked sandwich spread. I was not worried about missing any time to explore the island, for I knew, once 3 p.m. arrived, the campers and fort staff would be the only ones left. Boy, did I take in a healthy serving. I stayed at the lunch spread until 1 p.m., when it closed, then took a walk along the fort's barrier. I had to get rid of the food baby somehow.

Sounds of children gleefully playing began to dissipate. The herds funneled their way back to the ark. The time for exploration was upon me. The crowds were gone and the VIP party was just beginning. Entering the desolate walls of Fort Jefferson, a feeling of exclusivity overcame me as if I were on a private tour. I became the giddy child I had been hearing throughout the day. Leaving no stone unturned I covered every nook and cranny of the Civil War prison. It was an invigorating experience with the ability to pose for pristine photos. The historic brick structure was my playground.

Blessed to have seen a monumental sunset atop a three-tiered structure, I left the walls to return to my camp. The long and restless day was coming to an end rather quickly. I was content and ready to greet the new day. Anticipation grew inside me, like a child lying awake on Christmas Eve. And, just like that child, eventually grew tired enough to lay my head to rest.

Whumps and thumps rained down from the seaplane overhead. The sputtering engine came to a halt as I pulled my head from the sand. It was too early for this shit. Rolling over and hoping for more sleep, my anticipation grew, clearly proving it was too late. The damage had been done and I was now awake.

A cloudless sky and a warm ocean breeze welcomed me to the second day at my new-found paradise. Thanks to the early-morning rumbles, I had the whole day ahead of me. Hankering for somewhat of a private day, I asked about kayaking over to Loggerhead Key. The on-site ranger traded me a marine radio for a float plan, which gave me the go-ahead.

Prior to shipping off, Roger swung through my camp with morning pleasantries. Mentioning I was headed across the channel, I invited him on the paddle, but he had his own agenda for the day and declined. After he left, I was approached by two guys from Philadelphia, Chad and John, who had overheard our conversation, asking for help getting across the channel. Their novice paddling experience, they claimed, limited them from attempting the three-mile paddle. Before I accepted, I laid down a few safety precautions and reiterated that if they broke any of them, they would be on their own. With the stipulations agreed upon, we set sail across the channel.

Somehow, for some reason, I assumed a role of responsibility. I was out here to escape all that nonsense and there I was, right back in the middle of it. I kept a close eye on the guys and often found myself waiting for their slower rent-a-yaks to catch Lola. During these times, I encouraged them to keep their arms moving and taught them lessons on navigating open water.

Open water has a funny way of playing a trick or two on the inexperienced paddler. The water is always moving and, if you're not careful, it can swiftly send you off-course. It may seem like you are still tracking, but before you know it, your three-mile paddle becomes a four- or five-mile paddle. The Philly boys impressed me with their willingness to follow instruction. As a result, we were able to arrive safely on the vacant shores of Loggerhead Key.

The largest of the Tortuga Islands was now ours to traverse. Appealing white sands encouraged me to stretch my legs. During my visit to the Loggerhead Lighthouse, I met Ray, the volunteer keeper. If you were to look up "lighthouse keeper" in the dictionary, this guy's photo would be right there. A white scruffy beard stood out from his well-tanned face as he greeted me with a smile. We immediately hit it off and he gave me a tour of the grounds. He showed me around the keeper's house, then onto the desalination area. In that room, solar energy is used to remove the salt and minerals from sea water to produce fresh water for the islands. Ray was great company, but, in time, I had to bid farewell as Little Africa was waiting.

On the west shore of Loggerhead Key is one of the finest snorkeling reefs in the Tortugas. Groves of soft coral, purple and red sea fans, sway in unison with the current. The surrounding gardens of the hard, stony corals are a playground for the schools of reef fish. As I watched the fish travel through the formidable maze, a juvenile barracuda decided to grace us with his presence. The glare from my camera brought the predator within arm's reach. I had to stow the GoPro in my pocket until he lost his interest. At the same time, I started shadowing a trigger fish snacking among the polyps. Yes sir, the Little Africa reef is a magical place.

Time flew by while I was in the water. The Philly boys were watching the time -- I was not. I spent hours immersed in the underwater ecosystem mesmerized by the fluidity of it all. Heartbroken, I left the reef behind only to receive more unpleasant news. Hypnotized by the reef, I had burned away the time I had allotted to visit a nearby shipwreck. This was the price I paid for being the responsible party. We had to start making our way back to Garden Key; there are too many variables that come with guiding the inexperienced.

The tide was on the move and the wind picked up the swells, but we held our own. I saw the boys were feeling a little more confident, so I paddled ahead of them for a bit. Next thing I know, I turned around and saw they were back a couple hundred yards, drifting off course. I got a little loud, reminding them about the tricks we had talked about earlier. They tried their damndest to close the gap, but it was no use. I had to paddle back and lead them like a mother hen. From that moment on, they did very well and tracked my path back to the camp.

In camp, the brothers and their successful fishing excursion was all the rave. As they were cooking up fresh-caught groupers over the fire, I congratulated them and we swapped war stories about our day. We were joined shortly by the Philly boys, who came bearing gifts. They were grateful I had guided them across to Loggerhead Key. I took the opportunity to praise them and boost their confidence by explaining further it wasn't as easy as it seemed and they should be proud they made it. I was super-stoked for them and glad I was able to provide the experience for them. Before it got too sappy I started to turn away, but they had some kryptonite in their pocket -- a semi-cold beer. My mouth dropped and now I was the one giving thanks.

The beer was gone and the moment passed. It was my turn to give the fish hell. The brothers gave me some bait and I was off to try my luck. I threw in my line at the calmer, lee side of the fort. Left and right, I was pulling in all sorts of fish having a whale of a time. Sure, I was enjoying myself, but everything I caught was nothing more than cut bait. I grew tired, so I kept the last grunt for shark bait and returned to camp until nightfall.

I had heard through the grapevine the dock was where to fish once the underwater lights kicked on. When the time was right, I grabbed the bait, rigged my rod with heavy tackle and took off for the dock. Minutes passed before I got my first hit. The line didn't run like I was accustomed to -- the fish hit, but then pulled the line straight to the depths. The drag was running like the shark in "Jaws" had taken the bait. I knew I had a monster. There was no skill to it at all -- I had the beast and now it was all up to my tackle. Pulling, reeling, sinking and repeat became the game. I was patient, by slowly wearing the creature out I felt like I was winning the fight. The brute strength of this fabled white whale was toying with me. I was able to get it to the lights and saw it was a Goliath grouper. Then, in a blink of an eye, he ran back to the depths, but not before showing me his ass and snapping my line, thus ending my evening of fishing.

As I was leaving, I saw a fort employee walking up the dock with a rig I knew could handle such as fish. Curious, I hung out to see if he could land the bastard. Within minutes, he hooked the Goliath. I watched in amazement. He obviously knew a bit more about landing such a monster. His buddies cheered him on as he worked the fish around the pylons and down the boardwalk. Shocked, I followed alongside. We were making our way to the beach like he knew exactly what to do. He finally got the fish floating on its side, completely beat. He handed the rod to his buddy, walked in about waist-deep, tapped the fish on the head and released the newly tamed beast. I had to ask -- turns out he catches the same fish three or four times a week. It was almost like he kept tally marks for wins and losses. Once he told me that, the innocence of it all was lost and I returned to my camp.

Oh, but the evening was young. The moon was shining through the blankets of clouds. I took the opportunity to capture the moment with a few still shots and meditated while sitting in the sand. At peace once again, it was time for me to bring the day to an end.

Enjoying Ft. Jefferson   **Paddle across the channel**

Loggerhead Key Lighthouse

Stranded

There was a buzz going around the camp. The ferry was out of commission and was not going to make it that day. For me, it made no difference, but for others? Some had been out there for a bit and had to catch returning flights, including the Philly boys. I was happy about the ferry not making it; it meant we campers had the island all to ourselves. We came together rather quickly over morning coffee. It was amazing how everyone pulled resources to make sure we all had water and food to eat. We were slowly becoming a community from the '50s, where neighbors talked to neighbors, and I dug the vibe.

Once the commotion settled, the vacation continued like any other day. I decided to take a lazy day reading more about the fort's history. Fort Jefferson was an old Civil War prison for Union soldiers who abandoned their posts. Post-Civil War history included the imprisonment of Samuel Mudd, Edmund Spangler, Samuel Arnold and Michael O'Laughlen, who had been convicted of conspiracy in the assassination of President Abraham Lincoln. Mudd escaped twice to Loggerhead Key.

A yellow fever epidemic at the fort in 1867 killed many prisoners, including O'Laughlen, and Joseph Sim Smith, the 5th Artillery's surgeon. Mudd helped provide medical care during the epidemic, which allowed him to work off his debt. He later was pardoned by President Andrew Johnson.

The U.S. naval fleet was docked at the fort during its coal station days in the late 1890s. One of the ships that was moving coal was a ship we all remember from history. The infamous U.S.S. Maine left the fort on its fateful trip to Havana, where it was either blown up by a mine or spontaneous combustion of the methane gas produced by the coal -- a question still debated to this day -- in February 1898. The explosion became one of Hearst's most famous newspaper headlines, "Remember the Maine." It also helped lead to the start of the Spanish-American War in April 1898.

Bored yet? Don't worry; I'll spare you any more details. I had had enough of the fort as well. I returned to the ranger station and asked about a shipwreck off the shores of Bird Key. The ranger talked me out of exploring the wreck, claiming there wasn't much left to see after recent hurricanes and the site was difficult to find. There went that idea, right out the window.

I returned to the frantic Philly boys and irritated workers, but I soon grew tired of the angst in the air. I retreated to the water with my rod once again. The fish were still biting. It was all in fun -- the groupers I caught were too small and the snappers I kept for shark bait. The hours of the day disappeared quickly. I saw the brothers paddle back from Loggerhead and met them at the beach. They claimed they had had a very relaxing day and I filled them in on the updates. Not long after, the ranger called everyone over to the picnic table. He said the ferry was not going to return the next day as well. Somehow, I was able to hold in a "Hell, yeah" or a "Yippee!" I was ecstatic. Others began to worry. The ranger informed us he would bring water and food in the morning to help us get by, then left us to our conversations.

With the exception of the Philly boys, everyone accepted the fact we would be stranded. It didn't take long for the "Gilligan's Island" jokes to start flying around. Overall, we were in high spirits and went about our business. The only thing that could have made me happier at that moment was if we had had some rum to share around a fire.

The ferry wasn't running, but that seaplane sure as hell flew over again. The mere fact it was available sent the Philly boys running. They paid the pilot to fly them back to Key West, leaving the experience behind.

When I unzipped my tent the next morning, Patrick, a volunteer firefighter was at my site with a pot of coffee. He had been calling me the "whollyburger," which I could only assume was some sort of Bigfoot creature. My longer hair and scruffy beard usually brings that sort of nickname around.

Over coffee, he filled me in with the newest updates. The Philly boys left a box of food and the ranger had brought drinking water and MREs. Before returning to his post, the ranger let us know he had a working satellite phone if anyone needed to reach out to travel agents or relatives.

Since Garden Key was left to the campers, I chose to explore the reefs along the mote walls. The waters were super calm in the morning, making it a perfect day to do some snorkeling. After I ate breakfast from the communal box, I geared up and swam around the mote walls. It was no Little Africa, but I saw a ton of pompano and huge sea urchins. I grew tired of all the swimming, called it quits and returned to camp.

156

At lunchtime, we gathered as a group at the food box. Spirits remained high and I got a little too creative with the food choices. Snorkeling took a lot out of me, so I packed together a couple peanut butter and tuna sandwiches. Don't let the mix fool you. I needed the protein and, believe it or not, it was pretty tasty. While we were eating, the ranger greeted us again. This time, he claimed the ferry would be returning the next day and we would all be leaving the island. Some cheered, others praised God; I was bummed.

In a short amount of time, we had grown close to one another and relied on each other's positivity for morale. Since we still had a big box of food, someone suggested we have a family-style grill and chill. The brothers and I volunteered to catch the fish, some offered to cook and others to clean. We each had a role to do and we were all proud to chip in to make the party happen. The one thing missing was the rum.

The brothers took off in their kayaks to the fishing hole off shore. I stayed on the island to try the surf fishing. We were the first step in making this all happen, so there was no time to waste. Thankfully, I was able to land a few snapper and the brothers returned not long after with a porgy and a few snappers of their own. Our main course was ready to be prepared for the fire.

Although my job was done. Instead of sitting idle and watching the others work, I took a moment to do some reflecting on the point of the island. Ryan, one of the brothers, saw me taking off and asked if he could join me. He seemed like a pretty cool cat, so I invited him along. A professional photographer in Seattle, he said he wanted to get some photos around the island with me in them. I had no qualms about it and off we went to explore.

Along the walk, he staged some shots of me backlit by the sun, looking up, salty sea-dog profiles and one of my feet in the sand. Now, when I tell this story to my friends or to my long-distance hiker friends, I always joke about how I used to be a foot model before I started hiking. There I was, at the point of Garden Key walking through the Tortugas. A photographer named Ryan snapped a few shots of my well-manicured, tattooed feet digging into the sand. When he later returned to Seattle, he stamped the prints, had some luck at the gallery and made some money. By definition, I am pretty sure that makes me a model. And that, dear friends, is how I became that foot model. (For those who thought I was talking bullshit, this insert is for you -- and I want you to know I forgive you.)

Back in camp, after my name was on its way to stardom, the meal was just about ready. The spread came to the table one dish at a time. We grabbed our plates and made sure there was enough to feed everyone. Praise went around from the providers to the chefs. We spared no laughs or smiles. The feast may have come to an end, but not the gathering. The fire was refueled while the stories continued to circulate.

Eventually, the group dwindled. Joe, the other brother, asked me if I wanted to go shark fishing. Fuck yeah; I wanted to go shark fishing! He grabbed his rig and his kayak, while I grabbed my rod and the cut bait. We went down to the dock, set up heavy tackle and took turns kayaking out to drop the lines. Fishing is not always a win -- and this time we both took losses. One thing that did come from this shared time was great conversation -- not just chit-chat, but a deeper, more meaningful conversation. Even though we didn't get a shark, I was happy to have shared those moments with this like-minded individual.

We called it quits just after midnight. The air temperature had dropped, chasing us to our tents in the now-silent camps. I bid farewell to Joe and crawled into my much warmer sleeping bag. I didn't want to go to sleep. When the next day became the next day, I would have to leave this beautiful place. I fought it with all my might, but eventually I gave in to the calling of the sandman.

The 2014 Garden Key castaways   Photo credit: Ryan Duclos

One last hoorahh!!!   Photo credit: Michael Arbore

158

My Inner Hemingway

First came the seaplane, then, as promised, the Yankee Freedom came, unloading its fresh cargo. The stranded campers had a spring in their step when they saw the ferry dock. I had to force myself to smile that day. The community was broken down rather quickly. It was as if the patch of sand hadn't hosted a co-existing community the past few days. Before we went our own ways, Ryan gathered everyone for a group photo along the mote walls. This became our "beach life" moment.

Mobs of pasty bodies fluttered onto the island. I sat back and watched from atop a picnic table. The children were dragging the adults and the adults were dragging the children. It changed the atmosphere from the chill island I had called home to the hustle and bustle of a cruise port. Wanting no part of it, I moved into the air conditioning of the Freedom with the rest of the campers.

I found it funny all we wanted to do was hang out on the boat, but even there we were our own little clique. The staff started putting out the lunch spread and boy, oh boy, did I take advantage. Just as I was about to dig in, there was a buzz circulated through our group. The brothers were going to dive off the boat. This was a punishable offense, but what the hell were the powers that be going to do? Leave us on the island? I tore off my napkin, threw down my shirt and joined them on the escapade.

Desperately attempting to breach the top tier of the boat, we were denied access by the captain. One of us made it to the top, but was scolded immediately. Settling for the bow of the boat, the brothers sent their dad and camera ashore for photographic evidence. We watched from the bow as Mike made his way along the beach. The go-ahead was as primitive as my new lifestyle. He gave a thumbs up; we all looked at one another, grabbed the railing, counted to three, then climbed over in unison. Pause that thought right there. My heart was racing, I was filled with adrenaline, not from the height of the jump, but from the notion we were jumping out of protest. The "three" came, we stepped over the rail and dove off the fiberglass bow into the salty blue waters. Our child-like laughter filled the opening of the catamaran ferry below. As we were swimming toward the shore, a crew member hollered from the dock, "Hey, you guys can't be swimming there!" We played dumb and laughed the whole way to the shore. Mike met us there and showed us the photos. We got some good ones, but I had a couple of sandwiches to attend to. I left them and returned to the luncheon spread.

Back on board, we were now celebrities among the community. I was eating my meal when Robert from Miami and his wife swung by to confirm our rumored deed. He was as enthusiastic as we were. Then Roger came by, adding his endearing words and high-fives. Shortly after, Mike, Joe and Ryan came over and invited me for one last walk around the island. I felt privileged to be considered as one of the family. It was an intimate time -- a father who lived in one state, two sons reunited from both ends of the nation, and then there was me. It was not an offer to be passed up nor denied. We walked and shared memories. I hope one of the three of them will get wind of this book and read these words, for I am eternally grateful. Thank you for inviting me into your memories.

Enough of this sappy shit. The time came when we had to check in and return to the boat. We went topside to enjoy a cold beverage for the long ferry ride back. The ferry was once again loose from the grips of the dock. I leaned over the rail and said a private goodbye to the vanishing island. My mind had to make a switch back to work mode, but for now I would sit back and enjoy the salt-misted air upon my undying smile.

New obstacles were waiting to overcome when we returned to Key West. The ferry rolled in just about sunset and by the time everyone was unloaded, there was little time to spare before night fell. The castaways met one last time for information sharing and good tidings. The moment was similar to a heist movie -- we had just pulled the biggest job of our careers and now we should spend a spell apart. Knowing and hoping we would cross paths again, we enjoyed the camaraderie of the unique event. The ferry docked and the anomaly ended. The group dispersed like a bursting star, leaving Lola and me alone on the concrete loading dock.

This was just the beginning of the evening for this castaway. In the grand scheme of things, I look back on the events that ensued and can see it working out better, but then again, I wouldn't have these stories to share. You all know my theories about paddling at night. I wasn't going anywhere and I wasn't about to spend money on a room, so I decided to be homeless in Key West for a night. First things first, I had to find Lola a home. She was fully loaded, so I dragged her over

160

the rip-rap rocks and paddled back to the dinghy dock. The dock master had left for the night, so once again I packed a bag and left her up against a pylon in the back.

The Green Parrot was calling my name. There was nowhere else I would have rather have returned. The band was luring patrons in from the sidewalks of Whitehead and creating an atmosphere you wanted to be a part of. Claiming a barstool and ordering a hometown favorite, I came up with a game plan -- enjoy the bar for as long as I could before getting thrown out after "last call."

I kept to myself, drank some Rolling Rock beers and surveyed the room. I was approached by a stunning young lady from Russia, Maria. No, she was not a lady of the night; she claimed she was drawn to my aura. Her smile and big-doe eyes captivated me. We sat and talked for a while. Unfortunately, she had some "baggage" that was interfering with our connection. Her very drunk friend was -- well, the only way to put it -- a complete bitch to me. She kept saying, "Look at you and look at her" and telling me I couldn't support Maria and yadda, yadda, yadda. Maria was not listening to her. She liked my stories, bravery and willingness to grab life by the balls. She knew she was a little drunk and wanted to talk in a deeper level, sober.

We left The Parrot and walked to a sandwich shop Maria had suggested. She said she wanted a Philly cheese and claimed Danny Z's was the place to grab the best. Of course, I was going where she was going. She asked about my bag and if I was on the street. Once I explained the situation, she invited me to her house to sleep on the couch -- even before the kick-ass sandwich we destroyed.

If only it had been that easy. Her friend caught wind of the invitation and was having none of it. While we were eating, she called a cab behind Maria's back. Upon leaving Danny Z's -- which by the way, *did* have a very good Philly -- a cab pulled up and the bitch grabbed Maria by the arm and threw her in the backseat. Had I just witnessed a kidnapping? Maria apologized and asked me to call her the next day. I bid farewell and returned to being homeless on the streets of Key West.

Time check, 3 a.m. What was still open? I knew of a 24-hour Denny's on Duval Street where I could kill an hour. The doors were open and the waitresses were bored. There was only one other couple occupying a table. I grabbed a table in the back and smelled the bacon frying. My stomach was speaking to me, so I ordered some breakfast and tried to sober up. An hour flew by, but I was ready to keep moving. When I went to pay the tab, the waitress explained someone had felt sorry for me and had paid for my meal. It was a kind gesture, but there was no need to feel bad for me. I guess I was looking pretty homeless at 4 in the morning.

The streets were empty. The hustle came to an end. Street-sweeper machines filled the air with their whisking in the distance. Just like the island I left earlier in the day, Key West was mine to explore. I took a walk to the zero mile mark of US1, the lighthouse and ended up at the Hemingway House. I am not sure of the statutes of limitation, but I will confess to jumping over the wrought-iron gate and laying in his yard for a quick cat nap.

My sleep was abruptly interrupted by the irrigation system. I came to covered in the morning dew. The sun was eating away at the darkness, convincing me to stop trespassing and return to the sidewalk. After clearing the fence, I began the walk back to Lola and the dinghy dock.

Appalled at what I saw as I approached the dock, I picked up the pace. I was watching a skinny tan home bum jump up and down on top of Lola. These were fighting terms. I yelled over and broke his concentration. "What the hell do you think you are doing? That is my kayak!" He looked up, jumped onto the dock and started running the other way. A chase ensued, but he had crackhead-like speed. I was unable to catch the little fucker. By the way, where was the dock master? He was nowhere to be found. That's what really upset me.

Back on the water, I went to start the draining process just as before. Cursing and slamming the gear, I was hoping the dock master would come out and I could give him a piece of my mind. He never did throughout the whole process and I continued throwing a hissy fit. The task was complete, but all my gear was soaked yet again. At that point, I had had enough of Key West and was ready to get the hell out of there. I visited the public restroom and found a spot I could crawl under safely to get a couple more hours of rest.

The cubby was under the raised walkway of the restrooms. I squeezed under and found a homeless camp already prepared. The bed looked like a snuggle party of sandy blankets. It didn't smell too bad, so I curled up and let my mind rest.

The long day finally came to an end. When I woke up, I was ready to head north, ending my vacation in the islands. I had grown tired of the party of Key West and whatever situations came with it. The Tortugas had given me a once-in-a-lifetime experience with, hopefully, lifelong friends. I would press further and harder knowing more experiences await.

Time for a quick cat nap

Early morning stroll through the streets of Key West

Segment 15 (North)
Key West - Garden Cove
115 miles

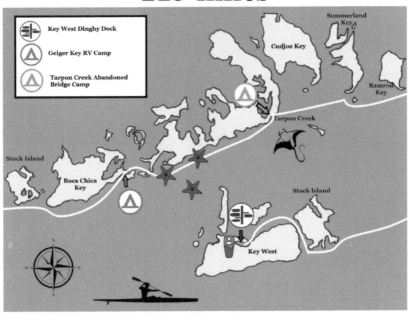

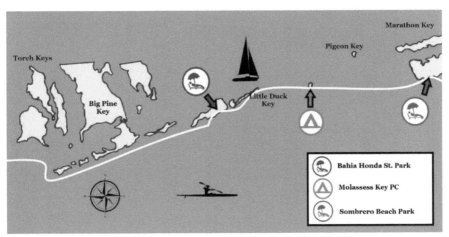

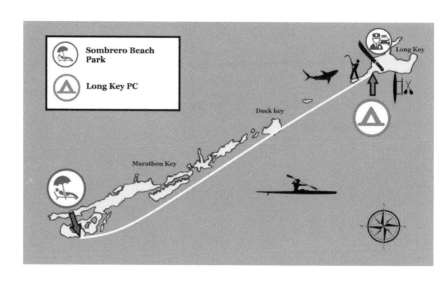

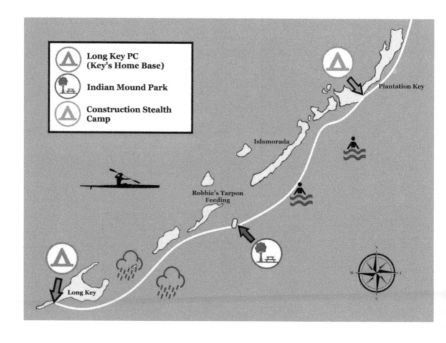

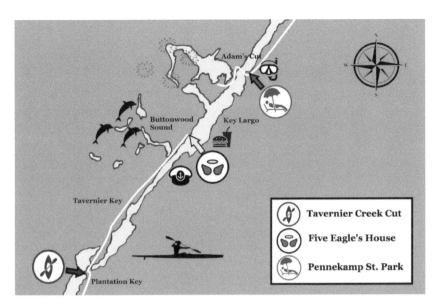

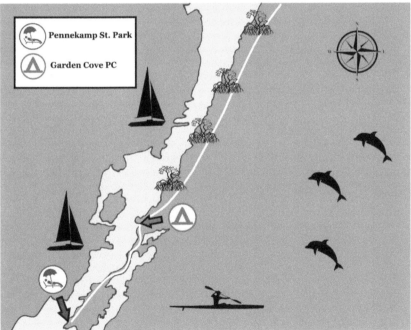

All maps were hand drawn and created by the author Jeffrey "Treehouse" Buncie

Northbound

It seemed like it had been months since I had crossed into the world of the Florida Keys. I had allowed its lifestyle to drag me down like a snapped anchor headed for the ocean floor. The moment came when I had to retrieve the broken lines and mend them back together to set sail. Just like the anchor, I hit hard, with a hesitation to repair the damage as I paddled north to Miami.

I had spent eight days covering the 95 miles from Long Key. Over the next 27 days I would battle obstacles and resistance toward returning to the mainland. These 115 miles had a gravitational pull that held me close to the bosom of the keys. Escaping that lifestyle soon became an internal debate I had to overcome.

Opening myself to the opportunities presented during the holiday season, I was able to prolong my time among the islands. Fighting an internal battle, I found myself stalling and jumping at any excuse not to continue north. Some of these experiences were unwanted; nay, uncontrollable, but others allowed me to kick off the New Year in high fashion. I made new friends, new enemies and reconnected with one specific sailor from the past.

I left the dinghy dock of the Key West Bite on the morning of day 100 of my odyssey. The skies threatened mid-day storms, cold winds and a significant temperature drop. The early morning activities left me exhausted, but eager to leave the shit show behind. My gear was still drenched from the home bum that had ravaged Lola a few hours earlier. These factors lead me to change the itinerary to a much shorter day than anticipated. I was headed back to the Geiger Key Marina to seek refuge and the comfort of amenities.

The lady tending the front desk remembered me swinging through earlier in the trip. I expressed my distaste for the locals, and she cut me a deal on a discounted site. The marina was happy to help. I was able to dry my gear, use the laundry services, set camp and grab a hot shower for a very reasonable rate. Choosing to skip the burger this go-around, I completed my chores and caught up on my sleep.

An early morning chill legitimized my choice to stop short the day before. When I stepped from the tent, I was happy to have dry clothes. I hit the water hard, making my way back to the bridge site.

Back in the flats, exploring the sea life, I made a new sighting -- Bahamian Sea Stars, large red starfish were lurking below the waters that day. I spotted a few and took some time to snag a few photos before moving through the mangroves. Around the mouth of Tarpon Creek, I came across the biggest manta ray I had seen thus far. He allowed me to paddle up beside him before turning on his jets.

When I got to the bridge, there were some hippie car campers hunkered down on the more popular side. They saw me tie up Lola, as I did before, and invited me to grab a beer in town. I told them I would be more than happy to after I set camp, but by the time I was ready, they had left me behind. It was going to be me and Lola, dinner for two once again.

Wouldn't ya know, those hippies never returned. The fire burnt well into the evening. Finally, giving up on a possible after-party, I crawled into my tent. My sights were on an island camp the next day, but 24 miles of open water stood in my way. It was time to call it a night and turn in.

I had one of the best nights of sleep I'd had in a long time. Well rested, I joined the sun for a fantastic day of paddling -- the wind even decided to cooperate. The one bone I had to pick was with my choice in breakfast. I had one of these granola-and-berry, freeze-dried meals the Philly boys had given me. It was unappetizing, to say the least.

During the past couple days, I'd been following bread crumbs left behind through familiar territory. That day I crossed the 1,000-mile threshold and celebrated with a burger at Bahia Honda State Park on Bahia Honda Key. While I was there, I met a couple live-aboard sailors and told them about my accomplishment. One claimed that now I had over 1,000 miles on the water, I had earned a blue sparrow tattoo, a sailor tradition, but he wasn't 100-percent correct. When I fact-checked him later, I found it was symbolic to get one when you hit 5,000 miles. Needless to say, I was a little bummed.

I made my way back to the island across from the Seven-Mile Bridge, Molasses Key. It was empty this time around and I had the prime tent spot. I had left over MREs from the Tortugas and I really have to say the armed forces had stepped up their game with the selections. Not only were the meals packed with calories, they took less than eight ounces of water to cook the entire meal. I am sure, over time, you would get very tired of eating the same meals, but if you liked eating Cracker Jacks as a kid, you would enjoy the little surprises they put in the MREs nowadays.

The world turns, therefore the sun sets. The weather must've been too perfect that day. The wind was unable to whisk the flying teeth astray as they came in waves. I had to run and hide. The tent site was good though, for I had an unobstructed view of the sunset over the causeway.

My favorite $8 campground was within reach. A long day would land me back at Long Key. High winds, choppy waters and swift tides were against me the entire day. Twice along the paddle I had to bail the excess water from Lola's belly. I felt like I was driving a car with the parking brake on for most of the day. Lola's drag was so strong I thought I was literally dragging a dead body behind her. When I stopped at Sombrero Beach for a snack, I opened the hulls and the rear was overflowing with saltwater. The seals were dry-rotted or I had a leak. Either way, if I wanted to make it to Long Key, I had to continue to paddle.

An hour out from the camp, I called the rangers to secure a site. They usually don't take reservations for the primitive sites, but I explained I was a paddler and they set me up. From Duck Key on it was a race with the sun to the park. My forearms were bursting through the skin; triceps were cutting glass and shoulders holding up the world, but I could not stop. I finally beached along the rental kayaks and dragged Lola to the sites.

Site F was taken yet again, but I was invited in by the camper upon arrival. Robert S., a Canadian, was enjoying a bit of wine. He threw me a beer, but I could tell there was something off about him. So off that I didn't finish my beer -- and that never happens. I excused myself and told him I would return after checking in with the rangers.

One of the most often questions I get asked while I'm out on these journeys pertains to carrying a weapon for protection or if I'm worried about getting hurt by others. After five years of long distance travel, I still don't carry a weapon, nor do I worry about these weirdos. I am usually pretty good with reading people or at least being able to feel out the vibe. I was right about the vibe Mr. S gave off ...

I returned with my camping permit and dragged Lola closer to get my camp set. As I was grabbing my gear, dickhead came over and started calling me the "kayak guy." He followed me to my camp and then said I "did not belong" there. I showed him my permit, then he left. After my tent was set, I received a phone call and while I was on the phone, he revisited. He had the balls to insult me again, so I told him he was beginning to aggravate me and to please leave me alone. He complied, leaving me again. I decided to take a walk to the store, hoping he would pass out, and I could get some burritos.

I returned to Lola in the dark of night. I walked up on what looked like a smash-and-grab. Lola was flipped over and my gear was

169

spread all over the pathway. At first, I thought it could've been some nasty raccoons, but I thought about how she had been flipped. The drunk was in his tent, but I called out to him to see if he saw anybody come through. I asked and he blatantly told me he did it because he didn't like the way I looked. I lost my shit from there. I had had enough of the bullying and told him that if he ever touched my shit again, I would drop him to the ground. Adding fuel to the fire, he yelled from his tent that he was grabbing his machete and was going to chop me down. Words crossed, I didn't back down and told him that if he threatened me like that, then he better be sure to put me down for good. I gathered my gear and walked back to the tent.

On the way back, I met another camper, Michelle. She told me he had been drinking all day and she had felt like he was a little off from the start. I was hoping he was too drunk to follow through, but I sat outside on the picnic table for a bit before heading into my tent. I eventually did and, sure as shit, he came by and called me out for a duel -- something out of the old saloon days type of duel. I unzipped my tent, saw he did not have his knife, but his shirt was off and he was still wielding his bottle of wine. I explained to him I didn't want to get arrested for fighting a senior citizen because, let's face it, he was retired and looking pretty old. It was a true pissing match, but he finally went back to his camp.

The night was not over. He returned within the hour and called me out again. Tired from the beating I had taken from the water, I was just looking for a good night's rest. I didn't even indulge him this time by unzipping the tent, I just told him to lay his old ass down. After another barking session, he left yet again. During his absence I decided to walk to the ranger's station to inform them about the situation. They were unreachable, but a sign with the police department's number was there and I gave them a call. They told me to hang tight at the gate to the campground and they would be by promptly.

Two cars arrived 20 minutes later, with the officers brandishing flashlights and on edge. I filled them in with the situation and they immediately thought the Canadian and I were buddies who had had too much to drink. Joking about not even finishing my beer, they finally walked me down to the camp. Doing their due diligence, they confronted the Canadian but could not find the machete. They asked me to move to a more expensive campsite. Declining that idiotic idea, I told them about my kayak and suggested they should move him. He was too drunk to move, so we had to trust each other with staying within our camps until morning. The cops helped me move Lola up to camp and that was the end of the Long Key Machete Debacle.

Sunset from Molasses Key

The return to Long Key

New Campers = New Opportunities

Long Key was my home base for quite some time due to Barry's piss-poor planning. My current phone did not have service there, and I had to sit and wait for Barry to get my replacement phone. I made daily trips to the post office, checking for the package. The post office was just beyond the convenience store, which I renamed Triple B after a few days. The store helped me survive by purchasing honey buns, burritos and beer. Clever name, right? The time spent waiting also allowed me to meet some pretty cool travelers, adding to the experience.

The first couple days, I stayed clear of the prick from Canada. I took advantage of the weather with a few hikes around the area. The Orb Trail on Long Key brought back a fond memory. When I was hiking, I recognized some landscape features that brought me back a few years prior. It took me a moment, but I realized I had had sex there before with an ex-girlfriend. This ah-ha moment lightened the mood and flipped a switch on a more positive spin of the current situation.

On another day, I decided to leave the key and hike north, along US1, to the neighboring keys. Ten miles away was the famous Robbie's Marina on Islamorada. I had all day, so I hoofed it to the happening spot. Robbie's has a day's worth of activities from renting boats, fishing vessels or snorkel gear. I stopped by for a burger and a beer, where I met a server from an AT town in Tennessee. I told her of my journey and, by the end of the meal, I had her number, a free dessert and a free beer. Too bad I lost her number. At least I had the tarpons. Pails of baitfish are sold nearby and you can feed the tarpons from the docks. These monstrous fish will eat right from your hand -- if you have the guts. Their intimidating mouths have the capability to swallow your arm whole. It's a quirky thing, but it is quite an experience.

On the hike back, I stopped at the palm-thatched Safari Bar, which had oversized animal statues designed to lure in tourists. Here, I met Chelsea and a man who went by "All Good." They refused to let me leave and bought round after round of drinks. We were having a great time welcoming people into the bar, dancing and even playing an occasional round of darts. Time eluded us for a while, but eventually they had to leave. I was free from my obligation of drinking the beers they had been buying -- it would have been rude to turn them down --

172

but it was well into the evening. I had about five miles left to stumble along the bridges and return to my sanctum. Thankfully, I made it back around midnight without any harm done.

The real fun started when I met Chuck and his canoe. His energy and excitement drew me in. On vacation from Washington, D.C., he had brought with him a canoe he just built outriggers for. I caught him at the beach, trying them out for the first time. The smile on his face when he saw his creation hold true was as pure as the sand below his feet. From that moment on, we decided to hang together while we were there.

Something changed from that day forth. The atmosphere among the primitive campers had a community feel. The asshole left early and in came Chuck and Erin, a solo traveler from Canada. Let's not forget about Michelle, the lady who had my back from night one. We gathered that night to have a sangria welcome party for all who wanted to participate. We shared stories and knocked off a few bottles of wine.

The following day, Chuck invited me to go fishing in the canoe. We shipped out early in the morning, some may say too early. I was still feeling the sangria, but Chuck had cold beer waiting in the cooler. We headed out toward the Long Key Bridge overpass. We trolled a line the whole way out, but had no luck. That was our theme for the day -- zero luck.

Drunk by the afternoon and bored, I rigged a shark rig -- heavy fishing tackle used for catching fish with teeth that features a steel leader, large hook and bloody bait. Moments later, I had my first shark hooked. Although I never actually got a shark on board, I hooked quite a few. It didn't dawn on me until I got them to the canoe where I would stash them if I actually did catch one. It was fun nonetheless.

That evening we gathered at Erin's camp for another session of drinking games. We had fun until the booze was gone. I said goodnight and went back to my site to cook some mac and cheese for a late-night snack. When I started cooking, I had a visitor invade my space. The biggest raccoon I'd seen in a long time was inching closer to my meal. In the state I was in, I had a little conversation with him, telling him if it came any closer, I was going to take my spear gun and shoot him in the head. I felt like he understood me for the moment; he disappeared, but came at me from another angle. I grabbed my spear gun, walked over and showed him I meant business. I cocked the band to the spear and laid it on the table as a warning. He disappeared into the palm fronds, but returned, coming from the shadows in front of me. He snarled, I grabbed the spear, pointed and warned him one more time.

I drew the line and he dared to cross it. He took his front paw and literally stepped onto my platform. I released the trigger. It was a direct hit. I had a raccoon on the end of the spear. He took off into the brush with the spear in him. I had to put my mac and cheese down and hold onto the gun with everything I had. I wrapped the braided line around my forearm and he was still pulling me into the brush. I had to get low, crawling through the muck to pull him out. Or rather, try. His force was overwhelming. We had a competitive game of tug-of-war for a good half-hour. I gave it one more wrap and a final pull before the tension was gone.

After a half-hour of lying in the muck and getting torn apart by the palmettos I couldn't help but think he won. I mean, he may have a pretty big wound, but he had gotten loose. For me, not only was I bleeding, but my mac and cheese was cold. It hit me once he was free -- I had speared a raccoon in a state park. Sound familiar? I didn't want to get scolded or fined by the ranger I met a few days ago. He seemed really cool and all, but I'm sure Alan didn't want to go down that road with me. I went back into the bush and looked for a blood trail. I had very little luck and my legs were scraped all to hell. I gave one last effort and walked the boardwalks looking for the carcass, but had no luck. I retired soon after throwing away half my meal.

Chuck had breakfast waiting the next morning. We were going to the reef five miles off shore to do some fishing. Unfortunately, the wind did not cooperate, so we spent the day goofing around and shark fishing. We had one very large visitor circle our boat a few times before calling it a day. Chuck noticed a large shadow and we checked it out. We came across a 12-foot nurse shark in the shallows. He was just as large as the boat and sorta freaked Chuck out. We headed back to camp.

The ladies wanted to meet us at the Sunset Bar for one last meal together. Chuck drove us to meet them at the Seven Mile Bridge restaurant. There, Erin extended an invitation to join her at Boyd's Campground for a few days. She already had a site and thought it would be a good time to share. After we'd had a few cocktails, she was able to sell us on a few days in Key West.

One conflict I had with taking a few days down south was with Lola. Where was I going to keep her? Michelle cleared it up in the morning, claiming she was going to hold onto her site and I could move her there. That seemed reasonable enough to me. We made preparations, loaded the cars and headed 67 miles south.

During check in, the lady at the desk remembered me and I Introduced her to my new friends. We set our camp and drove to the party along Duval Street. We dove head-first into the festivities, hitting

174

up Sloppy Joe's for our boardwalk beverages. Chuck and Erin were interested in visiting the Tortugas. I showed them where to buy the tickets and where to meet in the morning. We made a quick circle, hitting some of the more notable bars while waiting for the Mallory Square performers to get into place. We gathered around and enjoyed the acts at the Sunset Celebration as the sun disappeared.

On our way back to the car, we passed a drummer beating on some buckets. The ladies stood by as he continued his set. He stopped short, stood up and gave me a fist bump. I guess I had previously hung out with him at Willy Ts. He surprised me with stories that coincided with one of my evenings. The group joked about how I knew everyone and how I got around. I took it for what it was as we returned to Boyd's for an early night's rest.

Goin' fishing off Long Key

Photo credit:
Chuck Rich

Long Key mornings   **Chuck, Shelle, Erin & me**

Poseidon and a Bahamian Sea Star

Photo credit:
Chuck Rich

175

Another Holiday on Long Key

By the time I woke up, Chuck and Erin were already enjoying Fort Jefferson and I had no idea where Michelle had gone. I decided to take advantage of the cheaper resupply at The Dollar Tree. After the seven-mile hike, I decided to lay low at the pool and wait for them to return.

Eventually everyone made it back to the campground, where we decided to hit the town hard. We all pitched in for a cab, which allowed everyone to drink alcoholic beverages and not worry about getting home. Chuck was in a blissful state and invited us to start the night on him. His choice included an intimate tradition shared among his friends back home. He took us to Dirty Kevin's and ordered a round of Irish Car Bombs -- shots of irish whiskey, Baileys Irish Cream Liqueur and Guinness beer -- to set the evening aflame. We made our way to the Bull and Whistle, where the ladies wanted to see the Garden for themselves.

I warned Chuck about the Garden and its activities as I pointed them to the stairway. Chuck and I stayed on the balcony for a drink before joining them. When we made our way to the third story, I heard the DJ kicking off a party. The door opened to a full bar of swinging dicks and bouncing titties. I would say it was a little different this go-around. We found the two women having a great time on the dance floor and joined in on the fun. Nobody in our group ate the forbidden fruit and got naked, but we all made a few friends.

We chose to spend the majority of the time on the rooftop terrace. I was approached by a couple in their 40s, who obviously wanted me to join them for the evening. They were the type that had the money to spend, prided themselves in keeping tight bodies and enjoyed sharing. They almost had me, too. As we were making our way out the door, headed for the strip club, the wife grabbed me by the hand as if we were about to fly away to Neverland, but group loyalty made me decline.

I noticed Chuck had disappeared. I told the ladies I was going to search for him and went on the mission. I found him at a neighboring bar enjoying a live band. We reached out to the ladies and had them meet us in a tamer environment. I watched as the alcohol took over. All three of them had hit their limit. I was able to talk them into one more stop for a road soda from Fat Tuesdays. We hailed a taxi and rode back to Boyds.

The newly deemed "Shelle Zell" was going back to Long Key to have some alone time. The three of us stayed one more day at Boyds, but went our own ways. I noticed our neighbors looked to be on their own journey. One younger guy with party-anthem hair was wearing ATC (Appalachian Trail Conservatory) socks, so I asked him about hiking. Mello and his dog, Yello, were there with three other southbound thru hikers. They had just completed their hike and wanted to escape the cold. They rented a car and drove as far south as they could. Our conversation was brief, but he said we could catch up a little later if I was still around camp.

Later in the evening, I had the opportunity to sit and chat with the hikers. Mello introduced me to a couple, Blueberries and Sage, who had joined him in the north, and Barstow, who had met them a little later. Their stories were very similar to my own; it was almost like they had had the same journey. The difference was they had finished their trek and I had another coast to paddle. I told them about the cheaper sites at Long Key and invited them up if they got tired of paying money to sleep on the rocks.

Chuck came by to hang out one more time before calling it quits. When Erin showed up, they explained they would drive me back to Long Key the next day, but they were going to continue north to the Everglades. The night wound down, I said goodbye to the hikers and thanked them for including me in their adventures.

Morning came and our bags were packed. Chuck drove me to Long Key, dropped me off and we said good-bye. I was finally able to secure site F, which turned my frown upside down. For a moment, I was feeling a little bummed out, but site F was what I needed. Lola was waiting at Shelle's camp, but when I walked down, there was no Shelle. Oh well, I had my own camp to set. In the meantime, I got a call from my sailor buddy, Mark. He had been keeping tabs on me and said if I could be in Key Largo for New Year's Eve, I was invited to a house party. That was a no brainer -- I told him I'd be there.

I sat down and refigured the float plan according to the new arrangement. Christmas was two days off. If I stayed at Long Key for a few more days, I could time it right to be in Key Largo for the festivities, regardless if I ever saw the phone or not. So there it was, I was to spend another holiday on the grounds of Long Key.

Not only was my body recuperating from the lively Key West atmosphere, my bank account had taken a hit as well. Thankfully, I had the foresight to resupply at The Dollar Tree. I was able to eat very cheaply, at roughly $3 a day. Although new campers were in and out of the sites, I kept to myself for the next couple days -- I was afraid I would allow myself to get side-tracked again.

Christmas Eve was my last shot to get the phone before the post office closed for the holiday weekend. I took one final walk and, of course, it was not there. You know you've been in a spot for too long when the postmaster knows you by name. She wasn't the only one -- I had come to enjoy daily conversations with a ranger, Alan.

The day started slow, but I kept myself busy with infusing coconuts with rum for the New Year's Eve party. I had three shucked, drilled and infused rather quickly. There was still time to fill, so I explored another nearby RV campground. I saw some familiar faces when I walked in. The hikers I had met at Boyd's were chilling in their hammocks.

I yelled to Mello and he popped up, happy to see me. We hung out, shared more stories, threw around a Frisbee, drank a few beers and shared some weed. I finally had to say good-bye to my new hiker friends, but not before Blue gave me a little baggie of weed as a Christmas present. I was so thankful. We exchanged contact information, then I left them to their hammocks.

Christmas morning in the keys was not all that it was cracked up to be. There were no presents, no family, no holiday ham or parades on TV. Emotional turmoil roiled around in my head. Loneliness crept in every once in a while, so I tried to keep busy preparing Lola to set sail. I would return to the water the next day. I wasn't sure what kind of shape I would be in, but, come hell or high water, I was going to be back at it.

Once I fixated on Lola, the day flew by in no time. Since it was Christmas, I decided to splurge and cook a feast. I had a can of raviolis, a pack of mashed taters, a honey bun for dessert and a hot toddy to wash it all down. Between the food belly and the bugs, I welcomed the night of rest ahead of me.

Meeting the Guys

That day I would leave a place that had become near and dear to my heart. An asylum that had brought several kind-hearted people into my world. We had had our challenges, but overall I was proud to call Long Key my home.

Alas! I was on the move. Bear in mind, once I left the island, I had all new water ahead of me. The unknowing became a driving force. Within an hour the rains hammered Lola and me. It has been far too long since I had paddled last, but thanks to the storm, I was thrown back into the ring. I was reminded shortly after how miserable it can be out there on the water. My triceps caught fire, my ass grew numb and I was already famished. Yep, it was exactly how I remembered it.

After I had lunch on Indian Key, the rains showed some mercy. Both Islamorada and Plantation keys had a slew of privatized beaches along the Atlantic route. It was my first day back on the water and I already dealt with the rain, lingering pain and now I was forced to take those damn sandbar breaks. I continued chipping away at the miles though -- I had a party to attend.

I was minding my own business on the flats of Plantation Key when I was suddenly upended. One moment I was in a zone just paddling away and the next, I was under water. Something caught me slipping -- I wasn't paying attention and wasn't on top of my game. More importantly, I was easily five football fields off shore and couldn't reach the bottom. I tied Lola's tow cord around my waist and swam her to shore. Five hundred yards don't sound like a lot, but when you are dragging a sunken ship, it's something else, I tell ya.

By the time I had Lola drained and ready to go, I didn't have anything left in the tank. I shoved off and began looking for somewhere to lay my head. There was nothing but private houses overlooking their slice of heaven. Around mile mark 87 I got lucky. I came across a house that was being renovated. Don't worry, I didn't break in, but I found a large dirt mound that hid me from the neighbors on both sides. I hid until it was dark enough to slide in and set camp.

Interior lights reflected off the sand, illuminating the surrounding areas. I swear I was being watched as I ducked and weaved among the shadows. Every crinkle or flap of the tent seemed to echo through the darkness. As the Geto Boys once said, "My mind is playin' tricks on me." That's what stealth camping does to you. Lights out, special ops-type shit. I was so paranoid, I only allotted two zips the entire evening. Those damn zippers always get you; therefore, I minimized it to one to open the fly and the other to close. From there on out, you could've heard a church mouse fart.

Stealth camping is at least a two-part exercise. The first was handled the night before, but the most important, I believe, is waking up in time. You would've thought I was a member of The Animals the following morning, taking "The House of the Rising Sun" to heart. Speedy Gonzalez didn't have anything on me as I broke camp. But when I had Lola all packed up, I chilled hard behind that mound, munching away at another stoveless breakfast.

Per usual, the wind was my biggest enemy that day. The Atlantic threw white caps at me the entire way. I admit, I may have become agitated and started to punch the side-swiping waves. It was my only joy until I reached the cut of Tavernier Creek. The tide pushed me through the cut and into the heavily trafficked Buttonwood Sound.

I was back in the Gulf, but for very good reason. Mark's friend, Jeff, owned a house off the sound, where the party was about to go down. As instructed, I called Mark and asked for directions. When he answered, he gave me some news I wasn't ready to hear -- the boat they were coming down in had an engine problem. Basically, he was saying they weren't going to make it that night. Thankfully, he had a solution. He asked Jeff, whom I had not met, if it was OK for me to stay on the property. Based on one fact, me being an Eagle Scout, he granted me permission. But where was the house?

Mark stayed on the line and directed me to the beach of the Five Eagles. The well-kept house was as blue as the waters of Islamorada and as white as the powdery sand below. Jeff may have trusted me to stay, but not as far as giving me the alarm code. But who needed the inside when I was supplied with a hot water shower, hot tub, dart board, electricity and hammocks abound on the back patios and in the yard? Hell, I felt like I had won the lottery.

After Lola was secured and the chores were done, I took a shower, started the hot tub, and scoped out the digs. The vacation home had two stories, plus a rooftop bar. I climbed the outside spiral staircase and sat at the bar. As I was sitting there, I couldn't believe this gift that had landed in my lap. But that was a fleeting thought. My stomach grumbled, I grabbed some things and went in search of some yummy town food.

Google on my cell phone led me to a Domino's two miles from the house. See ya fellas! I was off like a duck on a june bug. By the time I got to the storefront, I had two medium two-topping pizzas waiting. On my way back to the house, I saw some possible breakfast options and got my bearings for a resupply.

I made it back just in time to possibly see the phenomenon known as a "green flash." Neptune's wink, as it is also referred as, has been turning heads westerly for thousands of years. Some say it occurs when a soul has been returned from the underworld; others say it's caused by some hoity-toity scientific word, like refraction. Regardless of the cause, the allure brings moments of silence as the sun spends its last seconds above the horizon. The flash occurs when the sun reaches its last breath before shooting a flash of green into the sky. Would I be one of the fortunate to see Apollo meet Poseidon at the water's edge? That day I would have to call it bullshit. There was no such flash, not on that day, but I didn't allow it to stop me from eating my pizzas.

Those pizzas didn't have a chance. Gluttony, at that point, was no longer a deadly sin. My body required the caloric count of a Michael Phelps-like character. Now that my stomach was full, I let the hammock down on the rooftop bar and swayed myself to sleep. Mid-way through the night, I was forced to leave my hammock in a hurry. Jumping out and duck-walking down the spiral staircase, while clenching my ass, was quite a challenge. The property did not have an outdoor toilet, so I had to think on my toes. I grabbed a grocery bag and barely made it behind the hedges before dropping trow. I've never been so close to shitting my pants in my adult life. The lesson to learn is quite simply put -- never trust a fart.

After discarding the wag bag the next morning, I walked back to check out the town. There was breakfast at Waffle House, brunch at Burger King and lunch at the local cantina. By lunch, I was making plans to become a professional like on that "Man vs. Food" show. I was also able to resupply and checked out the local dive shops to kill some time.

When I returned to the house, I got a text from Mark that they would be there around sunset. I enjoyed the hot tub and waited for them to show, but they didn't -- not at the time they claimed. Mark reached out again, reporting more engine problems, but they said they were on their way. Jeff gave me some chores to do to prepare the outdoor areas for the party.

The crew pulled in around midnight. Mark introduced me to the master of the house, Jeff; Bill, an old college buddy, and Mark's brother, Rick. We had the meet-and-greet around a table drinking some rum cocktails. They were pretty beat from the sail down, but that didn't stop them from divvying out preparation tasks. When we got up the next morning, we all had jobs to carry out to ensure we had a great week.

Jeff's kids and friends would join us the next day. Jeff felt bad about the situation, but he asked me if I could sleep outside. I was like, "Oh, no!!! I have to sleep outside? What a catastrophe!" From there on, he knew I was going to fit in.

The guys were close and if they weren't, they were like-minded. We spent a lot of time bickering back and forth, busting balls and trying to get a rise out of each other. Jeff, Mr. South Florida, a stocky guy, fit and in his 60s. He was always busy or moving onto the next task. He had a way with words and getting people to help. He reminded me of a manager at a restaurant, approaching an employee with a compliment before asking to follow through on a shitty task. Bill, the old frat brother, was silver-haired, tan and had a skinny physique. He won you over with sarcasm and a smile. He was a constant pain in Jeff's ass, in a good buddy way, spending most of his day razzing the hell out of Jeff. Mark's brother, Rick, was a good guy to join around a table. His calm nature and intelligent conversations were a highlight of my day. He was a stocky guy, who loved paddle boarding and adventures. Mark, who I had met at Manasota Key, had tasks that seemed to never end. He was the workhorse. He spent most of the days working on the boat and in the kitchen cooking up master spreads. His meals were fit for royalty. Joe was the Gary Cooper, silent type. The first mate of the Midnight Strait was a knowledgeable sailor. He stuck to himself, but when he did add to the conversation, he was spitting out gems. Rounding out our group was Pilot Dan, an intelligent 29-year-old live aboard who had a brain like a sponge.

Jeff's kids and their friends came down from their Florida colleges for the holiday weekend. When they arrived, it felt like I was in the middle of an Abercrombie and Fitch photo shoot. They pretty much kept among themselves, unless Jeff put together an activity or outing. The vibe changed when they were around Jeff, who catered to them as a good father does. I spent most of the time cleaning up after them to help preserve Jeff's sanity. They were good kids, but I preferred to hang with the guys.

New Year's Eve was spent on a 60-foot catamaran, the Midnight Strait. We took it to Blackwater Sound and caught the fireworks show. This boat had everything you could imagine -- satellite TV to an on-board hot tub. We had the sound system pumping as we drank shot after shot. The fireworks illuminated the night sky over the rippling water below. Most of the evening was a blur, but I recall a grand scheme I built up in my head. At the stroke of midnight, I jumped off the top of the boat and into the water. Lt. Dan in "Forrest Gump" would've been proud of me as I cleansed 2014's wrong doings and brought in 2015 as a new man.

When the kids left to return to school, it was back to the guys and our antics. The quips, razzes and debates returned. The debates were the best. We would have some of the stupidest, but hilarious arguments. One, that remains unsettled, lasted two and a half days and was over the origin of the Rum Runner cocktail. In the keys, the Rum Runner is a hot topic, on which often people get up in arms about. I didn't care where it had started; I just wanted to drink them.

The last night was spent among the beach bars and dives of Key Largo. We gassed up the Bayliner and hit Gilbert's, a standard beach bar with over-priced cocktails, palm-thatched chickees, cornhole and tiki toss. We then hit a couple others and ended up at The Crib, a dive that was more my style. The stench of stale beer and cigarettes made me feel right at home. It was said to have been the bar where Humphrey Bogart's movie, "Key Largo," was filmed. It was our final stop, closing out a magical week with some kick-ass guys.

Another morning where I felt like a complete bag of shit arrived, but I had to keep moving. The guys were prepping the boat and closing up the house. I had Lola ready to go and paddled out to the Midnight Strait. The guys were going to give me a hitch to Adams Cut. Along the ride, we were followed by a pod of dolphins playing in the boats' wake. Their playful manner made me smile and provided motivation to move forward.

At the cut, we unloaded Lola, said good-bye and wished everyone safe journeys. I watched the boat sail into the distance, leaving me and Lola alone in the cut. There was a swift incoming tide that had a grip on us. I had to dig deep and keep it in mind we were moving forward. Eventually, we were back in the Atlantic and onto John Pennekamp State Park for a break.

This luxurious state park is world-renowned for its snorkeling and diving. The nearby reefs offer the best opportunity to see the underwater treasures of the keys. That day, the park was bustling with tourists. I didn't have it in me to hit the reefs, choosing to explore the mangrove channels and taking a nap on the beach.

The nap helped with my hangover recuperation process and allowed me to continue the paddle. I took a path through the backwaters along the mangroves and into the Atlantic. The serene paddle was what

I needed. Shortly after, I arrived at a gravel ramp leading to Garden Cove campsite.

It was a short six-and-a-half-mile day, but I felt every bit of it. I set camp on the rocky opening, dried my gear and heated up some Chef Boyardee. Around 3 p.m., I was joined by a couple of paddlers just starting the Overseas Paddling Trail. I told them my favorite camps and added they would have a great time. Next we had the gear talk; they had all the gizmos and gadgets. They were a little taken aback when I told them about my lack of gear. They couldn't believe I had made it that far without a spray skirt, hand-held GPS and bilge pump -- to name just a few.

As night fell, we continued to talk before splitting off to our tents. I laid down, thankful for making it through the rough patches of the day. Another thought hit me like a two-by-four across the jaw. Garden Cove was the final camp along this section of the trail. Although I still had the northern part of the keys to wrap up, I could finally say I had escaped the party-lifestyle of the keys.

Always a fight

Green Flash dinner

Morning coffee at The Five Eagles

Saying goodbye to the pirate brethren

Segments 16 & 17
Garden Cove - Marina in Pompano
95 miles

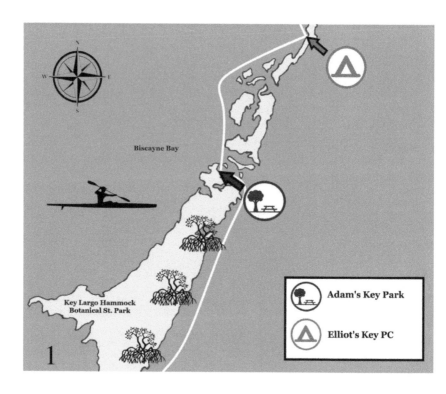

Biscayne Bay

Key Largo Hammock
Botanical St. Park

1

Adam's Key Park

Elliot's Key PC

As I make my way north the maps will be in reverse order starting with the next map at the bottom of the page. Follow the numbers to remain in order

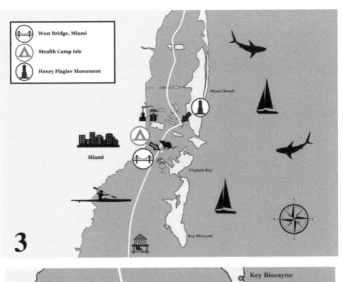

West Bridge, Miami
Stealth Camp Isle
Henry Flagler Monument

Miami Beach

Miami

Virginia Key

Key Biscayne

3

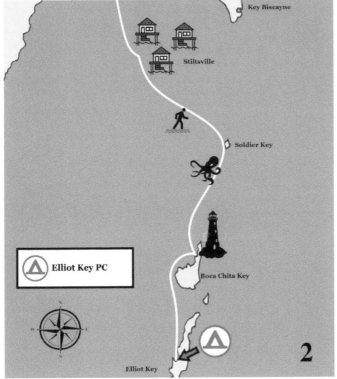

Key Biscayne

Stiltsville

Soldier Key

Elliot Key PC

Boca Chita Key

Elliot Key

2

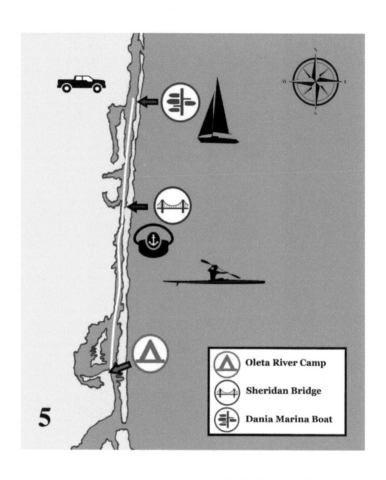

5

△	Oleta River Camp
bridge	Sheridan Bridge
marina	Dania Marina Boat

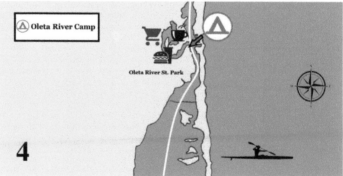

Oleta River Camp

Oleta River St. Park

4

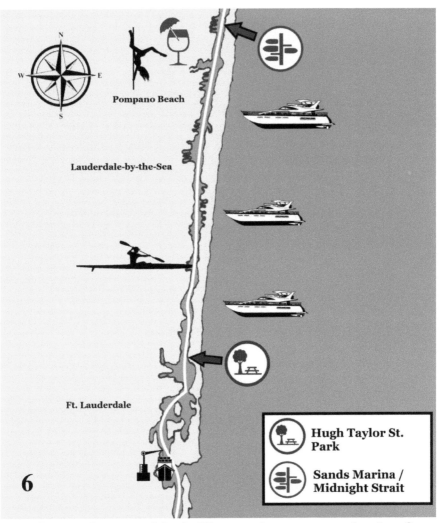

Pompano Beach

Lauderdale-by-the-Sea

Ft. Lauderdale

6

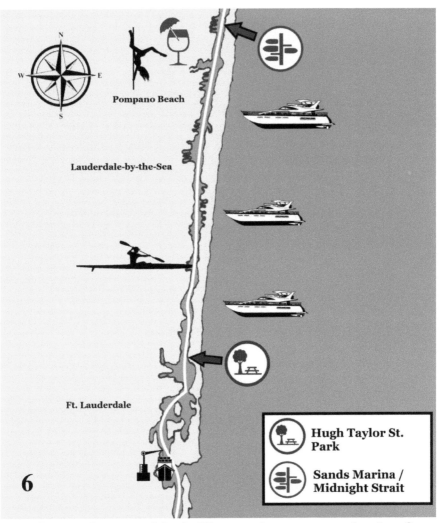	**Hugh Taylor St. Park**
	Sands Marina / Midnight Strait

I know, it sort of feels like you're on an episode of "Blue's Clues," but I hope I made it nice and easy for you.

All maps were hand drawn and created by the author Jeffrey "Treehouse" Buncie

Back to the Mainland

Watery expanses and tropical oases draw paddlers to the Biscayne Bay Preserve. Through this section, multiple routes allow exploration of the southern Florida landscape. Gliding by the historic homesteads, interesting lighthouses and botanical gardens, you'll find yourself in the less-populated areas of the Intracoastal Waterway. This narrow corridor presents a more intimate paddle along the smaller, esoteric state parks. Once north of Port Everglades, the second section of this chapter will take you into the yacht capital of the world.

From Hollywood to Fort Lauderdale the heavy boat traffic tests balance and patience. It took everything I had not to curse the folks who didn't follow the "no-wake" rule, but I pulled through and met Jeff at the Midnight Strait. That's right -- for some reason I was welcomed back. That's how I would wrap up another section, hanging with Mark and Jeff upon the catamaran that called the docks of the Sand's Marina its home.

It began with an early wake-up call at Garden Cove. I wasn't used to hearing people camp next to me. The tent zippers and rustling about woke me from my slumber. I had no intention to converse that early in the morning, so I laid in my tent until they had gone. Once they had left, my day started with a healthy breakfast of honey buns and coffee. A grueling 24 miles separated me from the campsites of Elliot Key and there was no time to waste.

The miles flew by like the sands of an hourglass. Tailwinds catapulted me in record time. The sun was shining and I was regaining strength. Most of the paddle was within Pennekamp's mangrove-lain beach parks. Adam's Key, just beyond the park, marked 20 miles on that day. The only real break I had landed me at the picnic area where the Cocolobo Club had once been. The club was a highly regarded retreat for U.S. presidents, such as Harding, Hoover Johnson and Nixon. A luxurious two-story building, which held 10 guest rooms, was built alongside a separate recreation lodge in 1922. The club, named after the local pigeon plum, had its downfall during the Wall Street Crash of 1929, but was resurrected by a Florida banker into a fishing club. By 1973, the National Park Service acquired the land, adding it to the Biscayne National Monument. Bad luck ensued the following year, when the main lodging caught fire leaving only the recreation lodge. Since Hurricane Andrew in 1992 all buildings have been wiped from the island leaving behind open landscape.

Leaving the historic landmark, I felt every muscle twinge as I pushed farther. I don't know what it is, but there is something to be said about the 20-mile mark that makes you feel every ache and pain.

An American flag flew high above the grounds of Elliot Key. The vacant camp was mine to commandeer. If I had a pirate flag, it would've flown under the colors. Instead, I had to settle for grabbing a site, hanging my gear and exploring the camp. Behind the restrooms I found a covered hiking trail that led across the island. Time wasn't on my side and I didn't spend too much time away from my campsite, but from what I did scout, the trail seemed worth further investigation.

Another big paddle was on the docket for the next day. By crossing over the shoals of Biscayne Bay, I would be bridging the gap from the keys to the mainland. Evening rains were in the forecast. With a prospective open-water paddle, I began to fear monger the crossing. I put together a contingency plan, then let the sound of the rain lull me to sleep.

All the fear mongering was unnecessary as the morning brought calmer seas. To prepare for back-to-back, high-mileage days I carbed up with a healthy three-serving breakfast. I ate my usual Pop-Tarts, then combined my snack and a mac-and-cheese lunch to ensure my body was not going to give up on me. After eating, I broke camp, filled my platypus bags, then shipped off to Boca Chita Key.

Five easy miles brought me to a cement ramp on the most northern key I would visit. A historic lighthouse sat on the northern end. The Boca Chita lighthouse is now an ornamental figure, but in its heyday was once operational. The "little lighthouse that isn't" was illegally built in the 1930s by the owner of the island, Mark Honeywell. A few hours after Honeywell lit it, the Coast Guard deemed it a navigational hazard. Goes to show -- you better inform and register your beacons. I never heard of Gatsby (of F. Scott Fitzgerald's book "The Great Gatsby") having an issue with his infamous green lantern. What the hell?

While I explored the island, I met a volunteer watching over the campground. He joined the fan club (I had started calling the people I met who seemed excited about me doing the journey my fan club or the BNC Odysseia fan club), supplied some snacks and, most importantly, told me about an island across the bay where I could camp.

We cross-referenced his charts to my maps in order to locate the island. Supplying me with one last waypoint he told me to look for The Rusty Pelican. I bid him farewell and talked myself up to make the crossing.

Biscayne Bay was a difficult paddle. Not because of the ripping tides, but for the time I chose to cross. At low tide, the shoals became so skinny I had to get out and walk Lola across from time to time. Boats full of people were running the channels and passing by as I dragged Lola through the middle of the Biscayne. If I had been on one of those boats, my mind would have been blown. Eventually I had to walk her to the channel and, in doing so, cut my feet to shreds on the submerged limestone.

One mile south of Key Biscayne is a historic treasure dating back to the Prohibition days. A man, Crawfish Eddie, took it upon himself to build a shack atop stilts among the flats. He allegedly did so to facilitate gambling, which was legal a mile offshore. He was more known for his crawfish chowder, bait shop and a spot to buy beer. Not long after, his buddies built their own shacks and drew the attention of the newspapers, which deemed the community "the shacks." In the 1940s, the well-connected Miamians began building social clubs, such as The Calvert and the more widely known Quarterback Club.

As the economic tides turned, the shacks began evolving into lodges in the 1960s, bringing the frontier era to an end. Hurricane Betsy of '65 was the nail in the coffin. It demolished most of the lodges and the government had had enough. It made sure not to issue any new permits to build or rebuild the campsites. By 1976, lease renewals issued were valid until '99, but even if they were in perfect condition in 1999, the structures would be removed at the owner's expense. When 1999 arrived, Miamians spoke up for the community, known as Stiltsville. The people won and a trust was created, handing the responsibility for the structures over to the National Park Service and the original lease holders. Today seven out of the 27 original structures still stand.

On my paddle, I had the pleasure of canvassing these structures from the water. I was told by many it was possible to stay at one of the renewed structures. As I investigated, I became intimidated by the number of "No Trespassing" signs, thus deterring any notion to stay. I later learned that it is possible to stay in one, but a very pricey reservation would have to be placed. Also, if you chance not getting caught, the fines can reach upward to $5,000. Needless to say, I believe I made the correct decision to skip stealth camping on one and hunt for the island.

Beyond Stiltsville was the backdrop of the Miami skyline. The West Bridge became a mirage for the remainder of the paddle. I swear, the harder I paddled, the bay sucked me back in, like I was flailing around in quicksand. As always, the bay allowed me to paddle under the causeway and into the calmer waters of the Intracoastal Waterway. Immediately on the right of the bridge I saw The Rusty Pelican, alive with the Miami nightlife. I was able to pinpoint the small retreat I would call my home, perpendicular from the restaurant.

I approached the island, but saw a large boat anchored off the beach. The boat was occupied by three gorgeous Brazilian women and their boy toy. They waved to me as I passed by looking for a different point of entry. At the point, I found a pocket beach, where I landed and sought out a more hidden tent spot. Trying not to broadcast my intentions, I dug in deep behind the palm trees.

Once my camp was set, I revisited the beach where the boaters were partying. A voluptuous Brazilian came over and introduced herself. I wasn't expecting this at all. They barely spoke English, but they were very friendly. These women were way out of my league financially. We had a simple conversation, then the ladies brought me a wheel of brie, olives, chips and sodas. I thanked them before they returned to their vessel and left me to my island.

I retreated to the camp to enjoy my snacks and watch the sun set over the city skyline. The views of the city were made for postcards. I sat watching the city lights brighten the starless sky. After taking a few snapshots, I went back to the tent and prepared for the new day. While looking ahead and journaling, I was reminded I did not inhabit the island alone. The island mice scurried in hoards, but that night I showed zero interest. My body was too tired to care. Sleep was my number one priority.

Foghorns and airplanes flying overhead pulled me out of a lethargic coma as the Port of Miami imposed its will upon me first thing in the morning. As I left the furry creatures behind, I went toe-to-toe with an incoming ocean liner. Sitting beside this ship on the water really made me understand how an ant feels in its daily life. After the liner passed, I stood ready for the wakes to challenge Lola and me. It wasn't as bad as I thought, but the sheer size of these ships scared the piss out of me.

Navigating around the port's many inlets and islands kept my wits about. The barges cut around the corners, kicking up monstrous wakes against the seawalls. The early-morning turmoil worked my brain to a frenzy. Mentally drained, I stopped by the Henry Flagler Monument to pay respects to the oil and railroad tycoon. The small man-made island nestles between the rich and famous houses of Palm, Star and Venetian Islands.

I was joined on the beach by Eric from Pompano, who was on the water giving his sleek handmade kayak a trial run. We swapped stories about our journeys and gear.

Eric is a multi-generational boat builder and his skills prove it. The stream-lined teak kayak held true, but we both agreed it would not hold for an extensive journey, like Lola had. Before parting, he gave me money for lunch and some cold water. Accepting money is against one of my rules, but he would not have it any other way. He was adamant and firmly stated that if I would not do him the honor, he would leave feeling disrespected. I had no intention of doing such a thing, so I accepted the gift, shook his hand and left him on the beach.

The rest of the day I was inside my head, counting the bridges of the ICW. Outlandish yachts cruised by one by one. Their curious crews waved and shouted pleasantries from aboard. Their friendliness kept my spirits high, but I was green with envy. I questioned what I was doing and why was I not on one of these yachts? It would be way easier for me to cruise the coast on a vessel under power. The internal battle only ceased when I put in my headphones and got lost in the music.

Oleta State Park, in 2014, accommodated paddlers with a primitive site built as an Eagle Scout project. It was a little difficult to locate, but I was able to circulate the landing to find the clearing. From the bank, you can follow a path to an overhang with a picnic table and barbecue-pitted fire ring. I continued to follow the path to the highway, where I found restaurants, a grocery store and a movie theater. I used Eric's gift to buy a stromboli and returned to the camp.

The day toyed with my sanity and the evening was no different. I was forced to hide once again within the safety of the four polyester walls. I finally cracked -- the no see-ums were the final straw on the camel's back. Eric's stromboli was the only thing that kept me from entirely losing it. Drained, hoping for better days, I spent the remainder of the evening forcing myself to sleep.

**Docking
on
Elliot Key**

A piece of Stiltsville

Boca Chita Light

**Welcome
to
Miami**

Pirate Brethren

Attempting to kick the day off on a higher note, I walked to town for a resupply and a coffee. While enjoying the coffee, I charged my electronics and was approached by an elderly woman in her late 70s. She was concerned and worried about me.. After explaining I wasn't homeless and describing the journey I was on, I saw her worry change to enthusiasm. She grabbed a seat and leaned on my every word. I saw the change in her eyes, which, in turn, reminded me why I was out there. My electronics charged, we split ways and I returned to Lola with a renewed attitude.

Everything began to click when I left the banks of Oleta. Mark was meeting me 10 miles north at a marina in Dania. The paddle was smooth and swift. I came across Sheridan Bridge, where I saw Mark's silhouette. He was standing overhead with directions of where to go. He snagged a few photos and took off on his bike to the marina.

I was confused when I found Mark standing next to a boat that was not the Strait. Turned out I still had 14 miles to get to the marina, where she makes berth. Instead, I was unloading at the boat owned by Mark's friend, Dave. We met briefly, but the owner and his lady friend, Wendy, were having a little riff. Mark and I looked at each other and agreed we did not need to be there for all the drama. Dave allowed Lola to stay next to the boat and Mark and I got in his truck and headed to Pompano to see Jeff.

There was no ticker-tape parade, but Jeff and Joe welcomed me with a hot meal. After the New Year, they had gone on a 5-2 diet -- basically only drinking on the weekends -- and that night was a weekday. I was a little bummed they didn't want to party, but we still had a good time catching up with each other on the boat.

The Sands Marina offers muffins and coffee for the patrons in the morning. I took full advantage as Mark introduced me to the lady running the desk. After a healthy serving, Mark and I returned to Dave's boat. This time, the couple were on good graces and we had a good conversation. I thanked Dave and Wendy for keeping a close eye on Lola, said, "See ya later," to Mark and headed down the waterway.

To get to Pompano, I had to make my way through Fort Lauderdale, which is known as the yacht capital of the world. I became intimidated early in the day by the multi-million dollar boats entering and exiting the waterway. The watery path ran pretty tight through there with seawalls kicking back the deeper-hulled wakes. It was a

195

whirlpool of disaster awaiting the strongest of paddlers. I couldn't muscle my way through, I had to outsmart the unstable waters.

My wisdom and talent came into play as I rounded the corner of Hugh Taylor Park. An inconsiderate boater whipped through the no-wake zone, causing the water to react like a thresher shark tearing through its prey. A crowd formed as it was my time to shine. Water ricocheted off the seawall and a steadfast tidal wave was approaching. I leaned hard to the port, kicking in the right pedal as I felt the recoil go limp. I broke the rudder. Backstroking to head on the collapsing swell, I pushed forward, all in, straight toward the opposite cemented seawall. The boaters watched from behind, laughing, Lola shattered the crest and broke the plane. She did her job, it was now on me. I had to reach far behind and put on the brakes. I leant back against the seat forcing an abrupt halt. It was a success. Bobbing inches from the seawall, I won applause from an older couple watching from a bench.

After that, I was furious, but confident. I muttered under my breath as I saw new boats approach -- daring them as they came closer "Try me, go ahead and try me." For the remainder of the day I was not provoked any further. I paddled into the docks of Sands Marina with an ear-to-ear grin to meet Jeff at the Midnight Strait.

My paddle was done for the day. It was a weekend and this time we shared adult beverages upon arrival. The mood was surf, sun and soak. Joey had some family members join topside and Bill Bell showed his tanned face. We had a great day kicking back a few and bull-shitting. Mark had to house sit, Joey hit the bed and Bill did whatever he had to go do. The evening was in the hands of the two Jeffs.

We first visited the marina bar for good eats and rum runners. Jeff introduced me to the owner, who bought a few rounds before I met another yachter, who invited us aboard The Margaret. The boat, named after his mother, was easily the most beautiful boat I'd ever stepped foot on. He had just had it refitted and decked out to the nines for the journey back to New Jersey. Jeff grew restless, so we rolled over to Bilney's, which was filled with beautiful ladies and fraternity brothers. It wasn't my cup of tea and I think Jeff felt the same way. We returned to the docks to take one last venture to a gentlemen's club down the road.

Jeff took the liberty of driving us down in his yellow H1 Hummer. Every time I meet this guy, he never ceases to amaze me with his outlandish toys. We arrived and Jeff was all about keeping me occupied. The girls were pros, to say the least. You could tell they took pride in their work. I don't know if Jeff was sliding them cash on the side, but I often caught him whispering in their ears before they came and shook their goodies in my face. The time flew by and, all too soon, the club was closing for the night. We jumped in the Hummer for a breakfast run before returning to the marina.

I spent the next couple days hanging around the marina taking it easy. Jeff had put me through the wringer our first night aboard, so we tended to the hangovers. Joey made sure we were fed and Mark swung through every once in a while to see how we were getting along. Sunday was a day for football and Joey's famous chili. We shared one more cocktail before calling it a weekend.

I spent my last night on the Strait topside, devoting most of my time thinking of how blessed I was to have been invited into this realm. Two more sections were complete and I reminded myself it had all started with saying "yes" to a rum bought by a stranger. I no longer called them strangers -- they were brothers. Nope, that doesn't do it justice. We shared too many tales and rum cocktails; we were now a class known as pirate brethren. You guys know how I feel, and I thank you for taking me in as part of the crew.

One tired paddler on the ICW

Segments 18, 19, 20 & 21
Pompano - Middle Cove
149 miles

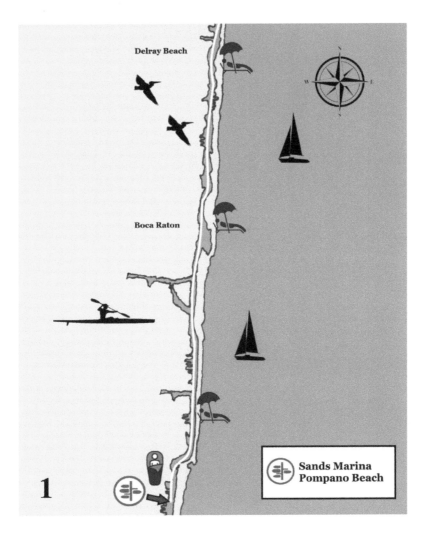

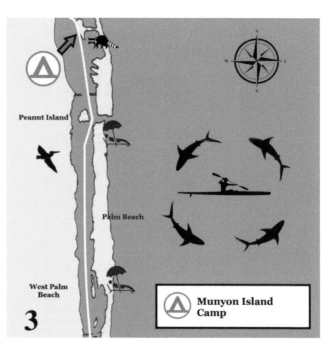

3

Peanut Island

Palm Beach

West Palm
Beach

Munyon Island
Camp

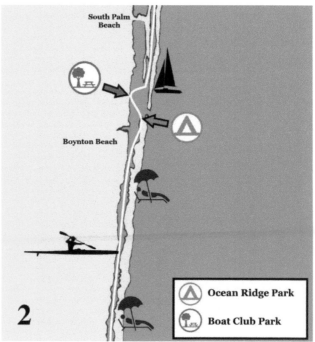

South Palm
Beach

Boynton Beach

2

Ocean Ridge Park

Boat Club Park

199

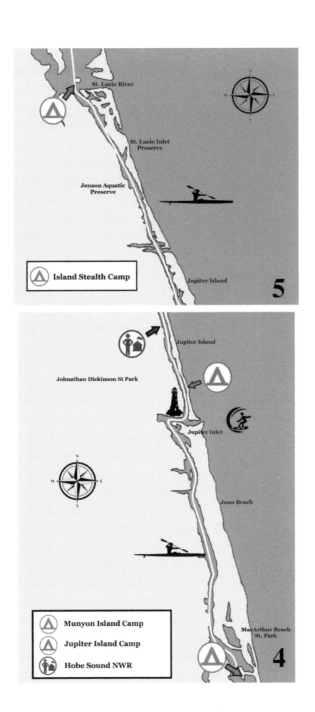

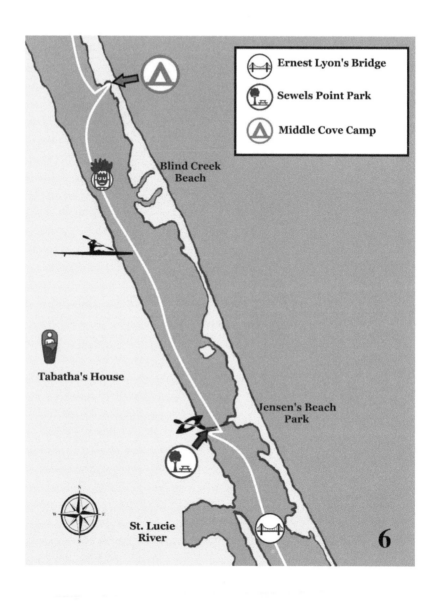

All maps were hand drawn and created by the author Jeffrey "Treehouse" Buncie

A Change in the Winds, Says I

January was now upon us. Cooler temperatures and strengthening trade winds would add to the daily challenges. Over the next three sections, the changing winds forced me out of the Atlantic and into the Intracoastal Waterway. I turned my focus toward scouring the dredged spoils and empty state parks for stealth spots. Hoping to cut costs and improve efficiency, I realized my playtime was coming to an end. From Pompano's yacht-lined marinas to the more environmentally sound Indian River, I faced the changes with a fire lit from within.

Leaving behind the crew of the Midnight Strait, I plowed through the remaining miles of segment 18. The morning flew by with smooth cuts through Delray and Palm beaches. I was blessed with music the entire way and used bridges as waypoints. I found it useful to keep track by counting the bridges on the ICW and also using them for motivation. Often I would be tired, but I would talk myself into pushing until "the next bridge." This became my replacement for the crab trap game, almost guaranteeing my mind to wander.

The game worked to its entirety placing me 20 miles north without a blink of an eye. I pulled over at Ocean Ridge Park to keep tabs on some approaching thunderheads. The park was completely empty. I found a boardwalk leading to covered picnic tables, in case the weather turned. Keeping an eye on the satellite images, I sat and ate some dinner. I didn't see a soul the whole time I was docked. The storm missed, but the sun was retreating. I couldn't see any reason why I should leave a shelter, so I gathered my gear and set camp under the awning.

Two old biddies speed walking during the early hours of the morning woke me up. I heard them mention Lola's physique and capabilities. When I greeted the morning air, I was swarmed by the flying teeth lingering in the humid surroundings. Worried that the ladies might reach out to the ranger, I broke camp and paddled to Boat Club Park, where I had a chance to eat in peace.

The waterfront parks supply long-distance paddlers with all the amenities needed. Most of them have working outlets, overhangs to escape questionable weather, restrooms and usually a gas station within walking distance. That day, I utilized the parks for the aforementioned reasons and to break out of the easterly winds.

Counting bridges became few and far between, so I leaned hard on another favorite pastime. With hopes of being a future live-aboard sailor, I sought out the mooring sailboats. Always curious to see the names, I began to come up with my own back stories of how the ladies received their berth rights. The names that stuck out were the ones that made me laugh. Naming a boat is a serious matter, but not at all serious. I remember the "Had it all, Lost it all." My mind took me to the wild investment opportunities that the online investment firms promise buy quick, sell hard or something along those lines. At one time, I was sure he owned a 300-foot yacht and a multi-million dollar mansion, but the crash came and left him with all that he really needs, a 38-foot sailboat.

Another I recall was my absolute favorite -- "Achieving Average." The 36-footer, in my estimation, was just average enough to survive. It was lightly aged, with a kayak tied following behind for a dinghy. Down to the hammock sitting topside and the reggaeton echoing from the cabin, this guy was doing just enough.

Some of my closest friends have called me a tumbleweed blowing through the wind. I do believe this guy was living up to that standard. But you know what? While coming up with these stories the mind wandered just enough and it did the job -- I was soon circling the unusually clear waters of Peanut Island. I was able to locate the PC I planned on staying the night, but I felt like I could push another three miles to Munyon.

I approached the vacant docks of Munyon Island at MacArthur State Park. The hidden docks among the tropical hammock provided another opportunity to stealth. Two nights in a row I was able to find the shelter of a pavilion on a quiet oasis. The best part of the evening was the sunset view over the barrier island. But once the sun went down, I had visitors rummaging nearby. I made sure to batten down the hatches and secure my inventory.

Over the past few days, my triceps had been ripped and torn from my body. Not willing to give in, I pushed onward to Jupiter. Not the planet, but Jupiter, Fla., home to once-renowned actor Burt Reynolds. The wind played its dirty little tricks on me until I found the shelter of the inlet. I docked to explore another lighthouse along the Atlantic.

Located on the north end of the inlet stands the Jupiter Inlet Lighthouse, one of six lighthouses a young George Meade planned and developed. That's right, the one in the same General Meade who defeated Robert E. Lee in the Battle of Gettysburg. Construction was overseen by a civilian, Edward Yorke, through the completion in 1860. The light remained dark throughout the Civil War until five years after the Confederates surrendered. The longest tenured keeper, James Armour, maintained the light for 40 consecutive years until finally retiring in 1906.

Even with Armour's 40 years, the light had 70 different keepers from 1860-1939, at which point military personnel kept watch until 1987. To this day, the light remains as an active navigational beacon for the inlet. After refusing to pay the admission fee required to climb the 105-foot lighthouse, I searched the grounds and watched the wicked breaks from the pier. A notable surfing break was a little rough for the soul searchers today, but the fishing was good. During a short walk along the pier, I could feel the anglers' excitement.

Satellite images brought me two miles north to a beach on Jupiter Island. My shoulders gave in to the ongoing battle. Fearful of tearing another muscle, I took heed and set camp behind the palmettos. Social media had put me in touch with a former neighborhood friend, Tabitha, a childhood crush, who saw a picture on the internet and reached out to invite me to dinner. She planned to drive over, use GPS positioning to locate me and take me into town for a hot meal. Damn straight -- I accepted that invitation!

There was one catch, however -- I would have to paddle across the waterway to the mainland and stash Lola in the grass. I waited until nightfall, broke a rule and crossed the channel in the dark. I dunno how she did it, but Tabitha found me right away. She did me one better and dropped off a resupply from the Dollar Tree. I stowed the food, stashed Lola and jumped into the car to head to town.

We caught up with each other while eating Mexican food and kicking back some Yuenglings. Before the meal was over, she invited me to stay in St. Lucie if I needed any further assistance. St. Lucie was about 20 miles north, but she already had done me the favor of resupply. At that point, I politely declined, but told her I would keep it in mind. She took me back to the bank where Lola awaited. We said good-bye and I returned to the darkened water of the intercoastal.

A full dinner, eight beers and a muscle relaxer later, I was crossing a waterway in the later hours of the night. I took the paddle with a grain of salt. Nice and easy, easy does it, all the cliché sayings. Thankfully, traffic was minimal and I was able to reach my tent safely.

Shorter Days and Longer Miles

The following day, the wind was even more ferocious. I put everything I had into moving forward into the blistering gusts. My skin was no longer sunburned, but now wind-burned. The only relief came from the Hobe Sound NWR and its wildlife exhibits.

A hidden gem along the mainland on the northern end of Dickinson State Park, the wildlife refuge had plenty to explore. After docking at a small pocket beach, a trail leads to the nature center with its interactive exhibits and information center. When I entered through the glass doors, I took a gander at the model of a Florida coastal habitat and checked off all the wildlife I had seen along the way. I turned around and noticed an exhibit, "Winged Warriors," that included a red-tailed hawk and a barred owl. I thought these were very detailed and lifelike. My brain wasn't quite firing on all cylinders and then I questioned how a small wildlife refuge had the money to buy animatronic birds like Disney World. Once I realized they were real birds, I hysterically laughed loud enough to bring a staff member over to see what was going on. After that incident, the staff allowed me to charge my electronics and hang around a bit out of the chilling wind.

I paddled until I couldn't lift my arms any longer. I was able to locate a camp on a small unnamed island before the Ernest Lyons Bridge. A bundle of blooming sea grape trees had just enough coverage to shield me from the aggressive winds. Forced to eat a cold meal, I digressed to fear mongering once again. The winds were to continue into the next few days. My body was spent, my mind was flustered, but I had an out. I phoned a friend for a lifeline that had been extended the day prior. Tabby would rescue me four miles north the next day.

The Windfinder app did not lie. Sustained winds kept me landlocked until the mid-afternoon. It took every ounce of mental stability I had to muster up the strength to get back on the water. As always, I worked up the motivation, but was not happy about being out there. Four difficult miles across the mouth of the St. Lucie River and into the Jenson Aquatic Preserve kicked the crap out of me. I kept my head down and fought the uphill battle until I reached a small beach, Seawall Park, on the mainland.

A cluster of trees along the pocket beach gave Lola a secure hiding spot. I picked through and grabbed a bag full of my valuables, then walked to the park. Upon first sight, the park wasn't quite the typical seaside retreat. I walked into a playground filled with local children and their mothers watching close by. I am not afraid to say I'm used to feeling out of place, but for the first time I really felt uncomfortable. Soon, a cop creeped by nice and slow. Can you guess how many other times after that I saw a cruiser? Their prevailing presence was felt. I started to believe I was going to be on an episode of "Cops" or "Live PD." To reduce the possibility of that happening, I retired to the beach until Tabby pulled into the parking lot.

On the way to her apartment, a plan was concocted, allowing for a zero. I spent the time doing tasks needed to increase mental and physical morale. I purchased a new iPod and replaced my charging cords due to the corrosion from salt water. There is nothing worse than trying to charge your lifelines, but are unable to due to rusted or crumbling ports. I was also lucky to procure a used wetsuit jacket to help with the incoming colder weather. The one bone I had to pick was with my inability to sleep indoors. Both nights led me into early morning, begging for a few hours of rest. I suppose my body was too used to hearing the sounds of moving water for I was not granted the luxury of getting any sleep.

Tabby's family drove me back to Lola's resting place. She was still there, but not so unscathed. Someone had found her, broken my fishing rod and drank both bottles of water. Weird choices of thievery, but I was glad I had gotten back when I did, who knew if they would return with a vehicle capable of transport. A thorough inventory inspection ensued and I extended my gratitude before paddling into the calmer waters.

It was a day of ebbs and flows. Morning winds were kind, but progressed into afternoon gusts. Music kept my spirits high, but something went array. A moment came where I felt a part of me become dismantled. Call it a sixth sense, but when I turned my head I saw Wilson floating a couple hundred feet back. In a fury, I tried turning Lola into the wind, water spewed into my lap, this was not good. Attempting again, more water lapped over, immobilizing another turn. Sitting uncomfortably, I gave it another go, only to somehow keep upright. My entire right arm went into the water. I had to make a decision, just as Chuck did when he lost his buddy, I gave out a merciless cry, "WILSON!"that the fishermen could have heard from the docks and said goodbye. It was heart-breaking, but WIlson's and my time together came to an end as he drifted away with the tides.

At the lowest point of my day, the winds chilled my core, causing me to add an extra two miles crossing the preserve. I took advantage of the land blockade until I arrived at another stealth camp,

Middle Cove. A couple of docks led to an opening that allowed me to claim a patch of land for the night.

Days were being cut shorter, forcing me off the water earlier. With the warmer days behind me I would have to allow time for additional nightly routines. Nightly fires were no longer recreational, but a necessity essential to survival. Lola's hulls flooded regularly, submerging my gear. The fires warmed my chilled core and dried gear to at least a comfortable dampness. I resorted to storing a pair of dry clothes inside a small cooler, which was my only saving grace.

With seven days and 95 miles ago, I left Jeff, Mark and guys at the Midnight Strait. Successfully finding multiple stealth spots, pushing harder miles and not getting caught in any tomfoolery, I was now three segments closer to the end of my journey. I'd lost a companion and tended to the wintery woes. Every day felt like I was stepping into the ring with a heavy-weight boxer, but I still pulled myself off the ground and made a go at the goal. Onward and upward as they say, the Space Coast awaited.

Fire in the sky

Daily battles on the ICW

Artistic parks of the ICW

Ponce Inlet Lighthouse

Segment 22
Middle Cove - Daytona Beach
82 miles

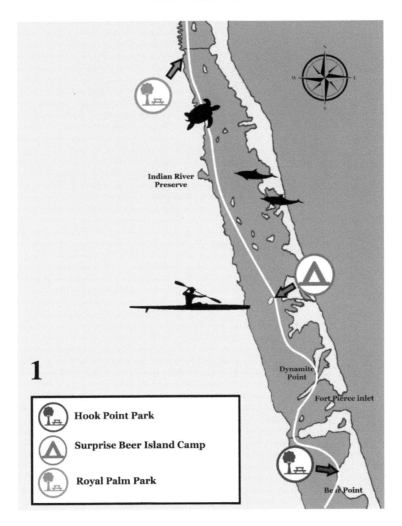

Indian River Preserve

Dynamite Point

Fort Pierce inlet

Bear Point

1

Hook Point Park

Surprise Beer Island Camp

Royal Palm Park

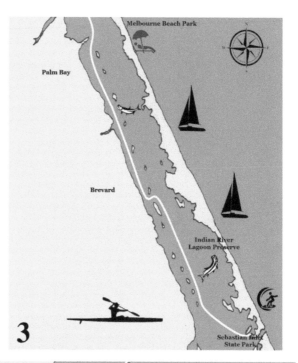

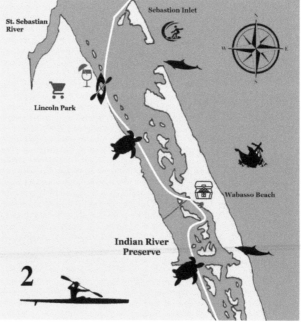

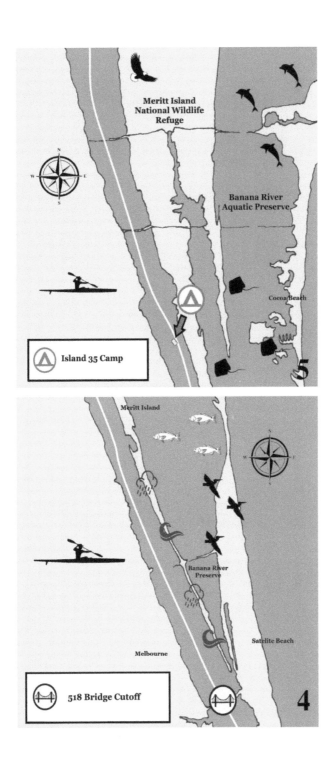

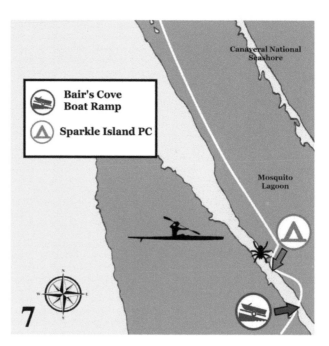

Bair's Cove Boat Ramp

Sparkle Island PC

Canaveral National Seashore

Mosquito Lagoon

7

Manatee Hammock Campground

NASA Parkway Bridge

Kennedy Point Park

Merrit Island National Wildlife Refuge

South Titusville

Cape Canaveral

6

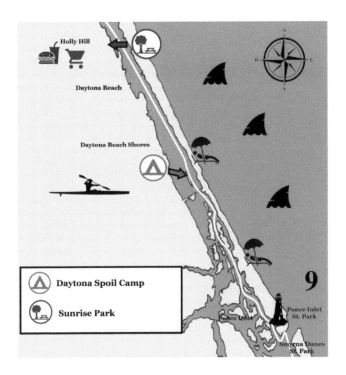

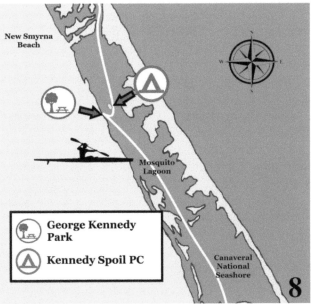

All maps were hand drawn and created by the author Jeffrey "Treehouse" Buncie

By Land, Sea or Space, There's Sparkles All Around

Overlapping boundaries of tropical and sub-tropical climates help create one of North America's most diverse estuary systems. Found along the Space Coast of Florida, the Indian River, Mosquito Lagoon and Banana River are of importance ecologically and economically. Some estimate the revenue stream creates upward to $800 million a year toward the local economy. The inviting nurseries provide oysters, clams, shrimp and many species of fish found in nationwide grocery stores. Abundant wildlife among the labyrinth of tidal creeks and spoil islands make for a very unique paddle.

Something about Central Florida, no matter which side of the coast you are on, allows for these rare ecosystems. The abundance of spoil island campsites fit right into line with my ideas. The next two sections provided ample options, allowing me to choose between the thriving island campsites. Paddling without set goals granted me more freedom to do what I pleased. Less structure, as we both know, could go either way here, but I believe I had the willingness to continue in more of a timely manner. I'll leave it up to you to judge how I did this time around.

Between the splintering planks, protruding nails and soggy burrito-like sleeping bag, there was very little sleep to be had sleeping on the boardwalk at Middle Cove. A mosquito-infested tent fly inherited a daunting buzz. The hum intensified like an ignored alarm clock daring me to greet the day. The troops were in position, holding the higher ground and biding their time. It was me against the blood-thirsty hordes. Bagging my gear, I funneled the full bags out through a small slit of the door. Clothed and covered, I slid out undetected. There were too many. I approached the situation with a new strategy. Rather than giving away my position and releasing the hounds, I dropped the entire tent and decided to sacrifice cleanliness. Hundreds of red splotches would forever mark what I can do to the needle-nosed pests. I left the bodies so that all around the bug.net my name would echo in eternity.

A brisk wind filled the air. It was time for me to give the wet suit a go. I paddled just over a mile north to Hook Point. That was enough to tell the neoprene jacket was too thick. Not only constrictive, but in that mile I was already beading sweat. That is why it's called a trial run, I suppose, but at least there I was able to enjoy a peaceful breakfast.

Paddling by the rip-rapped rocks along Fort Pierce Inlet I saw no need to stop by the small picnic areas for a rest so soon. The Fort Pierce State Park had me excited to make a cut to Pepper Park for possible bobcat sightings. During my brief time at the park I didn't see any bobcats or any dynamite explosions from the point. "Dynamite?," you ask. Well, back in these waters during World War II the Navy trained the original "SEALS," known as Frogmen. It was here that over 100,000 personnel trained for the D-Day Invasion. The Navy Underwater Demolition Teams (UDTs) still refer to this as Dynamite Point that used these waters to explode ammunition. While appreciating the history and lack of wildlife I found ample campsites but the day was still young so I decided to move North with the winds.

The remainder of the day was spent passing spoil island after spoil island. When I stopped for a late lunch, I came to an island with a family in a boat docked in the shallows. Stating they had seen me earlier in the day, they inquired about my trip. Their two kids were into the encounter and stories. The father supplied me with a few beers over my swashbuckling tales and before they left, they gave me some snacks to enjoy. After the beers and a restless evening, I grew tired and decided the island was perfect to set camp.

I may have cut the day short, but I had to tend to a blood-ridden tent and a bunch of water-logged gear. The island was filled with dead palm fronds, which made for a perfect gear-drying fire. That night I would retire to a dry bag with dry socks and warm toes. A good night of sleep was on the horizon.

On back-to-back days I was blessed with beautiful paddling weather. Non-existent winds helped finish the Indian River section with smooth sailing. Quirky riverside parks, like Royal Palm, brought me to feeling like a kid again while running through their squirt fountains and enjoying the tile art mosaics. As promised, I was guaranteed sea turtle and playful dolphin sightings. Although the sea turtles remained elusive, dolphins were often skimming through the water mimicking a game of tag.

While embracing the nostalgic energy fired within, I took a moment on Wabasso Beach to harness my inner Goonie. They may never say die, but I was a long way from finding One-Eyed Willy's treasure. Found along the Treasure Coast, Wabasso Beach is one of the three top destinations for treasure hunters along this coast. No fancy skull key or map needed, although a metal detector could increase your

214

chances. After storms or cold fronts the coast here has been known to wash up peso de ochos (piece of eight coin) from the Spanish fleets of 1715. My luck did not change that day along the beach by unveiling any new found fortune, but I sat digging through the sand dreaming of discovering a piece of Spanish history.

Searching for the lost treasure of the 1715 fleet only fueled my childish spirit. When I came to Sebastian Inlet State Park Launch, I wished I still had the longboard I had found in the Glades. The inlet has been world-renowned for the two surfing breaks -- the "First Peak" and the "Monster Hole." Unfortunately, First Peak has been diminished due to the reconstruction of the jetties in the early 2000s, but I had to see it for myself. The glory was no longer there for the once ultra-consistent, right-handed wedge Kelly Slater and Lisa Andersen had fine tuned their professional careers surfing. Monster Hole, on the other hand, is still ripping about a ⅓ of a mile off shore, daring intermediate and expert surfers to surf the break among the sharkie waters of Sebastian.

My morale was at an all-time high with a supply of caffeine, canned pasta and bourbon, gained by docking at a bar, Squid Lips, and a quick resupply along the road leading to a small town, Lincoln Park.The next stop, north of the Banana River Preserve along Cocoa, Fla., would land me in the great beyond of the Space Coast Paddling Trail.

North of the 518 bridge, the Banana River merges with the ICW. At the confluence, I could either add seven miles by paddling up the river system or make a bee line on the narrower cut. I let the morning weather dictate the decision. When I arrived at the bridge, I was feeling good and the weather was on my side. I made the decision to stay in the ICW, therefore placing myself back on a schedule. The closest island camp was a long 18 miles from that point. I rolled the dice and went for the jugular.

Shortly after making the decision, Mother Nature turned on me, spitting a misting rain and blasting intense winds. I was soaked to the bones. The penetrating winds coerced my arms to spin like propellers. Invested with nowhere else to go, I begrudgingly forged ahead to a small spoil known as Island 35.

Sparring with Mother Nature's icy breath significantly strained my muscles. When I beached, I promptly built a fire to warm my blood. As I thawed out, my camp slowly came to fruition. A hot meal and a few shots of bourbon brought me back to life; a full belly and warm sleeping bag brought me to the tent. After journaling, I took a look at the maps, only to realize I was on my way to completing my journey. The light at the end of the tunnel was becoming a little more feasible. I was able to admit I could actually do this, it was possible. Less than 200 miles stood between me and the final mile.

The new day brought an imposing will from Aeolus, the Greek god and King of the Winds, as his mind was set on shifting the winds. Tail winds through the bay ambushed me from behind like a mountain lion stalking their prey. I felt their presence, but had no idea when they would pounce. Piercingly cold water was furling down my back and filling the cockpit. I was bullied into pulling over and bailing Lola out multiple times on our way to camp.

Across from Cape Canaveral's space center is a pier marking the Manatee Hammock Campground. Within walking distance of Titusville's amenities, the price was right and I secured a site. I was thrilled to be off the water. The camp provided electricity, hot showers and a laundry option. I didn't carry a lot of clothes, but laundry was a selling point. It had been a while, dating back to The Five Eagles, since last doing a load. It was time.

After starting a load in a washer, I had a few moments so I explored the nearby bar, Pinto's, where I spent the remainder of the day. The moment I walked through the smoky dive bar doors, I was approached by the curious day-drinking crowd. Chris, a stuttering drunk, took a liking to me. His regularity at the bar guaranteed knowledge of the day-to-day patrons. We shared a few beers before I returned to change over the laundry.

With nothing better going on, I treated Pinto's as a revolving door for entertainment. I had a good thing going with Chris, so after I changed over the wash, I made my second appearance. Hours flew by, the after-work crowd began to funnel in and the bartenders changed shifts as I told my tales. Getting caught up in congratulatory moments, I almost forgot to eat. They told me a McD's was a little over a mile down the road and, if I timed it just right, I could be back for the live band. Sounded like a solid plan to me and I strolled down the road for some double cheeseburgers.

Two and a half miles later, I became a third-time offender at the local watering hole. Chris had retired, the crowd was younger and the band had just started its first set. I couldn't have timed it any better. The classic rock cover band rocked the house, but in doing so, they took the storytelling out of the equation. I became just another guy stumbling across the dance floor in the bar. Becoming increasingly bored, I called it a night, crawling into my tent around 3 a.m.

When I was at the bar, a Boy Scout troop had moved in next to me. They were not shy as they banged pots and pans in the early hours of the morning. While investigating the noise, I met Miles, a friendly neighbor, who shared my lack of enthusiasm about the boisterous fanfare. He invited me for coffee and conversation. He was a solo traveler, who had recently retired from NASA. I found it ironic we were across the waterway from the building where he had spent most of his working days. He enjoyed the jokes I cracked about the view as I dove further into stories of my journey. I left on a high note, thanking him for the coffee before I searched out breakfast.

By the time I found my PopTarts, I had taken note of the winds. My app predicted sustained 26 mph with gusts reaching 38 mph. I quickly walked to the registration office to pay for another night. I would rather take my chances with the rambunctious Boy Scouts than be out on the water combating that type of weather.

Since my day had opened up, I took a walk to town for resupply and lunch. I had to say goodbye to a good friend that day replacing my long-tenured flip-flops. Together we'd seen things and traversed many town miles, but that day I had to chalk them up to the game.

During the evening, the temperatures dropped into the lower 40s. Moving forward, I mentally prepared myself for these temperatures to be commonplace. I separated a pair of clothes in an emergency bag as a back-up safeguard. I mapped out the remaining miles with the hope of finishing on Feb. 1 and started working on my ride. The evening was young, but I had missed a lot of sleep, so I crawled in my bag and caught some zzz's.

Miles had coffee for me in the morning. We enjoyed another coffee/talk session, but I told him I would be leaving at some point of the day. While finding a spot for my emergency bag in Lola, I found a pack of eggs from two weeks previously. I went out on a limb and cooked six of them for breakfast. The temperature was not expected to reach over 50 degrees that day ,so I had to prepare for cold-weather paddling. I cut the sleeves off the wetsuit, turning the jacket to a vest. I could then use the sleeves for leg warmers, if needed. While I was preparing to leave, I felt like every camper in camp came over to inquire about the journey. Indulging the Q and A's, I became a little annoyed, it was getting late and I had a solid day ahead of me. Eventually, they stopped probing and I was able to pull Lola into the water.

On my way to the third installation of the estuaries, I had a flat-water day along Kennedy Space Center. Before entering Mosquito Lagoon, I stopped at a boat ramp, where I joined a local kayak guide for a few beers. He informed me that seasonally the lagoon plays host to one of the largest bioluminescent blooms in Florida. Unfortunately, they are more prevalent during the summer months, but he said I might be able to see some staggered along the beaches. As we got acquainted, a tour group started to show for their night-time paddle. We had a meet-and-greet while the guides unloaded the boats. The head guide told me to look him up if I ever wanted to run tours after completing my journey. I gave it a thought, but only for a brief moment. It's hard enough to keep myself alive, let alone rookie kayakers on vacation. I decided the time wasn't right for me to assume such responsibility.

The sun was just about gone, I was out of beer and I still needed to get to a camp. Leaving the ramp, I paddled along the beach until I found an acceptable spot to claim. Setting camp by headlamp I began to notice twinkles up and down the beach. The sand looked like a stage at a strip club. Thousands of glittery sparkles lit up the beach. Investigating further, I realized the sparkles were reflections bouncing off the eyes of little spiders.

Deeming the camp Sparkle Island, I took a night-time paddle into the lagoon, hoping for the chance to see some bios. A couple hundred yards into the lagoon I shut off my lamp, sat for a bit, allowed the tide to drift and then reached down with my hands, interrupting the water. The first couple times I did not have any luck, but then I saw a few shimmers. Progressively, the interrupted plankton began to illuminate the water.

Little twinkles of phosphorescent green specks shone through the motionless water. Every time my hand broke the surface, more appeared, like I was building an army bringing more followers leaning on every swipe. I felt as if I had found the sorcerer's hat from "Fantasia" and was controlling them as Mickey hailed over the brooms. Before chaos ensued, I broke free from the power I held in my hands and enjoyed the remaining shimmers.

Having had enough of the water, I paddled back to lie among the spiders. Delighted, I was able to have solace knowing I had the best of both worlds -- by land or sea I was in the middle of nature's light show.

Clutching to the banks of the easterly beach propelled me through the lagoon the next day. Winds blew in surging bands, like waves of an invading Persian Army. The bombardment of the side-sweeping swells forced me into a game of chess. Every stroke was strategically timed and placed in order to stay upright.

Mentally exhausted, I finally gave in to the stalemate. While taking a sanity break on the grass by the park's pavilion at George Kennedy Park in South Titusville, I gazed across the water with a blank stare. These thoughtless moments occur when my brain becomes overworked by the exertion of reading the water. It may take a moment or two, but I eventually realize it and snap out with a shake of the head. Once I returned to the present, the solution seemed all so simple. An island sat directly in front of me and Lola, just beyond a capsized sailboat. Devising a plan surely enough not to paddle any farther I sought refuge on an unmarked island in the middle of the ICW. The impromptu site had ample space, plenty of firewood and a view worth toasting. Offering sacrificial bourbon to Mother Earth, I expressed my gratitude and hope of forgiving weather before retiring to my sanctuary.

Mother Nature must've wanted a little more bourbon, for she did not appreciate my offering. The next morning was the coldest morning to date. The chill in the air made me forget I was in the Florida tropics. Before I even thought of packing up, I had to make a fire to warm my body and appreciate the foresight I had had to purchase the wet suit.

A day filled with complications and disagreements wrapped up the last bit of the Space Coast. After four miles, I came to the notable Ponce Lighthouse Park. Back spasms forced me to take an involuntary break. I'd had my share of aches and pains, but these were a little worrisome. I spent the day paying close attention and not overworking when I could.

The northern point of Smyrna Dunes State Park wrapped up the Space Coast paddling trail. Standing atop the sand dunes, I focused my attention to the tide barreling through the inlet. Outwitting the surge of turbulent currents was going to take a calculated effort to land safely at the Ponce Inlet Lighthouse launch. Knowing I was fully capable of the crossing, I approached it with tenacity and practicality. The extended break allowed my back to recover as I dove head-first into the challenge. Choosing to take a diagonal cut into the approaching tide I figured if I worked twice as hard halfway into the pass I could benefit and cruise back using the momentum to my advantage. Sure as shit, my plan of attack worked and I was safely to the launch unloading Lola onto the ramp.

I was now just a hop, skip and a jump away from exploring the tallest lighthouse in Florida. Standing at an impressive 175 feet tall, the once-known Mosquito Light was lit in 1887. Seen across the Atlantic from 17 nautical miles (20 miles) out, this historic structure in times past has saved one of the most recognized American authors, Stephen Crane. On his journalistic adventure to Cuba during the Spanish American War, the SS Commodore sank off the coast. Crane and a number of crewmen steered their dinghy toward the inlet by the beaming kerosene light.

In 1927, Mosquito Inlet was renamed Ponce de Leon Inlet. Changes continued 12 years later when the newly abolished Lighthouse Service handed the responsibility to maintain the light over to the Coast Guard. By 1970, the USCG left the post unmanned for their new beacon at New Smyrna Beach. Deeded to the town, the abandoned light was preserved and placed on the historic registry by 1972. Ten years later, the light was placed back on active duty, thanks to the high-rise buildings blocking the New Smyrna Light opposite the channel. Today, the beacon remains active as a private aid of navigation and is run by the current museum staff. For a nominal fee, you can explore the museum and get a feel for the importance of these aids.

Beyond the inlet turmoil of oscillating wakes, bitterly cold breezes and cross-cutting gusts lay the groundwork for the perfect storm. I was strong-armed off the water one mile short of my prospective island. My body had had enough of a beating for the day. When I beached, every piece of gear was soaking wet, including my emergency clothes. I am not proud to admit it, but I completely lost my shit. I threw my gear around, yelled obscenities that are not worth reading and kicked up sand like a 5 year old. It wasn't one of my finest moments.

Eventually, I took a step back and accepted what needed to be done. A fire was the only way to survive the night. I focused on one task at a time to get through the unproductive thinking. Somewhere in my travels I remembered hearing an answer as to why people die in the woods. They die of shame. The explanation always stuck with me and I used it more than once to pull me through shitty situations. Find the solution -- and that night the solution was a fire.

One task led to another, bringing me closer to mental stability. I was able to dry most of my gear well enough to stay warm. I also boiled water for a makeshift foot warmer inside my sleeping bag. Slowly, a calming presence came over me while I sat on the sand and took in the evening lights. The Daytona Beach skyline shone through the darkness. Something about it made me feel like I was right where I needed to be.

The Space Coast awaits   **Nightly drying gear**

Manatee Hammock Campground

Tile art at another ICW waterside park

Segments 23, 24, & 25
Daytona Camp - S. Nassau River
151 miles

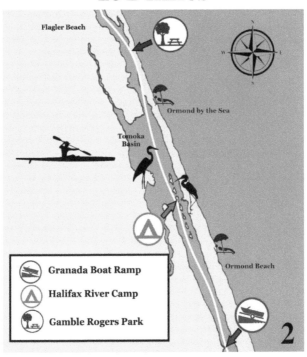

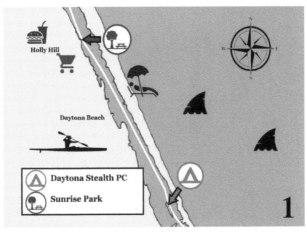

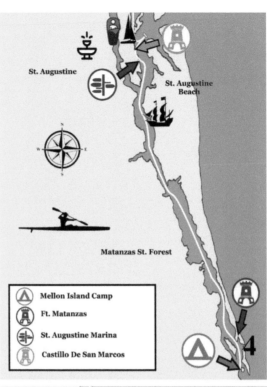

St. Augustine

St. Augustine
Beach

Matanzas St. Forest

Mellon Island Camp

Ft. Matanzas

St. Augustine Marina

Castillo De San Marcos

4

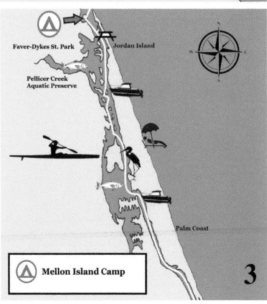

Faver-Dykes St. Park

Jordan Island

Pellicer Creek
Aquatic Preserve

Palm Coast

Mellon Island Camp

3

223

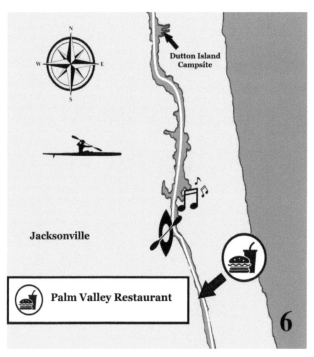

Dutton Island Campsite

Jacksonville

Palm Valley Restaurant

6

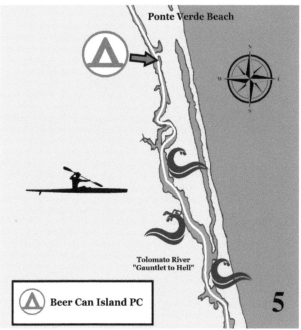

Ponte Verde Beach

Tolomato River
"Gauntlet to Hell"

Beer Can Island PC

5

224

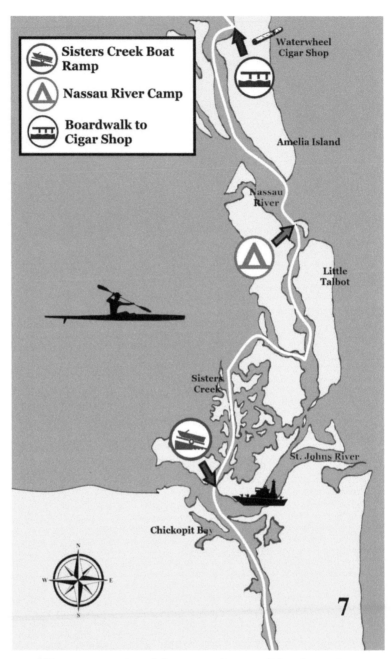

Sisters Creek Boat Ramp

Nassau River Camp

Boardwalk to Cigar Shop

Waterwheel Cigar Shop

Amelia Island

Nassau River

Little Talbot

Sisters Creek

St. Johns River

Chickopit Bay

7

All maps were hand drawn and created by the author
Jeffrey "Treehouse" Buncie

Living for Today

The secret to closing out the remaining four segments was staying in the present. Everything started to turn against me, daring me to push harder, faster and farther. I had to shut down the internal whispers and remind myself how I had made it this far; one day at a time, one mile at a time, one stroke at a time.

The first stroke started on a numbingly cold morning off Daytona Beach. Ruthless winds pierced me to my bones as I paddled to Sunrise Park. A few miles on the water led me to a dock, where I stashed Lola for one last resupply. Holly Hill housed a Dollar Tree and some nearby restaurants. After a stop at my favorite store, I had lunch at an Italian restaurant to replenish calories.

Back on the water, I occupied my mind by counting bridges as I crossed their thresholds. Back spasms slowed my momentum and encouraged the frigid drafts to threaten my core temperature. I was unable to stop shivering. The restrooms at the Granada ramp were the saviors of the day. The strong heating elements inside the hand driers brought me back. I must've hit that button 40 or 50 times, but, boy, did it feel good.

I was, indeed, back. Five more miles that day and I was set. A row of dredged islands in the Tomoka Basin welcomed me home, giving me the option of choosing where to stay. I chose a small unnamed island in the Halifax River, across from the heart of the Tomoka Basin. The bird-watchers' paradise and hardwood hammock provided ample scenery. I was ecstatic to be off the water for the day. A tree barricade, shaped like a horseshoe, blocked the wind and held in the heat from my campfire. Warming my toes at the fire I sat in a mixture of crystalized sand and pine needles. The crackling of cedar within the fire brought gratitude. Finally, I was able to enjoy a night without fearing hypothermia.

I thought I'd never be able to say that the weather would take a turn for the best. I suppose Mother Earth had sobered up after her hangover. Well, I wasn't going to waste the day, so I took full advantage of the calm seas and blasted some miles.

Intermittently spaced boat ramps supplied ample support for stretch breaks. The second ramp and the highlight of my day was named after a famous folk singer and storyteller of Old Florida. Gamble Rogers State Park and Memorial of Flagler Beach welcomes visitors to commemorate the Florida hero and enjoy the park's many amenities --

surfing, hiking, padding, camping and sunbathing await vacation goers on the quarter-mile strip of beach.

Gamble Rogers was known for his fictional stories of the old Florida county of Oklawaha. I referred to Rogers as a hero for he died tragically while attempting to save a father of a young girl stuck in the rough surf of Flagler Beach. Rogers grabbed an air mattress and swam out, but was unable to retrieve the man due to worsening health conditions. Regrettably, they both died in the surf, but the folk singer gave it all he could, thus earning his name to this enchanting beachside park.

During the initial 17 miles, using these ramps, a couple on their boat became a recurring sight. I began to notice them after leap-frogging them a few times in the early morning hours. We spent most of the day involved in this game along the ramps. When I left the impressive docks of Bing's Landing, the couple circled back and yelled over. "How much farther today?" I removed my earphones and paddled alongside their cruiser. We shared a few laughs before getting into serious answers. They were impressed with the daily account, never mind finding out I had started on the Floribama border. I hoped I was going to score a beer or two, but they sped ahead after wishing me good tidings.

Entering the Pellicer Creek Aquatic Preserve led me through the flats with an average depth of two to six feet. The pristine estuarine tidal marshes provide a unique paddling experience atop the monstrous Redfish below. From atop among the ecological communities, the egrets and white ibis were wading along the banks, while the wood warbler songbirds stuck out their colorful plumage in hopes of attracting their mates.

Two islands managed by the Favor-Dykes State Park were my next stops. Depending upon time, one of the three campsites on Jordan Island or Mellon Island would be my resting place that night. By 3 p.m. I was walking the sites on Jordan Island. The campsites were well-kept, manicured and supplied with picnic tables. I almost talked myself out of going farther to Mellon Island. But, it was still early in the day ...

Marked by two wooden pylons and a concrete sign, Mellon Island was hard to miss. I was happy to see the campsites were just as manicured and the picnic table was in good standing. The 24-mile day ended the 23re section and I had a table to eat at that night. What more could a guy ask? One could say, how about only 86 miles left to go?

One of my favorite towns in Florida has always been St. Augustine. My plan was to arrive around sunset, so I could pull into the marina after the dock master left -- and thus wouldn't have to pay to store Lola for the evening -- and explore St. Augustine's nightlife. I did one better, searching Google Maps, and finding an island north of the Castillo de San Marcos. The island appeared to be adequate for a stealth spot if I got a little too carried away. Before I get too far ahead, there was still 18 miles on the water I had to get through.

A mile or two north of my camp on Mellon Island, I came to a small Spanish fort, Fort Matanzas. A sister fort to the Castillo, the deteriorated structure once protected the back door of St. Augustine. From the water, I could appreciate the strategic location, but saw no need to explore. For an even more bleak history lesson, "matanzas" is a Spanish word meaning "slaughters," after the massacre of the French Huguenots in the first battle for St. Augustine. I get history and all, but the area has a river, state forest, monument and an inlet all named "slaughter."

The rest of the day, I pushed up the Matanzas River eyeing the time. I began to see the pirate cruise schooners and the lighthouse in the distance. I was making too good of time. Arriving at the marina by 3 p.m., I decided to act like I belonged. Honestly, no one batted an eye. I slipped into a spot along the docks and used the facilities. When I returned, I thought if I was able to casually pull up, what could someone do to Lola? It was time to move to the island.

I'd never been able to see St. Augustine from the water, so I took in different angles and played around with different photos. Passing the Castillo de San Marcos, I took a straight shot to the island. Upon beaching at the southwestern tip, I saw a dinghy tied ashore. The island was definitely suitable to camp. In the distance, I heard people laughing. A sandy path cut across the dune to another beach. Over the dune, I saw two locals enjoying some cold refreshments. They seemed like they would know if the island was permissible to camp on, so I introduced myself.

Steve was a hairdresser and Doug, a writer. I jumped right in, asking whether or not it was cool to camp on the island. They reassured me with a "Oh, hell, yeah, we've done it plenty of times." That was enough for me. Naturally, I wanted one of their cold beers, so I shared some stories. It worked and, by the end of the conversation, Doug did me one better. He claimed to own a sailboat across the river he wasn't going to stay on that night. I liked where this was going, I could almost bet on what he was going to say next. Then he did -- he offered it to me, just like that, stating again he was crashing at his girlfriend's. If I wanted to get out of the cold, the boat was mine for the night. All I had to do was follow them across the river to the dock.

228

Doug pointed me in the direction and I got a head start. When I was across, they came up behind me and led me to the Ibis, Doug's sailboat. Doug gave me the tour and a rundown of the rules. It was simple enough; clean up, use a wag bag, if necessary, and don't steal the boat. He left me to get comfortable and a specific thought went through my mind once again. I know live-aboards are a special breed, but how do I keep ending up in these one-of-a kind experiences?

Thrilled to have a sailboat as a house for the evening, I didn't even care about the nightlife scene. I planned on having a peaceful evening, listening to good tunes on the boat. If there was no bar for me to attend, I figured next on the list was food. I went for a walk through town and found an all-you-can eat-pizza buffet. They didn't see me coming -- I shut the place down as every thru paddler should do. After the buffet, all I wanted to do was lie down. I walked back to the warmth of the boat and enjoyed the solitude.

Fort Matanzas

St. Augustine Lighthouse

Castillo de San Marcos

The Ibis

The Home Stretch

A solid night's sleep led me to an early morning expedition. Everything was still closed, but I'd seen it all before. My first stop was the grounds of the Castillo de San Marcos. The Spanish built fort protected St. Augustine from western invaders. Claiming to be the oldest and largest masonry fort in the continental United States, it ran an unprecedented 251 consecutive years until decommissioned in 1933. In all of its time under military rule, the fort was never breached, yet it did change ownership six times between four governments, all peacefully. Figure that one out.

My next stop was Old Towne St. Augustine. It was a good little hike, but I had some fun along the way. I sat by the old jailhouse and watched the shop employees during their pre-work pep talks and motivation meetings and then explored the stores. I got bored with the gimmicky shops and candy stores, and moved on to the Fountain of Youth.

The Fountain of Youth was first explored by Juan Ponce De Leon in 1513 and is said to be the holder of the Spring of Eternal Hope. The archeological park, founded under the village name of Seloy, has been proven to be put on the map by De Leon, but the fountain remains a mystery. Later owner "Diamond Lil" MacConnell aggressively marketed the property as the fabled Fountain of Youth. Her lifelong quest to prove the tale would remain unrealized until her death. Not until 1927, when the land was sold to a Walter Fraser, who maintained the property to educate the public of Juan Ponce De Leon and his legendary spring. Believing in the historical traditions, he sought to secure the site's rightful place in American history. And so goes the mystical powers of the purest water that flows from the crevasse of the Earth's bosom.

The fountain is one of the biggest of all the gimmicks, but I figured with all the paddling I could use all the help I could get. It was the one attraction I paid admission for. I spent a couple hours on the grounds. I caught the shows, attended the planetarium show and yes, drank from the spring.

My hunger became unbearable. After the visit to the fountain I found a Denny's for breakfast. If there was one thing I had learned over the previous five months was to never leave a town hungry. I stacked up on the breakfast foods and drank enough coffee to kill a small animal. I wasn't in too much of a hurry, but eventually I made my way back to the Ibis.

I had to get paddling, but not before I left Doug a note thanking him for his trust and hospitality. An island a little over 15 miles north was my EOD goal. Once north of St. Augustine, I was on the twists and turns of the Tolomato River. This stretch of seemingly endless headwinds put me through the wringer. I left St. Augustine on top of the world and those miles beat me right back down. There was no sense to make of any of it. Both the wind direction and tidal movements had me confused, but I forged ahead one uncomfortable, patient stroke at a time. When I finally found the camp, I was so irritated I deemed it the gauntlet to Hell.

I was off the water and 15 miles closer to Fort Clinch. Actually, it turned out I was closer because I had overshot the camp -- it was only by a half-mile, but now I would have to build my own fire ring. There was, oddly, a bunch of aluminum cans around, so I got creative. I made a beer-can fire ring, built a fire and sipped some bourbon. Sitting by the fire's warmth, I thought it was all so surreal, that it would be one of my last fires.

The next morning, the weather was on my side and I was awake in time to take advantage. I was going for the gold that day, paddling for as long and as far as my body would allow. A protein-packed breakfast, supported by hot coffee, got me motivated and onto the water.

The friendly staff at the Palm Valley Restaurant in Ponte Vedra Beach, roughly 5 miles from the previous night's campsite, welcomed me with free coffee. I was expecting a second breakfast, but the restaurant was closed for the season. It has been awhile since I had heard anything about my fellow kayaker Mary, who was a bit ahead of me. They said she had been through not too long ago, so my chances of meeting her were no longer an option. She had come through a few days prior and I was only a couple of days from the end, I guessed she had already finished her journey. I was happy to hear she had made it that far and found motivation in her accomplishments.

After leaving the restaurant, I entered the Jacksonville segment of my trek, starting with a long and narrow shot to Jacksonville Beach. I put some music on and sang my way north. Getting lost in the moment while passing by the waterfront houses, I began to belt out some notes while listening to the earphones. There I was, singing loud and proud as Whitesnake came across the playlist. Smashing the lyrics from "Here I Go," I saw a family playing in a yard look over in shock. They all smiled and threw up their rock and roll devil horns, the hand symbol for rock and roll. With a lift of the paddle I returned the smile and sang even louder. At that point, I didn't care who heard me or saw me, I remember feeling like I was the freest person on the planet when I paddled through this stretch. There was no other feeling like it.

Dutton Island was the last camp before crossing the St. Johns River. I passed the point of no return, which forced me to get across before the day's end. The St. Johns wasn't shy about pushing me into the swift moving water, where the two bodies of water met, moving in opposite directions through an open corridor, dizzying and chaotic. I started the crossing for the not-so-faint-of-heart from Chickopit Bay. Rip-roaring currents and large boats accompanied the chaotic factors of the northerly flowing river. Coast Guard members in a raft kept an eye on me from afar as I pushed forward. I pressed on as every other crossing I'd notched in my belt, but the Sister's Creek launch couldn't come quicker.

If you've ever tried to balance across a high beam or cross a gushing river atop a downed tree, there really is a reason they say "do not look down". In the past, naturally I looked down and felt confidence slip away. The fear and uncertainty at this juncture interferes with your concentration. Just before I approached the north side of the shallower channel, I felt this confidence slip away. My nerves were racked and shook me to the bones. Fear was overcoming my confidence, but I continued to push beyond the unrest in order to regain poise.

When passing a river or channel, the water is shallower then deeper, then shallower again. When you get over the deep and back to shallow, the water calms down a bit and you can tell the worst is over and the water begins to calm. I finally hit that spot, slightly turned back to the USCG officer and received a thumbs-up. I was glad to know he had my back, but I felt better knowing I had won his praise. I still get anxious thinking about crossing that river.

At the boat ramp, I took a breather while looking back across the St Johns. A guy standing at his car came over and sparked up a conversation. He confessed to watching me for the last 30 minutes of my crossing. He couldn't believe I made it across without failing. Talk about a big ego boost, between the thumbs-up and that guy, I was flying high. I thanked him and told him some funny antidotes.

I pushed into the much calmer Sisters Creek. I had no goal as I had already exceeded where I had hoped I would make it that day. Two hours remained until the sun set and I decided to paddle until dusk. The surrounding islands and protected creek shot me through the chamber like a bullet leaving a gun. At that point, I was moving into the last segment of the entire trip. The compliments throughout the day, moving into my last set of maps, I knew wherever I ended up that evening, I would only have one more day of paddling.

Blasting through the backwater creeks, I was soon passing Little Talbot Island. It was nearing 5 p.m. and the sun was setting quickly. I went as far north as I could before the mouth of the Nassau River. There was a beach large enough for the tent, so I tapped out and set camp.

Looking at the maps after a much-needed meal, I realized I had covered a personal best of 34 miles. I had to get on the horn and set up ride options. The countdown continued with 18 miles remaining. The final camp was set and I was excited, thankful and exhausted.

Eternal youth

Saltwater vs. electronics   **One last sunset at camp**

Mellon Island

Segment 26
Nassau River Camp - Fort Clinch
20 miles

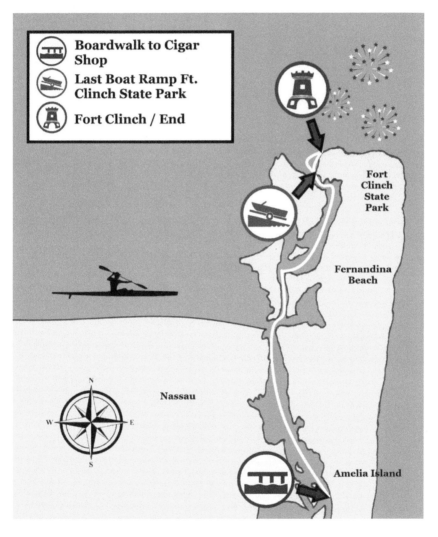

Boardwalk to Cigar Shop

Last Boat Ramp Ft. Clinch State Park

Fort Clinch / End

Fort Clinch State Park

Fernandina Beach

Nassau

Amelia Island

All maps were hand drawn and created by the author Jeffrey "Treehouse" Buncie

Day 155
A Thru Paddler is Born

By the end of the day, I could finally say there would be no more flying teeth eating away at my flesh or swarms of blood-thirsty mosquitoes. There would be no more unruly winds or tumultuous water to navigate. It would be a bittersweet end to an amazing experience pulling me off the islands and away from unforgettable encounters. A day to light the cigar, hang up the paddle and solidify my name as a thru paddler. Yessir, today was the day.

Trying to contain the excitement coursing through my body was a fool's errand. I received a text from my brother, Dan, confirming a ride back home by the day's end. A plan was in motion; there would be no turning back. It was time to unzip the tent and meet the day.

A brisk 55 degrees, 25 mph winds, and spitting rain waited for me on the beach. Wasting no time to get on the water, I broke camp and prepared for the elements. Crossing the Nassau River led me to Amelia Island, where I planned to stop for a cigar at a local shop. To this day, I have no idea how I managed to take a wrong turn into Walker Creek, but it happened. By the time I realized I was in the wrong cut, I had added an extra two miles to my day.

Pissed off, I returned to the ICW almost an hour later, searching for a dock to go ashore. I came to three lengthy docks jetting into the water. Using Google, I saw the buildings looked more like condos, and thought there would be no harm if I borrowed their docks. To save strokes, I left Lola halfway down the docks, climbing up and over the railings. An eerie feeling came over me, but I continued cautiously to the grounds. A ghost town trapped me behind a wrought-iron fence. I had to slide my hand between the bars and unlock the latch using a stick I found in the courtyard. I was free.

Two blocks away was the Waterwheel Cigar shop, a fancy cigar lounge. I felt bad walking into it as I dripped water everywhere. The salesman understood the circumstance, gave me a towel to dry off and a free cup of coffee. While I was enjoying that coffee, we got to talking, mostly about hiking, but nonetheless the time in the shop kept me warm and dry.

When I returned to the condos, I realized I had spent a little too much time at the cigar shop. I had made a rookie mistake on my last day. The tide had completely disappeared. Lola was sitting atop a muddy bank. The closest water was 30 yards from where she sat. I knew all too well this was going to be a dirty job.

Knowing what lurked beneath the swampy bank, I tried like hell to find my magic toe shoes. Hanging from the rafters, frantically stretching into her front hull, they were too buried. Faced with only one other choice, I slowly lowered myself into knee-deep mud. One leg at a time I tried pushing her, but Lola was not budging. I stepped around to the tow cord, cutting my feet something fierce. Nimbly pulling her inch by inch, adding to the cuts and abrasions, I made it to the end of the dock.

Prior to sitting back into the cockpit, I had to take the time standing in ankle-deep water to clean off the filth. When I got going, I paid close attention to the oyster bars so as not to make that mistake again. As I was weaving in and out of the shallow river basin, the rain returned. Temperatures dipped into the 40s and the sun disappeared behind the clouds. Bullied off the water at a boat ramp one mile before Fort Clinch, Fernandina Beach, the end of the trail, I ran for the restroom. Hiding in the restroom was the only way to escape the bone-chilling winds. Only this time, there was no hand driers. A father and his son walked into the restrooms. Seeing me shivering, the father asked if I was OK. I told him about everything and he could see how much pain I was in. He went to his car, and grabbed a windbreaker and a towel. He told me that was what he had and insisted I take them. I accepted, thanked him and watched them pull away.

Time was now my enemy. It was 5 p.m. before I left the ramp for my final approach. A new windbreaker beneath my vest kept me warm as I turned into the St. Mary's River. The winds picked up the open water, forcing me closer to land. Hugging the sandy banks, I saw the reddish-orange bricks of Fort Clinch standing tall behind the dunes. A smile that spread further than the mile I had just paddled was across my face. After the rock jetties, I beached, pulled Lola to safety and ran through the sand. Hooting and hollering, I held my head high and fell to my knees. All of my hard work was for this one pure moment. It was if nothing else mattered and I was the only one left on the planet. I reached high, gave one more yell and stood up to give it the ol' "Breakfast Club" fist pump.

During the final moments of the celebration, I was joined by three bystanders, who watched me from a distance. They asked if something was wrong. Smiling and with a gaspy chuckle I said, "Nothing is wrong, nothing at all." After a quick explanation, they threw around high fives and snapped a few celebratory photos.

You would think my paddling days had come to an end along that beach. Not the case. I had to return to the ramp to meet up with my brother. The celebration was rushed, but I had more paddling to do. I had already broken too many of my rules throughout the day and did not want to end on a sour note. I shoved off a beach one last time, peering into my last sunset.

I couldn't stop smiling. My mind went blank. Nothing but wholesome energy filled the air around me. I felt like I was invincible -- that is until I reached the ramp where I had left the bathroom, one mile from the fort on the grounds of Fort Clinch State Park, and stopped moving. Reminded again how cold the temperature dropped once the sun fell, I ran to the restroom to change into a dry pair of clothes. I prepared Lola for transport and finally lit the cigar.

An hour went by and still no rendezvous. My brother finally called to tell me, no kidding, that "he was at the coast waiting." Lowering my head, embarrassed for him, I told him it was all coast. What else could I have said? I mean, he was literally helping a brother out. He took another half-hour to locate the correct boat ramp and greeted me fondly. We loaded Lola on his car, strapped her down and left the ramp behind with the settling dust.

"What a long day," I said from the passenger seat. My then-8-year-old niece Kelsey, who was sitting in the back seat, bluntly stated, "Uncle Jeff, you need a shower." I couldn't help but laugh. Dan asked if I needed anything for the ride back to Ocala. Hell yeah, I needed six double cheeseburgers and some road sodas. We stopped for gas and bought some Yuenglings, then stopped at McDs. When inside, Dan listened to me order six double cheeseburgers, looked at me and laughed. There was nothing to laugh about -- before I got back in the car, I had eaten four of them. While standing at the soda machine, he saw me grab a handful of salt and pepper, straws, and ketchup packets, and put them in my pockets. Again, with another chuckle, he asked what I was doing. I had done it not even thinking about it; this was how I had gotten by on my trek, it was ingrained; it was now a part of my life.

My parents were waiting for my arrival back in Ocala. We made the trip and arrived home just about midnight to a warm reception. Before the Q and As I unloaded Lola and my gear. I left the stench in the yard for everybody's sake. I could say the chores were done one last time before the cocktail hour commenced.

Over a few stiff drinks, leaning on the in-house bar, I thought back to that ramp on the first day. I was a different person than I was now. Before I even sat in Lola's cockpit, I had to throw everything I thought I knew out the window and push the reset button. I was having difficulty putting my thoughts together, but I did know I was internally changed forever.

Perseverance and stubbornness helped me through the day-to-day challenges. I learned to channel the negativity and flip it into more positive outcomes. Every single day, my mind and body was put to a test. Just like the cuts and bruises, I, too, would heal overtime and come through renewed. Sometimes scars were left behind, but they reminded me of the lessons to be learned.

So many dreams became my reality. Priceless visits to places I held near to my heart allowed me to open up to many more. The opportunity to travel through the significant historic Florida coast and live in its culture was a treasure. Observing the diverse sea creatures in our planet's collected bodies of water left me speechless. I'd miss the sounds of fish feeding in the shallows, the crashing of waves and the smell of salt in the air.

From the first interaction with the fishing buddies at Fort Pickens to the last, sharing high fives and congratulations at Fort Clinch, I valued each one of them. Yes, even that machete-wielding Canadian. By remaining teachable, I gained the wisdom of so many righteous humans. They made my paddle a success in more ways than they will ever know. I came out a better person from their uplifting spirits and generosity. I was blessed to have shared cocktails with truly genuine people. I couldn't have become who I am today if I had never have met each one of them -- and just because I didn't think to record everyone's name doesn't mean they were not part of my journey. They were, I promise them that.

Before I leave you, from the bottom of my heart, thank you. This story is dedicated to every single one of you. Even if I never met you, and you purchased or borrowed this book, you continue to help the overall cause of the BNC Odysseia, 20,000 miles paddling/hiking. I may have earned every stroke, but each of you helped me experience the life I aspire to live.

That magic moment

My
"Breakfast Club"
fist pump

A thru paddler emerges

**Dan and Kelsey taking me
away from the water's edge**

The cigar has been lit

For More Information

The uses of two Florida websites were used before, during and after the paddle along the Florida Circumnavigational Saltwater Paddling Trail.

Office of Greenways and Trails- https://floridadep.gov/parks/ogt

Florida Circumnavigational Saltwater Paddling Trail - https://floridadep.gov/parks/ogt/content/florida-circumnavigational-saltwater-paddling-trail-segments-information

Author Jeffrey "Treehouse" Buncie Social Media

Facebook- BNC Odysseia- (Travel page) @BNCOdysseia
https://www.facebook.com/BNCOdysseia

Instagram- @treehouseog14

Email - jeffbuncie@gmail.com

Website- https://www.jeffbuncie.wixsite.com/website

* I would appreciate if you took the time to provide honest feedback from the outlet you purchased this edition. If you loved it, let us know. If you hated it, let us know. I am always willing to hear from the BNC's followers. Thank you again for your time.

About the Author

Originally from a small town nestled in the foothills of western Pennsylvania, Jeffrey "Treehouse" Buncie spent his childhood years learning early fundamentals of wilderness preservation. When it came time for his parents to hang up the snow shovel, they moved him and his two brothers to the centralized town of Ocala, Fla. During his young adult years, Buncie had access to a national forest and the Florida beaches an hour away, where he was able to enhance his appreciation for the outdoors and new-found respect for the ocean's power.

The childhood spirit of venturing off in the woods became misplaced as Buncie pushed his way through his high school and college graduations. Believing he must follow suit and get that haircut and get that real job, he was easily lost in the rat race of running a business and educating today's youth.

The age of 30 approached; it was time to ignite that internal flame with a spark across the pond at the Festival of San Fermin in Pamplona, Spain. The flame grew brighter as did the wanting to return to the simplicity of outdoor living. An opportunity struck and Buncie took it by the horns. A new life would ensue with the succession of a thru paddle of the Florida Circumnavigational Saltwater Paddling Trail.

Now, six years later, he has immersed himself in this long-distance community. Having completed a thru-hike on trails such as the Pacific Crest Trail (PCT) and the Appalachian Trail (AT), he spends his time either on trail or giving back to the trail community. As for Lola, she was taken by a thief along the banks of the Mississippi River on Buncie's paddle in 2016.

He has not looked back and looks further into enhancing the light that no longer only burns from within, but shines through as a beacon to other misguided souls.

Acknowledgements

I would like to say thank you to everyone who has contributed or assisted me along my journey. This section of acknowledgements could easily fill two or three pages. I personally would like to take some time and recognize these individuals for their exceptionality.

Barry Hoefling - Without the ride to Big Lagoon State Park I wouldn't have been able to start, let alone complete, my journey.

Barbi Johnson - You always had my back and came through with support when I was down and out in Naples.

Mike Sims - You took a chance on me at the boat ramp and accepted me into your family. Fun times, family vibes and my first spear gun.

Michelle Brown - While eating lunch you never gave up on me and negotiated a free stay during a pivotal point of my journey.

Charlene Prater & Linda Nichols - A house! You gave me a house and great conversation while showing me there are still good people out there.

Jacque Beech - All you need in life is a friend like you. Take me in, bring beer and McD's and still call me out on my shit.

Ashley Morgan - Your time and honesty was much appreciated, as with your efficiency when asked to review the pre-released edition

Captain Mark Reinhardt - Rum, insight and new friends all came about because of your thinking. You showed me more compassion than one could in a lifetime.

Jeff Wilson - You brought me off the water and into your homes. Thank you for your trust, camaraderie and stories.

Dan Buncie - It took you awhile, but you finally found the boat ramp, enabling safe passage away from the water.

Margaret Button - This entire book would not be out there if you didn't have the willingness or patience to help me through the literary process.

CPSIA information can be obtained
at www.ICGtesting.com
Printed in the USA
LVHW071101241120
672558LV00007B/562

9 780578 78542